# FIRE & SONG

ALSO BY ANNA LANYON

*Malinche's Conquest*
*The New World of Martin Cortés*

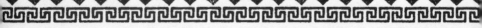

# FIRE & SONG

*The story of Luis de Carvajal and the Mexican Inquisition*

## ANNA LANYON

ALLEN&UNWIN

First published in 2011

Copyright © Anna Lanyon 2011

Allen & Unwin
83 Alexander Street
Crows Nest NSW 2065
Australia
Phone:  (61 2) 8425 0100
Fax:     (61 2) 9906 2218
Email:  info@allenandunwin.com
Web:    www.allenandunwin.com

Cataloguing-in-Publication details are available
from the National Library of Australia
www.trove.nla.gov.au

ISBN 978 1 74114 708 7

Consultant publisher: Jackie Yowell
Internal design by Emily O'Neill
Maps by Ian Faulkner
Set in 10.5/18 pt Aldus by Bookhouse, Sydney
Printed in Australia by McPherson's Printing Group

10 9 8 7 6 5 4 3 2 1

*For Jackie Yowell*
*And for*
*Adele P.,*
*a Carvajal survivor*

# CONTENTS

# LIST OF
# ILLUSTRATIONS

# PREFACE AND
# ACKNOWLEDGEMENTS

I CAME ACROSS THE CARVAJAL STORY FOR THE FIRST TIME DURING
the summer of 1994 while I was in Mexico City gathering
material for a different book. It was the kind of accidental
encounter that often happens in archives. We may not always
find what we are looking for, but sometimes we find other
treasures instead.

Although this work is subtitled 'The story of Luis de
Carvajal and the Mexican Inquisition' there can never be
just one way of understanding a human life. Two earlier
books—one by Martin A. Cohen, the other by Seymour
Leibman—have approached Luis's story in different ways,
and I have benefited from those meticulous works. I have also
been fortunate to be able to consult documents that were not
available when Dr Cohen and Dr Liebman were preparing

their biographies, in particular the trial transcripts of Leonor and Isabel de Carvajal.

Those forlorn manuscripts had long been missing from the archives in Mexico City. They are now safely housed in the University of California's Bancroft Library, in Berkeley, and in constructing this narrative I have used substantial portions of them, along with parts of Luis's own testimonies and personal writings. I did this because I wanted readers to 'hear' their words as directly as possible. I have, however, interposed myself into this process by selecting which passages from which hearings to include, and then translating those passages. For this reason I encourage readers who know Spanish to consult the original documents for themselves or, in the case of Luis's records, read the paleographic transcript referred to in the bibliography at the back of this volume.

In reality, every member of the Carvajal family deserves a book of his or her own: Luis's mother, Francisca; his sisters, Isabel, Catalina, Leonor, Mariana and Anna; his brothers— Balthasar who found refuge in Ferrara, Miguel who made his way to Salonika, and Gaspar, who chose a different path to the rest of his family. Most of the documents are there. All that is needed is time and patience to draw out the life stories they contain, with all their joys and sorrows, regrets and paradoxes.

The great American historian of the Mexican Inquisition, Richard E. Greenleaf, once wrote that counting and tabulating heresy trials can tell us nothing about the actual nature of heresy; that if we hope to comprehend the mental world of religious dissidents in colonial Mexico it is necessary to read their trial transcripts in full. I have borne Professor Greenleaf's advice in mind while preparing this book, and hope it will contribute in some small way to our understanding of what it meant to be a secret Jew in sixteenth-century Mexico.

But I wrote this book for another reason besides: because the men who sent Luis, his mother and sisters to their deaths four hundred years ago wanted no memory of them to remain. That desire to extinguish any remembrance of this tragic and courageous family inspired me, more than any other factor, to help ensure that they are not forgotten.

A great many people have assisted me in preparing this book. My friend and former teacher at La Trobe University's Institute of Latin American Studies, Dr Barry Carr, guided me through the early years of research and writing. Professor Peter Mathews and Professor Tim Murray, also of La Trobe University, encouraged me from the outset, and the university's School of Historical and European Studies provided me with financial support in the form of a scholarship and a research travel grant.

Professor Richard Broome, Dr Anthony Disney, Dr Claudia Haake, Dr John Hirst, Dr Ralph Newmark, the late Dr Stephen Niblo and Dr Heidi Zogbaum, all of La Trobe University's History Department, helped with advice and encouragement along the way, as did Professor Suzanne Rutland of Sydney University's Department of Hebrew, Biblical and Jewish Studies, Professor Eric van Young of the University of California at San Diego, and Professor Colin Tatz, presently a visiting fellow in the College of Arts and Social Sciences at the Australian National University. The staff at La Trobe University's Borchardt Library located books and articles for me throughout the world, and I am grateful for their expertise and dedication to their work.

In Mexico City my friends Elena Bouret, Malena Gurrola and Jorge Ortíz Moore looked after me with their usual generosity. Irving Reynoso helped with some last minute research at the Archivo General de la Nación, while Dr Alejandro Padilla Nieto kindly showed me through the Archivo Histórico 'Genaro Estrada' in Tlatelolco, which was once the Franciscan college where Luis de Carvajal spent the years from 1590–1595.

In Lisbon Dr Irmgard Heidler and Hans Heidler gave me a home during my research trips to Portugal and I am deeply indebted to them for their kindness. Also in Lisbon Marta Pascoa used her paleographic skills to transform sixteenth-century Portuguese into a script that I could read. Without her expertise I could never have deciphered the trial transcript of the first Luis de Carvajal.

Many people made my visits to the province of Trás-os-Montes in north-eastern Portugal memorable, but I especially want to thank Maria do Carmo Baptista of the Livraria Carvalho in Mogadouro for the interesting conversations we shared. In beautiful Fermoselle, across the river in Spain, Jorge Luis Garrido Sánchez, and Cristina and her family at the inn on the plaza were unfailingly hospitable.

In Medina del Campo Dr Antonio Sánchez del Barrio, director of the Museo de las Ferias, made me feel welcome in the municipal archives, while Fr José Manuel Caballero kindly showed me around the Church of Santiago which had once formed part of the Jesuit school where Luis de Carvajal studied as a boy. In Valladolid Padre Carlos Alonso Vañes of the Colegio de Agustinos Filipinos did his best to track down a member of the Carvajal family who had once been an Augustinian monk in Mexico City. At the Archivo Histórico Nacional in Madrid Esperanza Adrados Villar allowed me to examine letters from the Holy Office in Mexico City to the Supreme Council back in Spain, and provided me with copies.

In Toronto Professor Thomas Cohen, of York University's Faculty of History and Humanities, helped me try to trace Luis's Jesuit uncle, Domingo de Carvajal. In Pennsylvania

Dr Karl Gersbach, Director of Vila Nova University's Augustinian Historical Institute, assisted in the quest for the long-lost Augustinian Carvajal. In California Dr Walter Brem, former Curator of the Latin American Collection at the Bancroft Library, University of California, Berkeley, guided me to the trial transcripts of Leonor and Isabel de Carvajal.

In Peru Fr Leo Donnelly located the portrait of former inquisitor Dr Lobo Guerrero in the Archivo Histórico y Museo de la Catedral de Lima, and Fernando López was good enough to provide me with a digital image of it. In Bolivia María Pompeya Patzy Avilés, director of the Museo Ecclesiastico de Sucre, risked life and limb by climbing on a ladder to take a photo of former inquisitor Alonso de Peralta on the cathedral wall, and for this I thank her very much. In Rome Br Peter Gilfedder visited the Jesuit archives on my behalf to seek out information regarding Domingo de Carvajal. In Zurich my dear friend Monica Iseli helped me during a difficult time, and showed me the riverside shrine of the Anabaptist martyr Felix Manz.

The following friends have supported me in different ways during the writing of this book: Dr Guillermo Anad, Robyn Annear, Wendy Bell, Nanette Carter, Lorraine Crellin, Dr Alan Dearn, Catherine Freyne, Dr Hildegard Ford, Joseph Ford, Dr Farley Kelly, Adele Kenneally, Christopher Koller, Barbara Marsh, Janet Mathews, Dr Denise Desmachelier,

Dr Tom McCrae, Dr Ann Moyal, Marta Ortíz de Rosas, Adele Pinczower, Dr Rose Rothfield, Professor Christina Slade, Dr Peter Woodruff and Walter Struve.

My friend Carmel Condon and my daughters Anna and Lucie were brave enough to act as my common readers for this project, and I am grateful to all three for helping me make some sort of order out of chaos when I feared that I could not. Patrick Gallagher at Allen & Unwin in Sydney showed great patience as he waited for this book to finally turn up and I thank him for his forbearance. Christa Munns returned to her post as senior editor just in time to guide me to publication, and I am grateful for her perfect timing, as well as her intelligence and skill. I also want to thank Ali Lavau for her careful and sensitive editing, and Emily O'Neill for the beautiful cover design.

As consultant publisher Jackie Yowell spent many hours reading, discussing and helping me shape this work. I thank her for her dedication and for the many kindnesses she and Steve Rothfield have shown me over the years since we met.

Finally I want to express my gratitude to my family: to my parents, and to Anna and Patrick, Lucie and David, David and Ella—for their constant loyalty and affection.

*Anna Lanyon*
*Descartes Bay, October 2010*

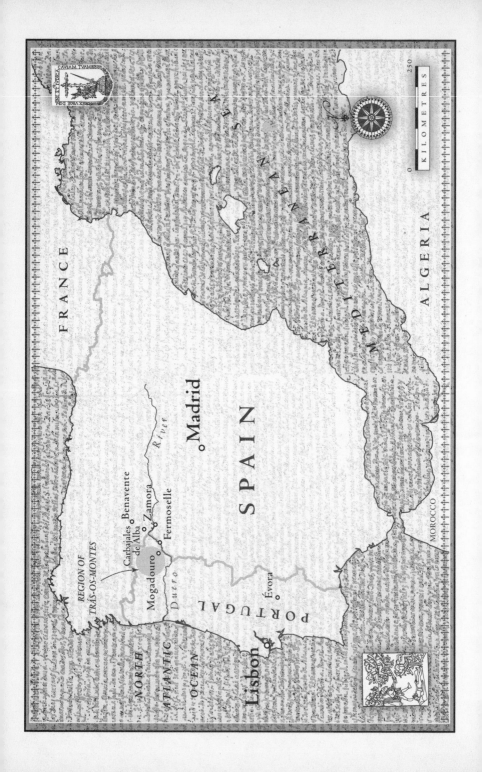

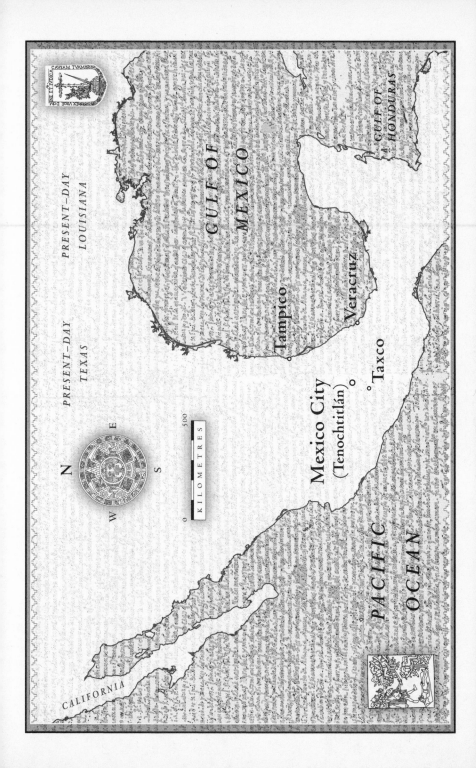

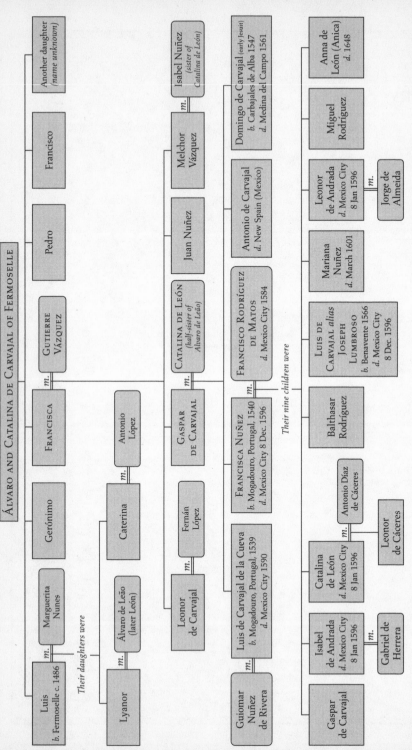

# Álvaro and Catalina de Carvajal of Fermoselle

**Their daughters were**

Luis, b. Fermoselle c. 1486 — m. — Marguerita Nunes

Gerónimo

Francisca — m. — **Gutierre Vázquez**

Pedro

Francisco

Another daughter (name unknown)

Lyanor — m. — Álvaro de Leão (later León)

Caterina — m. — Antonio López

**Catalina de León** (half-sister of Álvaro de Leão)

**Gaspar de Carvajal** — m.

Melchor Vázquez — m. — Isabel Nuñez (sister of Catalina de León)

Juan Nuñez

Leonor de Carvajal — m. — Fernán López

Antonio de Carvajal (d. New Spain (Mexico))

Domingo de Carvajal (early Jesuit), b. Carbajales de Alba 1547, d. Medina del Campo 1561

**Francisca Nuñez**, b. Mogadouro, Portugal, 1540, d. Mexico City 8 Dec. 1596 — m. — **Francisco Rodríguez de Matos**, d. Mexico City 1584

**Their nine children were**

Luis de Carvajal de la Cueva, b. Mogadouro, Portugal, 1539, d. Mexico City 1590 — m. — Guiomar Nuñez de Rivera

Gaspar de Carvajal

Isabel de Andrada, d. Mexico City 8 Jan 1596 — m. — Gabriel de Herrera

Catalina de León, d. Mexico City 8 Jan 1596 — m. — Antonio Díaz de Cáceres — Leonor de Cáceres

Balthasar Rodríguez

Luis de Carvajal alias Joseph Lumbroso, b. Benavente 1566, d. Mexico City 8 Dec. 1596

Mariana Nuñez, d. March 1601

Leonor de Andrada, d. Mexico City 8 Jan 1596 — m. — Jorge de Almeida

Miguel Rodríguez

Anna de León (Anica), d. 1648

*Note:* The surnames of the Carvajal family members altered slightly as they move between Spain and Portugal. Portuguese Leão becomes León in Spain, Nunes becomes Nuñez. Vázquez becomes Vaz, Carvajal can appear as Carabajal, Carvalho, Carvagalo. The Iberian naming systems permit siblings to bear different surnames, and wives are not obliged to adopt their husband's surnames.

*'The struggle of man against power is
the struggle of memory against forgetting.'*

MILAN KUNDERA
THE BOOK OF LAUGHTER AND FORGETTING

# A DISTANT SHORE

It is September 1596 in Mexico City. As night falls the people of the conquered Aztec capital wrap themselves in capes and shawls against the first chill of autumn. In a cell on a street not far from the central square a young man kneels to pray. His face is pale, his hair and beard are black, and he is thin from fasting. His cell has a tiny window and through it he watches the sky for the first light of day.

The young man is a prisoner of the Holy Office of the Inquisition. As dawn illuminates the space in which he has spent much of the past nineteen months he takes a quill, some ink and a small sheet of paper—his last—and begins to write. He is writing his spiritual testament. He lists the divine commandments by which he has lived and intends to die. He invokes passages from Deuteronomy, Exodus and Psalms, from the prophets Jeremiah, Ezekiel, Daniel and Job, to show his Christian captors that his religion is the true faith, that they are the heretics, not him. When he has filled every space on his precious sheet of paper he signs his name at the bottom: *Joseph Lumbroso*.

Next morning he goes upstairs to the audience chamber. The usual preliminaries take place. He knows them by heart now. He swears to speak the truth. The inquisitor asks whether he has remembered anything. He says he has not. The room is quiet; the only sound is the scratching of quill on parchment as the scribe records the proceedings. But then the Holy Office lawyer appointed to assist Joseph begins to speak. 'You are blind,' he tells Joseph and begs him not to persist with his blindness, 'because in following the Law of Moses rather than that of Jesus Christ you will be condemned'. The lawyer means condemned in the afterlife; they both know Joseph is already condemned in this world. But Joseph will not yield. He has brought his sheet of paper with him to the audience chamber. He presents it to the inquisitor and as he does he makes the following formal declaration: 'I have shown in a note written and signed in my name and by my hand,' he says, 'in which I have written the commandments that I obey, and my testament, that I wish to live and die in the belief of those commandments. And therefore I request and submit that this paper be placed with my trial documents, as my last will, so that it will be recorded for all time.'

The inquisitor's response is not recorded. Perhaps he nodded; perhaps he made no gesture whatsoever. But he did what Joseph asked. The spiritual testament has remained in Joseph's trial transcript all these centuries: a fragment of paper covered back and front with his beautiful handwriting. The scribe who placed it there entitled it 'the last will and testament of Luis de Carvajal, in which he says he wishes to die'. *Luis de Carvajal* was the baptismal name Joseph had received as an infant and by which he had been known for most of his life.

Who was he, this young man with two names who said he wished to die following the Law of Moses? He had chosen to call himself Joseph, but his captors called him Luis. He called himself a Jew but they did not. Instead they called him a 'Judaizer'. It was an old expression from the ancient world that signified a person who was not a Jew, but followed Jewish observances. As far as the inquisitors in Mexico City were concerned, Luis/Joseph was such a person. Not a Jew—they refused to grant him that self-designation—but a Christian so unshakeable in his heresy that they described his case as one deserving of their pity, *'una cossa de compassión'*.

He had indeed been baptised as an infant back in Spain; he had admitted this during his first Holy Office trial seven years earlier. The inquisitor who questioned him at that time had asked whether he was a baptised and confirmed Christian. 'I am,' Luis had replied. 'A bishop in Benavente confirmed me, although I do not remember his name.' So why did he call himself a Jew? Because his ancestors had been Jews and he wanted to be like them and live as they had lived, guided by what he always called 'the Law of Moses'. Four generations had passed since his great-great-grandparents had been forced to convert to Christianity, but he had spent his life trying to keep their original faith alive.

The transcripts of his trials are held today in the Archivo General de la Nación in Mexico City. They contain the story of his life as he told it to the inquisitors in 1589 and 1590, and later, in 1595 and 1596. Given the circumstances in which his words were recorded it is necessary to approach those documents with caution. When Luis/Joseph spoke in the audience chamber he tried to protect himself and his loved ones by disguising certain names and dates and the places where events occurred. It is an instinctive thing to do and we must never forget the predicament he was in as we read the testimonies he gave to his interrogators four hundred years ago.

There are other, obvious limitations to his trial records. They do not allow us to see his face or hear his accent or the timbre of his voice as he spoke. They cannot tell us whether it was soft and low, firm and self-assured, or anything like the husky peninsular Spanish of today. Yet despite these limitations his transcripts allow us to 'listen' as he talks about his childhood in the kingdom of Castile and his adult life in New Spain, as Mexico was known to Europeans at that time. They also reveal his complex religious beliefs which, although he did not know it, were unorthodox not just from the Catholic perspective, but from the standpoint of formal Judaism as well. Luis lived in a society that had outlawed his ancestors' faith and so he never experienced even one moment of rabbinic guidance in all his thirty years. He had to study alone and furtively as he sought to recover the Law of Moses, and at times, to his great sorrow, he sensed that his knowledge of it was far from perfect. Yet nothing—not even the threat of death—could persuade him to forsake it.

His mother and his sisters shared his tribulations. Like him they each endured two inquisitorial trials and their surviving records—some in Mexico City, others in the University of California's Bancroft Library—offer parallel versions of his story which is, after all, their story too. Their transcripts contain portions of each other's testimonies, and each testimony reveals a new door waiting to be opened and another thread to be followed, so that the problem for those of us who read them becomes one of when and how to stop.

The Italian scholar Carlo Ginzberg calls inquisitorial records such as these 'the archives of repression'. These remnants of past tyrannies, and harbingers of worse to come in the twentieth century, can be found in their tens of thousands wherever Europe's ecclesiastical courts existed, and they are filled with the stories of individuals, families, and sometimes entire communities. But, in the case of the Carvajal family, trial transcripts are not the only source of information available to us.

Luis/Joseph left a precious collection of personal writings to posterity; not just his spiritual testament, but an autobiographical work he called his 'book of miracles'. It is not a record of the great political events of the times in which he lived. You will find no mention of the failed Armada of 1588 in its pages, or of Spain's war against the Hugenots of France. Luis's memoir is a work of interiority—an intense and often mystical narrative in which he describes his family's joys and many sorrows, and the religious faith that sustained them throughout their troubles.

He also left a series of letters that he filled with consolation and advice to his mother and sisters during the penultimate year of his life, and theirs. Those personal papers—more intimate and far more candid that his trial transcripts—provide a rare touchstone as we seek to follow his physical journey to the New World, and his sacred journey to the Law of Moses.

Luis's writings survived because the inquisitors in Mexico City kept them as evidence of his Judaising heresy. It was their duty to do so. They acted within a legal and conceptual framework unthinkable to us today, but their tribunal was not a lawless, unrestrained and unregulated authority. It was a legitimate and properly constituted ecclesiastical court supported by the secular authorities of the day. That, perhaps, is the most frightening thing about it. Every inquiry its officers conducted, every letter they wrote, every ration sheet they completed and every arrest warrant they issued had to be recorded. Similarly, every piece of evidence they gathered had to be stored away in case it should be needed in the future. That is why, paradoxically, the men whose role it was to consign Luis's memory to oblivion did more than anyone else to preserve it. Of all the twists and turns and ironies of his story this is possibly the strangest.

The poet Deborah Masel recounts an old Hassidic tale in which, at a time when the world was cloaked in darkness, a mystic remembered the secret of light. In a quiet forest he kindled a fire, sang a wordless song and illuminated the world. Before his death he passed the secret on to his brightest student. This boy could not recall the song, but he lit the fire and restored the light. Years later he in turn gave the secret of light to another student, who found the forest glen, but did not know how to kindle the fire or sing the song. Yet light still flowed, because just knowing that a fire had been lit and a song had been sung was enough to bring light into the world. But what happens, Deborah Masel asks, when we forget the story? When we do not even know that we have forgotten? This, she says, is to be lost in oblivion, in nothingness: a terrifying fate, for 'oblivion is the root of exile, and memory is the secret of redemption'.

Luis de Carvajal alias Joseph Lumbroso had much in common with that third student; like that boy he knew that a fire had once been lit and a song had been sung. Luis wanted to recover that fire and that song and the secret of light, no matter how dangerous the search might be, rather than be lost forever in oblivion. This book is about his struggle to do that, and the risks he was prepared to take with his life, and the lives of those he loved, in order to restore the fire and the song, and find his way back from oblivion and exile.

Luis's life ended in the New World, but it did not begin there. The events that shaped him, and led him across the Atlantic to the fallen Aztec city had been set in motion long before his birth, and if we wish to follow his journey through life we need to understand something of those events.

In order to do this it is necessary to leave the Americas for a while and return to the former kingdom of Castile where he was born and raised, and where his family had lived for generations. That kingdom is now the Spanish province of Castilla y León and at its heart, not far from Salamanca, is the old walled city of Zamora. No human story has just one beginning but in a sense we could say that Luis's story begins in the district around Zamora because that is where, seventy years before his birth, his great-great-grandparents made their decision to convert to Christianity.

Their names were Álvaro and Catalina de Carvajal, and if you leave Zamora and follow the great River Duero west you will come to the village where they took that fateful step. On the way you will pass by fields crossed and scarred by ancient stone walls that lean into the wind like the standing stones of Ireland or the Orkneys. It is a remote and haunting landscape, especially in winter when snow envelopes the dovecotes and cork oaks on either side of the road.

The place where Álvaro and Catalina once lived is the last village in Spain. It is perched high above the border with Portugal and its name is Fermoselle. The word means 'beautiful' in the old Leonese tongue once spoken in these parts and Fermoselle is indeed a beautiful place. It was built long ago on a towering granite outcrop above the Duero, and on winter afternoons, when the fog clears and the sun comes

FERMOSELLE, SPAIN, JANUARY 2008.

out, its old people like to sit beneath their ruined castle and look out towards Portugal on the other side of the river gorge.

Álvaro and Catalina's surname suggests that they probably came originally from the village of Carbajales de Alba, much closer to Zamora. We know very little else about them; only that they were cloth merchants, the parents of at least six children, and that they were in Fermoselle when the bitter year of 1492 came around.

We remember that year because in October Columbus sailed into the Caribbean and his voyage ushered in an era of catastrophe for the peoples of the New World. But 1492 was a calamitous date for people in Spain too, if they happened to be Jews or Muslims. In January, after a long and terrible siege, Fernando of Aragon and Isabel of Castile took formal possession of the Islamic city of Granada; in March they delivered an ultimatum to the Jews within their realms: convert to Christianity or leave this land forever. Columbus himself recalled the royal edict in his logbook. 'After the Spanish monarchs had expelled all the Jews from their kingdoms and their lands,' he wrote, 'in the same month they commissioned me to set out on the voyage to India.'

The expulsion of 1492 still troubles and perplexes scholars. Some argue that the royal pair simply wanted an excuse to appropriate Jewish riches. Others counter that the presumption that the Jews of Spain were universally rich is wrong; that in reality most Jews possessed so little wealth that this could not have been the motivation. Besides, by sending them into exile the Crown would forfeit the taxes traditionally paid directly to it by Jewish communities. What does seem clear is that Isabel and Fernando were determined to shape their fledgling nation into an exclusively Christian polity. How else to explain the fact that ten years after forcing their Jewish citizens to convert or leave, they would offer the same ultimatum to their Muslim subjects: accept baptism or leave your homeland forever.

But this story, the Carvajal story, is not about the complex and infinitely arguable reasons why the spring of 1492 brought a dramatic end to the history of religious toleration that had for centuries set the Iberian world apart from the rest of Western Europe. It is about the resistance of one family and one young man in particular, and the ways in which they kept their faith alive in the aftermath of that catastrophe.

Expulsion had been a constant sorrow for Jews in other parts of Western Europe since medieval times. The English had expelled them in 1290, the French in 1302, and they had been driven out of countless other kingdoms and principalities on a deadly litany of pretexts, accused of poisoning the wells, or murdering Christian children, or mutilating communion hosts, or because their ancestors were alleged to have killed Jesus.

But the cluster of Christian kingdoms and Islamic caliphates that we now call Spain had always been different. Jews had lived there more or less undisturbed since Roman times. One legend claims that they arrived even earlier—around the sixth century BCE—as captives of the king of Babylon. That story turns on a reference in the scriptures to 'the exiles from Jerusalem who are in Sefarad'. *Sefarad* means 'a distant shore' in Hebrew and is thought to have signified the Iberian Peninsula in ancient times. It is this sonorous word, as melancholy as a sigh, that gives the Jews of Spain and Portugal their distinctive name: 'Sephardim'.

Whatever the truth of that appealing legend, Spain became a lasting homeland for people like Álvaro and Catalina de Carvajal. Not a paradise; there were bad times as well as good. But it was a place where they were able to live in relative if uneasy peace alongside Christians and Muslims. The Sephardim spoke Judeo-Spanish and wrote it in both Roman and Hebrew scripts. They spoke Arabic, too, and Catalan, and until the fifteenth century they were mostly spared the garish Jew badges, the tinkling bells, the Jew hats and other degrading costumes forced upon their co-religionists in Venice and Savoy, Salzburg and Arles.

The events of 1492 seem to burst without warning onto this tranquil scene, but that suddenness is an illusion. In reality life had been growing steadily worse for the Sephardim throughout the previous century as the kingdom of Castile, where most of them lived, was torn apart by plague and civil war. Those calamities unleashed a storm of anti-Jewish violence in 1391. Thousands of Sephardim were massacred while thousands more submitted to baptism in order to save their lives. During the decades that followed the surviving Jewish communities faced increasing harassment from municipal authorities. Then the Jew badges and other distinguishing signs so familiar in other parts of Christendom began to appear, like sinister warnings of what was to come.

What came, in 1478, was the Holy Office of the Inquisition. It arrived in the kingdom of Castile much later than in other parts of Western Europe. It had first emerged in France almost three hundred years earlier in order to prosecute the Christian heretics known as Cathars. In Castile it came into existence for the express purpose of examining the orthodoxy of the many New Christians whose parents and grandparents had been forced to abandon Judaism during the massacres eighty years before.

It is important to understand that Europe's inquisitions had no jurisdiction over Jews or Muslims or members of other non-Christian faiths. Inquisitorial power extended only to baptised Christians, and unless we comprehend this legal technicality we cannot fully appreciate the fear that gripped the Sephardim in 1492 when the edict of expulsion forced them to choose between conversion and exile. They knew that danger and degradation awaited them if they tried to make a new life in another European state. They might be tolerated for a while in Ferrara or Venice or Arles, but the Jew badges and hats and bells they would be made to wear would mark them out as pariahs. Their movements would be greatly restricted and they would be at risk of massacre or further expulsion at a moment's notice. On the other hand, if they accepted Christian baptism in order to remain in their

Spanish homeland they would become subject for the first time to inquisitorial investigation.

This was the dilemma faced by Álvaro and Catalina de Carvajal in 1492. We have no idea whether they made their decision to convert swiftly, or after weeks of anguished conversation, but contemporary accounts tell us that it was a time of indecision and confusion for the Sephardim in general: that while some decided to convert and stay, others decided to go, and that some began the journey into exile, only to return and accept baptism after all.

For all we know, Álvaro and Catalina de Carvajal may have been among those forlorn pilgrims who set out and later turned back. Perhaps they struggled down the steep and furrowed road out of Fermoselle with their children and walked on until they saw the strange, dark shape of the mountain called Pereña in the distance. Below it is an old stone bridge that fords the River Duero. Perhaps they turned back at that point, too frightened by the howls of wolves, or because they lacked the fees required by the Portuguese Crown—eight cruzados per family—to buy their way into one of the refugee camps on the other side.

All we can say for certain is that some time in 1492 this couple took their sons and daughters to the church beside the plaza in Fermoselle and did what their country asked of them: they abandoned their faith and joined the unhappy ranks of reluctant New Christians or *Judeo-conversos*. Yet their sacrifice brought them little sympathy or respect. Some of their co-religionists in other parts of Europe regarded them as traitors; Rabbi Eliyahu Capsali wrote later from the safety of Crete that many Sephardim apostatised during those 'days of desolation'. Meanwhile, in Spain, their Old Christian compatriots took to calling them *'marranos'*, or swine. It was a deliberately offensive term for a people who regarded pig flesh as unclean.

In recent times the historian David Graizbord has coined a far more sympathetic term for these unfortunate proselytes. He calls them 'liminal people'; liminal because they lived precariously on the limina or threshold between two religions. There is another term, a Hebrew word that captures an equally essential aspect of their tragedy: *anussim*. It means 'the forced ones'. Álvaro and Catalina may not have known that word, but it suggests the way they probably felt about their predicament. They were liminal people now, condemned to perch on the threshold between two faiths and, in their case, between two countries as well.

They raised their children as Catholics from that day on. They had to, if they wished to survive, and from time to time they may have asked themselves whether they had made the wisest choice. Many of their fellow Sephardim had settled on the other side of the Duero River, among the deep ravines and crumbling Templar castles of the Portuguese province known as Trás-os-Montes, and were living openly there as Jews. Perhaps Álvaro and Catalina should have crossed the river after all.

They would have learned within a few years that things would have turned out badly no matter what they did. In 1495 a new king ascended the Portuguese throne. He was known as Manuel I and at Christmas the following year he declared that all the Jews of his kingdom, whether native born, or refugees from across the border, must convert to Christianity. No choice this time between expulsion and conversion. With the stroke of a royal quill, amid an explosion of anti-Jewish violence throughout Portugal, the exiles from Spain were forcibly baptised. They became New Christians like the relatives and friends they had left behind on the other side of the river, and had to suffer the painful knowledge that their journey into exile for the sake of their Jewish faith had been for nothing.

Those were the bewildering 'days of desolation' through which Álvaro and Catalina de Carvajal lived. What is history to us was daily life for them. They were just two among the tens of thousands who endured all that hardship and we might never have heard of them if their son had not been arrested fifty years later by the Holy Office in Portugal. But he was arrested and because of his misfortune we know about the decision they made in 1492, and the chain of kinship that connects them to the young man in Mexico City a century later.

For many years the index in Lisbon's Arquivo Nacional da Torre do Tumbo was composed of little squares of cardboard threaded onto strings. They were nicknamed the *rosarios* because of their resemblance to Catholic prayer beads, but these rosaries were not intended for prayer. Instead they contained the names of people prosecuted by the Holy Office in Portugal for crimes which, from our twenty-first century perspective, are not crimes at all.

The rosaries are gone now but the inquisitorial records remain in the Arquivo, and the transcript of the trial of Álvaro and Catalina's son is among them. It is not an easy document to decipher—the handwriting has faded, and Portuguese spelling of the mid sixteenth century was very different from Portuguese today. Yet despite these palaeographic challenges the transcript tells us quite a lot about Álvaro and Catalina's son. It reveals, for example, that he went by the same name as his as-yet-unborn young kinsman in Mexico City—Luis de Carvajal—and that in January 1548 he was arrested during the first great wave of terror against the New Christians of Trás-os-Montes.

The Holy Office constables found him in the town of Mogadouro. They led him back down through the high dark mountains of the Serra de Estrela, and imprisoned him in the beautiful city of Évora where his daughter Lyanor, her husband Álvaro de Leão, and several other members of their family and circle of friends had been incarcerated some months earlier.

This first Luis was questioned on 8 January 1548. He told the inquisitor who interrogated him that his parents, who were now deceased, had been known as Álvaro and Caterina de Carvajal—he used the Portuguese variant of his mother's name. He said that he had been born in Fermoselle, in the kingdom of Castile, and that his brothers still lived there. He gave his age as sixty, which meant that he had been just six years old in 1492 when the edict of expulsion was promulgated.

When asked whether he carried the 'stain' of Jewish or Moorish ancestry this first Luis admitted that he had been born a Jew and was circumcised, but had been baptised as a small child in Fermoselle. He added that he had once had a Jewish name, although he could no longer remember what that name had been. He probably did remember, but in Portugal by that time the less said about one's Jewish heritage the

MOGADOURO, TRÁS-OS-MONTES, PORTUGAL, JANUARY 2008.

better. In any case, whatever his original name, whether Jacob or Joseph, Abraham or Judah, it had been lost to him in the little church in Fermoselle in 1492.

The transcript of his trial lists his crimes as *Judaismo*, *heresia* and *apostasia*: a complex trinity of charges, each one separate yet related. Judaism was a crime because the Portuguese Crown had prohibited its observance. Heresy was a crime because a heretic is one who chooses—that is the original meaning of this ancient Greek word—and Luis de Carvajal was not free to choose his faith. Why apostasy? Because at that time in Western Europe, not just in Spain and Portugal, church and state were considered one and indivisible.

It followed therefore that if Luis was guilty of abandoning the state religion—Catholicism—and reverting to his ancestors' faith, he had committed apostasy against the state.

But was this first Luis really a secret Jew? Or a sincere Catholic whose only crime was his Jewish lineage? From this distance in time it is impossible to say. Even if he had confessed to Jewish practices we could not be certain, because confession was often the wisest strategy for men and women arrested by the Holy Office for the first time. They might forfeit their goods, they might be made to wear penitential garments and endure house arrest for many years, but as long as they repented and asked for mercy they would live. Heresy was not like other crimes. It was a state of mind, an attitude that could be corrected, unlike rape or theft or murder. This idea is reflected in the sentencing rules of the Holy Office. They stipulated that repentant first offenders had to be given a chance to mend their ways, but one chance only.

Luis de Carvajal of Fermoselle did not have to use his single chance, however. His trial transcript is unusually slender because by the time he appeared before the inquisitor in Évora, a deputation of Portuguese New Christians had arrived in Rome to negotiate a general pardon for their fellow converts in Portugal: men and women like Luis who stood accused of Judaising. The papal authorities responded well to the financial inducements offered by the delegation. The pardon was granted and on 10 June 1548 the first Luis was released from jail. His daughter and her husband were also later freed, and as far as we can tell from the records in the Torre do Tumbo archives the Holy Office in Portugal never troubled them again.

The first Luis de Carvajal had a sister. Her name was Francisca, and her story, although fragmentary, provides a glimpse of the fear in which this family lived for generations. When Luis appeared before the inquisitor in Évora in January 1548 he explained that she had once been imprisoned by the Holy Office in Castile and had later come to live near him in Mogadouro. He added that she had left Portugal two years before his arrest and he had no idea where she had gone. He almost certainly did know but had no intention of divulging her whereabouts.

Francisca de Carvajal is important to this story because she was the great-grandmother of Luis/Joseph in Mexico City. The testimonies that he, his mother and sisters gave to the Holy Office many years later tell us that in 1546 Francisca fled from Portugal and returned to the kingdom of Castile, taking her daughter-in-law and her four-year-old granddaughter with her.

The precise route these fugitive women took is unclear. They had to cross the Duero at some point, however, and may well have gone to Fermoselle first because it offered the quickest escape route out of Portugal, and Francisca's family there would presumably have assisted them. But by 1548, when her brother was imprisoned in Évora, she had reached Carbajales de Alba, the Spanish village from which their parents seem to have derived their surname.

Carbajales is a very old settlement beside the River Aliste and in sight of the sinuous foothills of the Sierra de la Culebra. Francisca, her daughter-in-law and little grand-daughter remained in Carbajales until 1547, when the men of their family came from Portugal to join them. After that the family moved to the town of Benavente, a little to the north of Zamora. Benavente had once been known for the goodness and wisdom of its rabbis, but Jews were no longer visible in its streets or plazas, or anywhere else in the Iberian world.

The rabbis were gone, the synagogues had been turned into Christian churches, and the Torah scrolls had been burned or carried into exile. Everyone in Spain and Portugal was now officially Catholic and any converts brave enough to cling to their ancestral faith, whether Judaism or Islam, did so in secret. This was the shadowy, dangerous world into which Luis de Carvajal alias Joseph Lumbroso was born in 1566. His family and their friends looked and acted like the Old Christians around them. They had to if they wanted to avoid suspicion. What they felt in their hearts is more difficult to say.

A great fifteenth-century Spanish chronicler, who was himself of Jewish ancestry, described the diversity of beliefs to be found in New Christian families like theirs. 'And it happened,' he wrote, 'that in some households the husband kept Jewish ceremonies and his wife was a good Christian, and that one son and daughter might be good Christians while another son was of the Jewish faith. And within the same household there was diversity of beliefs.' He added that the members of such households often concealed themselves, 'one from the other'. As the Carvajal story unfolds we will see that at times they too concealed themselves, not just from the hostile world around them, but 'one from the other'. They were not unanimous in their religious loyalties and at critical moments the hidden tensions between them would erupt with disastrous consequences.

Francisca de Carvajal had three grandsons. The elder two journeyed to the New World as conquistadors, like so many young Spaniards at that time, while the youngest boy stayed close to home and embarked on a different kind of adventure as an early member of the newly formed Society of Jesus. None of these three young Carvajal men demonstrated any longing for their Jewish faith; or, rather, no longing worth sacrificing their careers for, or their lives.

Their sister was different. She had been named Francisca after her grandmother and, although she too would eventually be know as Carvajal, she went by the surname Nuñez during the early part of her life. The fact that she is absent from the inquisitorial records after fleeing Portugal with her mother and her grandmother in 1546 is a good sign. It means that when she and her family returned to the kingdom of Castile they managed to stay clear of the Holy Office.

This is not as surprising as it may sound. By the 1540s the Holy Office had ceased to be exclusively concerned with converts from Judaism. It had extended its reach to the thousands of Spanish Muslims who had been forcibly baptised thirty years earlier. Their orthodoxy had to be investigated and cases of alleged 'Islamicising' would eventually outnumber those of Judaising in the Holy Office records. Meanwhile, the beliefs of the fervent Catholics known as *Alumbrados*, 'the Enlightened Ones', had to be examined because their desire for a direct and personal relationship with God, rather than one controlled and shaped by priestly mediation, suggested dangerously Lutheran leanings. To add to its burden the Holy Office was increasingly obliged to inquire into the conduct of Old Christians whose blasphemy and sexual transgressions now made up the greater proportion of inquisitorial trials.

Young Francisca Nuñez grew up quietly and cautiously in Benavente. She married her cousin at an early age, and when she was forty she followed her brothers to the New World. Her attachment to her ancestral religion was deep and enduring. We know this because her son was the young man in Mexico City who called himself Joseph Lumbroso. And later, when he composed the narrative of his life for his book of miracles, he described the part she played in introducing him to the Law of Moses.

# 2

# THE CITY IN
# THE FIELDS

IT HAPPENED IN AN ANCIENT TOWN ON AN OLD ROMAN ROAD ON
the high plains of Castile. Medina del Campo is white with
frost in winter, burned by the sun in July. It began life long
ago as a resting place for shepherds as they moved their flocks
down from the mountains of Asturias to the warmer pastures
below. No-one remembers what those Asturian shepherds
called their primitive way-station, but it later grew into a
thriving township, and when a Berber king paused there
during the eighth century he gave it the Arabic part of its
present name; 'Metina', he called it: 'city'. Later it became
known as the city in the fields, 'Medina del Campo'.

In medieval times Medina was famous for its fairs, one
each May, a second each October. Merchants came from Paris,

PLAZA IN MEDINA DEL CAMPO, SPAIN, JANUARY 2008.

Florence, Ghent and Brussels to purchase fine merino wool, brocades and silks, devotional paintings and golden chalices. After the age of printing began in 1440 they came for printed books too, so that by 1561, the town had sixteen thousand residents and almost thirty guest houses to accommodate the visiting merchants. But Medina's mercantile glory faded as the sixteenth century waned. The merchants ceased to come, the population dwindled and the city in the fields fell into a decline from which it never really recovered.

As it did a shining thread of spirituality began to weave its way into Medina's history. The poet known to English speakers as St John of the Cross was educated in Medina and sang his first mass there. His close friend and confidante Teresa de Ávila founded her second Carmelite convent there. These renowned and fervent thinkers—the poet and the nun—were both descended from Jews. Was it their shared ancestry or their passion for reform that drew them to each other? Perhaps it was both. But Medina's past holds another, darker thread of religiosity. In September 1480, when the kingdom of Castile's first two inquisitors were formally inducted into their roles, their investiture took place in one of Medina's many churches.

There were Jews in Medina del Campo at that time. They had lived quietly in their *aljama* beneath the castle for many centuries. But in 1492 many left Medina and went into exile, while those who remained were subsumed beneath the mantle of Christianity. Nothing now remains of their old quarter, but if you arrive in Medina by train and walk from the railway station to the bridge across the river, the empty wasteland you will pass through is the space where that Jewish community once flourished.

Francisca Nuñez arrived in Medina del Campo in 1577. She was thirty-seven by that time, and probably looked like any other Spanish woman as she made her way through the cobbled streets in her elevated cork shoes and farthingale skirt. She came with her husband Francisco Rodríguez de Matos and they took a house in the mercantile lane then known as

Rua Salamanca. A black-and-white photo taken of this street during the late nineteenth century shows a jumble of old arcaded houses with iron balconies. Most of those buildings are gone now and the street is called 'Gamazo' these days, but in this quiet passageway just off the central plaza, Francisca and Francisco set out to make a living selling wax, beer, dried fish and olive oil.

They had seven children when they arrived in Medina del Campo, and all seven had been born in Benavente, that former 'city of praise'. Although the children would later be known collectively as 'Carvajal', they went by different surnames at this stage of their lives, as permitted by the infinitely supple Spanish naming system. Their names were Gaspar de Carvajal, Isabel de Andrada, Catalina de León, Balthasar Rodríguez, Luis Rodríguez, Mariana Nuñez and Leonor de Andrada. The eldest two, Gaspar and Isabel, did not accompany their parents and siblings to Medina, however. Gaspar was in Lisbon working for his uncle, and Isabel had settled with her husband in Astorga, in the far north corner of Castile.

After taking the house in Rua Salamanca, Francisca and her husband enrolled their younger sons, Luis and Balthasar, in the newly founded Jesuit school for boys. Francisca had a personal association with the school because her younger brother Domingo had once been a novice there. Young men

Arcaded house in
former Rua Salamanca,
Medina del Campo,
January 2008.

and women from *converso* families were officially excluded
from most of Spain's religious orders, but the Society of Jesus
was different. It openly accepted boys whose ancestors had
been Jews, because its founder, Ignatius Loyola, had ruled
that there should be no distinction 'between Jew and Greek',
a quiet allusion to St Paul's letter to the Galatians. We know
in retrospect that Domingo de Carvajal was not the only boy
of Jewish descent to study at Medina's Jesuit school. The
historian José de Acosta had been among its first pupils, and
the future St John of the Cross was a student there at the
same time as Domingo. Unfortunately Domingo died at the

age of sixteen and left no recollection of this mystical poet
who gave us the expression 'the dark night of the soul', or
of how it felt to be a member of Loyola's brave new order.

Luis was eleven when he entered the Jesuit school, Balthasar
was fifteen, and Luis would later write that they loved each
other like water and earth. Each morning they left their
parents' house in Rua Salamanca and walked together through
the arch that still leads into Medina's plaza: two slender
boys, one dark, one fair, carrying the quills and inkhorns
they needed for their lessons, and dressed, no doubt, in
hooded capes on winter mornings. From there they would
have turned into the street called Almirante and walked on
towards the Santiago gate in Medina's western wall where the
Jesuit College stood in 1577. Within its austere classrooms,
beneath the supervision of their black-robed teachers, Luis
and Balthasar studied Latin and rhetoric as well as classical
authors such as Cicero and Livy.

Latin was a precious gift to Luis. As the key to European
learning at that time it provided him with the translation
skills he would need in years to come. Theatre also formed
an essential part of Jesuit education at that time, however, and
Luis and Balthasar would certainly have taken part in some
of those sacred dramas. The famous episode from Genesis in

which Joseph, the son of Jacob, is sold into slavery in Egypt is known to have been a popular theme at the Medina school. Luis knew and loved the story of Joseph and may have learned it as a pupil of the Jesuits. He would retell it to his mother and sisters during the darkest hours of their lives, and when he eventually adopted the name Joseph it was the son of Jacob that he had in mind.

Many years later, when Luis began to write his book of miracles, he said that his introduction to the Law of Moses took place in Medina del Campo one September, 'on a special day we call the Day of Pardon, a holy and solemn occasion for us that falls on the tenth day of the seventh month'. He didn't mean Ash Wednesday, that day each year when Catholics are encouraged to reflect on their transgressions. Luis's 'Day of Pardon' was the Jewish Day of Atonement, which falls on the tenth day of Tishri, the seventh month in the Jewish calendar. He did not use its Hebrew name, Yom Kippur, however, and seems never to have been quite sure of it. The closest he ever came was to call it '*el Quipur*', but that was much later.

Luis said it was his mother, his brother, his sister and his cousin who revealed God's truth to him. The brother must have been Balthasar. Gaspar was far away in Lisbon, and in any case he had already turned his back on his family's faith. The sister was either Isabel or Catalina. As for the cousin, Luis did not name him. We know only that he was a *'primo'* rather than a *'prima'*: a male cousin, in other words. Presumably this little group chose somewhere safe to reveal their secret to Luis—a room in Francisca's house perhaps, or a field outside Medina—and once they were sure no other ears could hear, they began to speak. We do not know exactly what they said to Luis, but we can infer some of what they told him from the beliefs that he would expound as a young man, which were, as it happens, typical of the beliefs held by secret Jews in Spain and Portugal at that time.

To begin with they must have explained that although they appeared to live as Christians, in their hearts they followed the Law of Moses, just as their ancestors had done until 1492. After that they may have appealed to Luis on the basis of ancestral loyalty, and implored him not to break with their traditions. They undoubtedly told him that Jesus Christ was not the Messiah promised in the scriptures, as Christians believed, and that the true Messiah had not yet come. It was, and remains an irreconcilable division in Jewish and Christian thinking, and a belief that Luis would cling to as an adult. There is one other critical point that he repeated often in years to come and that his family almost certainly explained to him that day in Medina del Campo: that the Law of Moses was the only true path to salvation, and that if he wished to be saved he must follow it. Otherwise he faced the prospect of eternal torment in the fires of hell.

That dual anxiety about personal salvation and damnation comes from Christianity, not Judaism. The Jewish faith recommends that a virtuous life be lived for its own sake rather than as a means to reward after death, or as a way of avoiding brutal punishment. But Luis's family had been cut off from formal Jewish learning for many years and in their isolation they had inadvertently absorbed many of the teachings of the Christian world around them. They were not alone in their confusion. When the historian David Gitlitz was compiling his definitive work, *Secrecy and Deceit: The Religion of the Crypto-Jews*, about the clandestine Jews of Spain and Portugal, he found countless examples of liminal people like the Carvajales who saw themselves as Jews but shared the Christian fixation with heaven and hell, redemption and damnation. They believed that only one spiritual path could save their souls from eternal torment, and for them that path was the Law of Moses. Luis, like other secret Jews, believed this for the rest of his days.

He was a boy of eleven when he arrived in Medina and fourteen when he left, so he was somewhere in between when he learned his family's secret. The revelation should have frightened him, and perhaps it did, at the time. Yet when he wrote about it years later he said that 'God's truth is so clear and pleasant' that he had understood and accepted it without hesitation.

His family's decision to disclose their dangerous secret at that time suggests a conscious mirroring of bar mitzvah, that rite of passage when Jewish boys are called to read the Torah in the synagogue to demonstrate their moral awareness and sense of responsibility. But whether inspired by lost tradition or innate caution, early adolescence seems to have been the moment when mothers like Francisca sought to reclaim their children for their faith.

Francisca could not have read the ancient Jewish scriptures that Christians refer to as the Old Testament. The Bible was still forbidden to lay people in much of Europe at that time, and although translations into various vernaculars existed, they had been banned and were consequently hard to find. The only volume Francisca could have got her hands on was the Latin translation St Jerome had made eleven centuries earlier from the original Hebrew and Greek. She had no Latin, however, so she could not have read it anyway. Yet, in spite of these obstacles, she seems to have remembered the commandment to Jewish parents laid down in chapter 11 of Deuteronomy: 'And ye shall teach them your children . . . in thine house, and when thou walkest by the way, when thou liest down, and when thou risest up.'

Francisca, and parents like her, must have needed great patience as they waited for a safe moment to tell their children that Jesus was not the Messiah promised in the Hebrew Scriptures, and that the Law of Moses was not obsolete, as the Church of Rome insisted. While they waited they had to hope and pray that when the time came their children would accept what they told them and not denounce them to the Holy Office, even though the law obliged them to do so. In the case of the Carvajal family, Luis's older brothers had probably experienced moments of disclosure just like his. Neither left an account of what took place, but the paths they chose in life suggest that they responded very differently to what they heard: Balthasar embraced the Law of Moses; Gaspar rejected it. At thirteen he left his parents' home in Benavente to enter the Dominican monastery in Salamanca. He was expelled within a few months. After that he tried for the Franciscans in Medina del Campo. They too expelled him, and later, in Mexico City, when he told the Holy Office about those rejections, he attributed them to his Jewish ancestry.

Gaspar often sounds like the loneliest member of his family. He wanted no part of his parents' secret faith, and they had no legal means of forcing him to adopt it. Yet like many New Christians he found it hard to make his way into the Catholic fold.

•

The right to choose or change our religious faith, or choose no faith at all, is such a cornerstone of secular liberal democracy that it is easy to forget that our ancestors did not enjoy this freedom if they happened to live in sixteenth-century Christendom; that for them to follow a faith other than the one the state had sanctioned was to walk a dangerous path. When young Luis embraced the Law of Moses in Medina del Campo he chose that path. By the very act of choosing he became a heretic and a traitor in the eyes of his society.

There were many categories of heretic during that violent age of faith when Luis lived. The nature of one's heresy depended on the kingdom or principality in which one lived, and which mode of Christian faith it deemed legitimate. That could change from time to time. These were the years of Reformation and Counter-Reformation when you could be condemned as a Protestant heretic in Catholic England, a Catholic heretic in Protestant England, a Lutheran heretic in Catholic Bavaria, an Anabaptist heretic in Switzerland and the Low Countries.

The Iberian world, as always, was different. There, where the three great Abrahamic faiths had lived side by side for centuries, and where Protestant influence was slight, the role of heretic and enemy of the state had fallen to the many 'New

Christian' converts from Judaism and Islam. The fact that baptism had been pressed on these reluctant proselytes did not excuse them in the eyes of the ecclesiastical and secular authorities. Technically they were Catholics, which meant that if they returned to their former religious observances they could be accused of Judaising or Islamicising, and suffer the consequences, as thousands did.

Within the space of one day, therefore, perhaps even just one hour, young Luis became both a Christian heretic and a secret Jew. It was a perilous double burden for a boy to adopt, for if fear of heretics has a long lineage in Christianity, hatred of Jews is even older. Some Catholic theologians, like Rosemary Radford Ruether in *Faith and Fratricide*, have argued that Jew-hatred is a foundation myth so essential to Christianity that it can never be eradicated. So when Luis accepted the Law of Moses in Medina del Campo he shouldered an additional strain of prejudice that Lutheran, Catholic and Anabaptist heretics in other parts of Europe did not have to face: the ancient prejudice that echoes through the syllable '*Jude*' that lies beneath the label 'Judaiser'.

Fortunately the society in which he lived did not yet know what he had done, because after that Day of Atonement in Medina del Campo he assumed the double life his mother, his brother, his sister and his cousin had been leading for some time. Everything was different for him from that point on;

not so much because of what he did, but because of the way he thought about himself. He could not go to synagogue or attend a rabbinic school as he might have done if he had lived a century earlier. There were none. And he was not permitted to search the scriptures for clues to his ancestral faith because he was neither a monk nor a priest and had no access to the Bible. On the outside nothing changed. In church and at school he recited the Catholic prayers he had said every day of his young life—the Apostles' Creed, the Lord's Prayer and the Hail Mary—but in his heart and mind he turned away from Christianity and committed himself to the Law of Moses.

He may have sensed before that day in Medina del Campo that his ancestors had been Jews. Ever since those waves of forced conversion in 1391 and 1492 Jewish ancestry had become a commonplace in ostensibly Christian families. But as far as we can tell Luis knew no Jewish prayers at that time. He certainly did not know that Jewish boys were expected to be circumcised; that knowledge would come to him much later. The things he learned about the Law of Moses in Medina del Campo concerned the domestic realm of women rather than the masculine world of the synagogue. He understood for the first time why his mother and sisters used olive oil instead of pork fat in their cooking; why they removed the blood and sinew from the meat they cooked, lit candles and dressed in festive clothes on Friday evenings, placed clean linen on the beds, and kept the next day's meal warm overnight in a pot above the fire so that they could abstain from work on their Sabbath. He would also have understood why his mother and sisters did none of these things if Christian guests were present.

This was the interior life he and his family lived in their home in Rua Salamanca and it is possible that Luis questioned Balthasar about it, quietly and carefully, as they made their way through Medina's streets to school each day. Meanwhile, on Sundays and Holy Days of Obligation, when he heard the church bells ring, he walked to mass. During Lent he appeared to fast like a good Catholic boy, and in spring he celebrated Holy Week in public, while at home with his family he was secretly observing Passover, which often falls around the same time.

It must have been an anxious existence. Francisca remembered fleeing Portugal with her mother and her grandmother when she was a little girl; one of her own daughters would recall her talking about their escape. Francisca also knew that the Holy Office had pursued other members of her extended family in Portugal: all those names on little squares of paper threaded onto string in the Lisbon archives. Her grandmother, her aunts and uncles and cousins had all survived, and some had settled in Medina after their release from the Holy

Office jail in Évora. But the memory of their experiences remained with them, and Luis would later recall that as a child he sometimes heard his parents talk of leaving Spain and going to a community in Italy or France where they could live openly as Jews.

Many of the 'forced ones' had followed that path during the decades after 1492. They had made their way to Jewish communities in Venice or Ferrara or Lyon, or to cities in the Islamic world like Salonika or Constantinople. Luis believed his parents had thought of doing the same and perhaps they might have done, if Francisca's older brother had not returned from the New World at the end of 1579 and come looking for her in Medina del Campo.

He was yet another Luis—Luis de Carvajal de la Cueva. At forty he was a year older than Francisca, but they had seen little of each other since their childhood days in Portugal. She had fled Mogadouro with their mother and grandmother when she was four; he had stayed on there until, at the age of eight, their father took him to Spain. At nine he had been apprenticed to his great-uncle in the slave trade on the Guinea coast, and later, as a young man, he had found his way to the newly conquered land we now call Mexico. He had made his name there by capturing a fleet of English pirates and fighting the Chichimeca people of the north as they struggled to resist the Spanish invaders. In return the Spanish Crown had made him governor of the Chichimeca realm. It stretched as far north as San Antonio in present-day Texas and, as conquerors tend to do, the Spaniards named it after a province in their own country—*La Nueva Reina de León*—the New Kingdom of León.

Francisca's brother is still remembered in those northern parts of Mexico. A bronze statue of him looms above the Avenida Constitución in the city of Monterrey and he stares into the distance, a giant man on a giant horse. His chin rests on one hand, in the other he holds his horse's reins, and his iron helmet is by his side. He looks massive, indestructible, and he had every reason to feel invincible late in 1579 when he came clattering on horseback into the plaza at Medina del Campo with his young adjutant at his side. It was a scene taking place in many parts of Spain at that time, as long-lost sons and brothers returned from across the sea with tales of hardship, adventure and, for the few lucky ones, riches.

The governor—we shall call him that to distinguish him from young Luis—found his way to his sister's house in Rua Salamanca. Whether he knew or suspected that she was a secret Jew is never clear. He would always deny having known; when the time came he would also deny his Jewish ancestry. As a young adventurer he had adopted an Old Christian identity in order to make his glorious way in the New World, and he had no intention of letting his undesirable past rob him of the wealth and power he had gained.

Given all this, Francisca must have adjusted her domestic habits while her brother and his adjutant were guests in her house. Perhaps she cooked with pork fat instead of olive oil. She may even have served pork and bacon at her dinner table. And if she and her family dared to observe the Sabbath they would have done so with great care, in order to conceal their forbidden faith. The governor spent seven days with them, and during his stay he suggested that they return with him to New Spain. After that he set off for the royal court in Toledo, leaving them to consider what to do. Should they go with him to the unknown world of New Spain, or make their way to a Jewish community in Italy or southern France, as they had often thought of doing? Yet another generation of Carvajales faced a troubling choice.

They probably knew that in the Italian states they would be permitted to live openly as Jews, go to synagogue, observe their dietary laws and circumcise their infant sons. They would pay a heavy price for their religious freedom, however. Jews were tolerated in cities like Venice and Ferrara, but only just, and that precarious tolerance could vanish without warning. Francisca and Francisco had no doubt heard about the recent expulsions from Bologna and Savoy, about the growing unrest in Ferrara, and the restricted life of the Venetian ghetto. They would certainly have known about the degrading sumptuary laws that compelled Jewish men to wear yellow hats and badges, and Jewish women to place ornate earrings in their ears, like prostitutes.

Compared with these indignities and uncertainties the governor's proposal must have seemed quite promising. It offered Francisca and her husband an escape from the turmoil of the Old World. If they went to New Spain with the governor they would have to continue their duplicitous existence, but they had never known any other way of living. And besides, in the New World they would enjoy comfort and security, possibly even luxury, beneath the protection of a high Crown official.

There are moments in the Carvajal story when, looking back at them across the centuries, we wish that they had chosen a different path to the one they did. This is one of those moments. Francisca and her husband accepted the governor's offer, and in May the following year, as spring was beginning to warm the icy plains of Castile, they said farewell to Medina del Campo. They travelled slowly south to Seville, the departure point for ships leaving for the Americas. They had nine children now. Francisca had given birth to two more infants, Anna and Miguel, in Medina, and all nine were going with them to the Americas.

It was, however, a time of grief for their eldest daughter Isabel. Her husband had died a few months earlier, and in her sorrow she cut off all her hair and announced that she wanted to enter a convent. Perhaps Isabel was not yet committed to the Law of Moses; or simply wanted to be left alone, in solitude, to mourn the husband she had loved and lost. In any case her father, Francisco Rodríguez, refused to let her become a nun. He insisted that she go with them and so, with her cropped hair and her broken heart, she prepared to leave for the New World.

While they were waiting in Seville for their ship to be made ready, Isabel became close to her aunt, the governor's wife, doña Guiomar Nuñez de Rivera. At some point in their many conversations doña Guiomar confided to Isabel that she observed the Law of Moses, but the governor did not know her secret and would probably kill her if he found out. Despite this doña Guiomar worried about his spiritual welfare, and as she was not going with him to the New World she asked Isabel to do her best to persuade him to follow the Law of Moses. Isabel promised her aunt that she would try. She pledged that when they reached the New World she would find a way to warn the governor that if he did not return to that law nothing would go well for him. And she promised to convey the same urgent message to the governor's young adjutant, who happened to be doña Guiomar's nephew.

Meanwhile, in the world beyond Seville, momentous events were taking place. Felipe II, the king of Spain, was making a concerted effort to win the Crown of Portugal, to which he had a legitimate claim through his mother, who had been a Portuguese princess. In August 1580 he succeeded in his quest and the twin kingdoms of the Iberian Peninsula were joined beneath his rule. This new dynastic union unleashed a fresh wave of persecution against *Judeo-conversos* in Portugal. Many fled back across the Duero River into Spain in the hope that life would be safer there. They were tragically wrong. Their increasing presence in Castile and Aragon upset the fragile calm of previous decades and provoked a renewed burst of inquisitorial activity there as well. But, by the time those new terrors began, the Carvajal family had turned their backs on the Old World and its prejudices and were on their way to the other side of the Atlantic.

## 3

# THE PLACE OF OTTERS

THE GULF COAST OF MEXICO CURLS UPWARDS LIKE A LEAF TOWARDS
Texas and the shores of Louisiana. In September 1580 the
ship carrying the Carvajal family to their life of hope in the
New World made its way along that coast to the mouth of the
Pánuco River. There the air was nothing like the dry, clear
air of their homeland in Castile. It was warm and moist and
salty and a foreign wind bent the palm trees to the ground,
causing their little ship to strain at its moorings.

They disembarked at Tampico. This was nothing like the
great and exuberant seaport that Tampico has now become;
in the sixteenth century it was a small, uneasy outpost. It
had begun life as a Franciscan mission, but by 1580 that
spiritual quest had faltered and the village had been taken

over by Spanish settlers and their African slaves. Sultry rain fell constantly in Tampico. Mosquitoes, frogs and serpents flourished in its marshes and otters slithered from its river banks—the name *Tampico* means 'place of otters' in the Huastecan tongue indigenous to these parts. The haemorrhagic fever that Native Americans called *cocolitztli* or *matlazáhuatl* was raging the year the Carvajales arrived, and out beyond the township's barricades, in the region the Spaniards called Pánuco, the still unconquered Chichimeca people, whose land this was, lay in wait for the invaders.

Luis would later write that when his parents saw what they had come to they reproached the governor for bringing them to such an alien shore. They had little choice but to accept their fate, however. They moved into a rudimentary timber house in Tampico and said farewell to their eldest son, Gaspar, who was leaving them to pursue his own separate life, as he had in Spain. Gaspar went south down the gulf coast to the port of Veracruz, then up through the mountains to the former Aztec capital of Tenochtitlán. It was now an emergent Spanish city known as *México* in an allusion to the Culhua-Mexica, or Aztecs, who had built it, and Gaspar apparently hoped to enter the Augustinian monastery there. But instead, he became a Dominican once more. And this time he was not expelled.

Meanwhile, back in Tampico, the governor began the task of trying to take control of the vast New Kingdom of León over which he was meant to preside. He headed out into the hinterland, towards the beautiful Sierra Madre Oriental, and he took Luis and Balthasar with him. The Luis we shall later come to know through his writings and his trial transcripts seems such a spiritual person that it is strange to think of him galloping across the plains with a sword and dagger and harquebus, sleeping rough beneath the stars and pursuing the people he always called 'the savage Chichimeca'. But that was how he spent his adolescent years in Mexico, and the governor, who had no children, seems to have treated him as his heir and protégé, and loved him like a son.

Two years after the Carvajal family's arrival in the New World the Christian calendar changed from the Julian to the Gregorian count with the loss of several days. This strange and sudden restructuring of time would have made it more difficult than ever for them to keep track of the Jewish ritual calendar. It must also have added to the sense of alienation they felt in their wild frontier home.

Luis wrote later that his parents could not forgive the governor for bringing them to a place of such desolation and exile. Their resentment seems to have simmered beneath the surface for some years, however, without ever quite erupting; until the day arrived when Isabel decided to keep the promise she had made to her aunt in Seville. She had vowed to persuade the governor back to the Law of Moses. She tried, and her actions exposed a hidden fault line in the Carvajal family that once revealed was never able to be closed.

Several of the family members involved in this incident later described what happened. The governor said he was sitting in his sister's house, praying from his Book of Hours, when Isabel approached. She asked to speak with him. He assented. She said she had something to tell him that he must promise to keep secret. He promised he would. 'Christ never existed,' she told him, 'and if you wish to be saved you must do so through the Law of Moses.' The governor leapt from his seat and struck Isabel. 'She fell to the floor,' he said, 'and I charged towards her, to kick and kill her. I called her an enemy of God and the saints, and demanded to know who had taught her such a thing.' The trembling Isabel replied that her husband had taught her before he died.

When Isabel herself described this episode she said that as the governor leapt at her he pressed his hands over his ears and shouted that she was a disgrace to her lineage. 'I tried to tell him that I was fulfilling a promise to his wife,' Isabel added, 'but he would not listen, and so he never knew who had told me to say those things.' Meanwhile Francisca, her husband Francisco, and their younger daughters Catalina and Mariana heard the shouting and rushed into the room to find Isabel cowering on the floor and the governor standing over her. Francisca said he was pulling at his beard 'like a fierce lion' and shouting that no greater ill had befallen him than this. Catalina said he was calling Isabel a traitor. Mariana said he was threatening to kill Isabel and shouting that if her husband had taught her the Law of Moses, he must be burning in hell.

What happened next? According to the governor, Francisco asked him what had caused the uproar and he, still seething, had replied, 'She said that Jesus Christ had never existed, and that if I wished to be saved, I must do so through the Law of Moses.' A pause. Francisco had looked at him and said, '*Y vuestra madre?*' And your mother? Another pause, a stunned silence, as the governor understood what his brother-in-law was insinuating: that his own mother, Catalina de León, had observed the Law of Moses.

The governor had been very small when his mother fled Portugal to escape the inquisitorial tribunal in Évora. He and his father had joined her in Spain when he was eight, but soon after he had gone to the Guinea coast with his uncle and had never seen his mother again. He had hardly known her, but the path their family had followed, from Spain to Portugal and back to Spain, was a typically Jewish trajectory at that time. The governor would have known this. He would also have known that in Spanish, the language he spoke each day, the word 'Portugués' had become a synonym for 'Jewish' because so many Jews had settled in Portugal in 1492. Given all these signs it would be strange indeed if he had never wondered about his mother's religious allegiances.

Isabel's comment that he pressed his hands over his ears when she tried to tell him about the Law of Moses is interesting. It suggests that what angered him most in their encounter was the voicing of a suspicion he could not bear to hear. But whatever the governor knew or did not know, he told Francisco, 'My mother was a good Christian, and if anyone says anything different he is lying.' With that he had pulled on his boots and spurs and stormed from the house.

We know about these conversations—about who said what to whom, and where and how and why they said it—because some years later the family members involved in them were questioned by the Holy Office in Mexico City, and as they gave their separate accounts of what had happened in Tampico, the Holy Office scribes, those constant witnesses, recorded what they said.

It is difficult to know exactly when this violent argument took place between the governor and Isabel. It must have been before the end of 1583, however, because Francisco Rodríguez left Tampico late that year and never returned. Whenever it occurred, it placed the governor in a difficult position. He was duty-bound to report Isabel to the Holy Office tribunal in Mexico City. But how could he report her? Family loyalty aside, the suggestion that his niece, his brother-in-law, his wife and even his own mother might have observed the Law of Moses would destroy the Old Christian facade he had invented in order to stake his claim in the New World. The governor could not denounce Isabel. Instead he removed himself from the scene, and any semblance of harmony between himself, his sister and her husband was shattered forever. He saw little of them after that. 'Just now and again, from year to year,' Isabel said.

The governor kept his distance from them, but not from his nephews Luis and Balthasar. They continued to ride with him and one day when they were crossing the plains Balthasar confided in the governor that he had some doubts about the sacrament of communion and the nature of the consecrated host. He asked what he should do about those doubts. He was testing, perhaps, to see whether Isabel's words had made any impression. But the governor had no intention of entering this theological quicksand with his nephew. 'Go and denounce yourself to the Holy Office,' he told Balthasar, and the two of them were estranged from that day on.

Luis made no such dangerous overtures to his uncle. Instead the governor broached the subject with him. It happened one day when the two of them were riding with a company of men towards the village of Cuzcatlán. The governor suggested that they ride ahead. They galloped forward together and when they had left the other men behind the governor asked Luis, 'Do you know that your father lives in the Law of Moses?' Luis began to weep. 'Yes,' he sobbed, 'and it is a great evil.'

Relieved, the governor told him, 'Well, that is why I love you more than all your brothers and sisters. Because you know that your father tried to deceive me into returning to the observance of the Law of Moses, but the Evangelical Law that Our Lord Jesus Christ gave us is the true one; and look how the popes, kings and wise men of the world observe it, and every one of them desires to save his soul.' Soon after this they reached Cuzcatlán and parted there. The governor headed for the villages of Tamapache and Luis returned to Tampico.

Several years would pass before the interrogations took place from which we learn about these conversations. Meanwhile the Carvajal family suffered a profound loss.

Towards the end of 1583 Francisco Rodríguez de Matos left Tampico on a business trip and Luis, who went with him, later described what happened. 'I came to Mexico City with Indian slaves that my father brought to sell, which occupied us for a year, because six months later my father became ill.' Francisco did not survive his illness. He died in Mexico City early in 1584. Luis washed his father's body. Then he and several friends carried it to Gaspar's monastery in the Plaza de Santo Domingo, and buried Francisco there, in consecrated ground.

Luis was eighteen when his father passed away. He left the city and returned alone to Tampico to mourn with the rest of his family, and in the tearful aftermath of Francisco's death he bought a Bible from a priest for six pesos. By law the priest should not have sold this restricted text to an unordained youth like Luis and when Luis wrote about this purchase later, in his book of miracles, he still felt astonished that such a precious gift should come to him amid the sweltering heat and cruel mosquitoes of Tampico.

The volume Luis acquired was a copy of St Jerome's translation from Hebrew and Greek. Luis had no interest in the New Testament. He knew his best hope of recovering his ancestral faith lay within the books of the so-called 'Old' Testament. He opened his second-hand volume and saw, *'In principio creavit Deus caelum et terram'*: 'In the beginning God created sky and earth.' That first line of Genesis marked a beginning for Luis, too. With the help of the Latin the Jesuits had taught him in Medina del Campo he began his life's work of discovering what he could about the Law of Moses.

He read on, and in chapter 17 of Genesis he learned for the first time about the covenant God had made with Abraham in ancient times. He learned that God had commanded Abraham to circumcise himself in order to seal that pact, and had warned that any uncircumcised male child in Abraham's household would be cut off from his people for having broken the covenant. Luis wrote later that his heart had been struck with terror as he read those words. He had not known until he came across that passage that if he wished to be a proper Jew he must be circumcised. Now that he knew he burned with desire to receive 'this holy sacrament'.

Judaism has no sacraments in the sense that Catholicism does; circumcision is an obligation—the symbol of a covenant, rather than a sacrament. Luis, who had never experienced Jewish communal life, knew nothing of this distinction, yet if we think about the circumstances in which he lived, we can understand why circumcision seemed a sacred act to him: not just because Christian religious concepts had influenced his thinking, but because for him circumcision required a solemn and conscious commitment to his faith. It was a commitment he made for himself at the age of eighteen, not one that others made for him in infancy, as in formal

Judaism. In any case, he wrote later in his book of miracles that he had leapt up from where he was sitting without even pausing to close his Bible. He found a pair of shears, rushed to the river bank and although the shears were blunt and worn he managed to slice off his foreskin until only a little flesh remained. He felt the pain, he bled, but he survived, and with that irreversible act of self-mutilation he expressed his eternal allegiance to the Law of Moses.

In March the following year his sisters Catalina and Leonor married. Their bridegrooms, Antonio Díaz de Cáceres and Jorge de Almeida, were wealthy New Christian merchants. They appeared at Francisca's door dressed in velvet clothes, with golden chains around their necks, and a troupe of loud musicians to trumpet their arrival.

Luis wrote later that the governor had been trying to marry his nieces off to men of his own choosing. He could do nothing to prevent their weddings to Almeida and Díaz de Cáceres however, because he was far from Tampico when they took place. Luis, who was with him at the time, shed tears of quiet joy at the news, for he had been secretly involved in the marriage negotiations. And when he heard that the gentile women of Tampico had described Leonor and Catalina as roses among thorns he wrote that they were roses indeed, even though their beauty was slight, because the Lord had blessed them with great virtue.

Catalina was twenty-one when she married and her husband, Antonio Díaz de Cáceres, was in his forties. Leonor, on the other hand, was only twelve and her extreme youth comes as a shock to us, especially when we know that her bridegroom, Almeida, was in his mid thirties. Yet early marriage seems to have been common among secret Jews like the Carvajales, not just in Mexico, but in Portugal and Spain as well. Francisca said later that she had been nine when she married her cousin Francisco Rodríguez. The fact that she did not bear her first child until the age of sixteen suggests, however, that juvenile marriages such as theirs were not expected to be consummated for some years.

The weddings of Catalina and Leonor improved the family's material fortunes. Luis wrote that his sisters now began to dress in silk and velvet gowns and wear golden jewels, whereas before they had walked about in bare feet and tattered skirts. More importantly, the marriages enabled them to say farewell to Tampico, which they had never learned to love. They went south to Mexico City. All of them, except Luis. He was not free to go because his uncle the governor still needed him in his wars of conquest against the Chichimeca. These courageous people had never ceased to fight for their land and liberty and their determination to resist the invaders seems heroic to us now. But Luis did not see them as we do. He regarded the Chichimeca as hostile, barbarous and savage enemies and wrote that he longed to leave their embattled territory. He stayed by the governor's side, however, for another year yet.

Mexico City in 1585 was not a small and wretched outpost like Tampico. It was a great metropolis of around one hundred thousand souls. Earth tremors shook it many times each day, the volcano known as Popocatépetl hurled frequent showers of ash into its streets, and the remains of the temples of Tlaloc and Huitzilopochtli were still visible in its central plaza. But Spanish houses and churches were rising amid the ruins of the Aztec city, and whereas in Tampico, the place of otters, Francisca had been one of just a few hundred Spaniards, in Mexico City she was one of fifteen thousand.

Yet she and her compatriots were still in the minority. A census taken ten years before her arrival shows that around eighteen thousand African slaves were living in the capital at that time and that the city's original indigenous inhabitants still made up the greater part of its population. Their numbers had fallen catastrophically since the Conquest sixty-five years earlier, however; and their scribes had developed a sinister new glyph to depict the diseases that now stalked them. That glyph expresses their tragedy with great poignancy: it shows a skull attached by a line to an upside-down Amerindian figure, dead or dying, and bleeding from the nose and mouth.

Francisca settled into the house of Antonio Díaz de Cáceres in the San Pablo parish of Mexico City, a few blocks south of the great central plaza. And at Christmas in 1587 her brother the governor arrived there as a guest. She had seen little of him since his fight with Isabel some years earlier. But that December they found themselves together again and one night, after everyone else had gone to bed, she went to his room and they talked for a brief and painful moment about the subject that had enraged him in Tampico.

'We were alone,' Francisca said when she recalled this incident later. 'He had just finished praying, and I asked him what he had prayed for.'

'For your conversion,' the governor told her, 'because ever since the incident with Isabel I have known that you observe the Law of Moses.'

'Pray for your own conversion,' Francisca had retorted. It sounds like a terse exchange, and it probably was. But she said that her soul had ached to see how blind the governor was because he was her only brother now. The other two had died years earlier, one in the Jesuit college in Medina, the other in the wilds of the Mayan realm. 'I had no other brother,' she lamented, 'and he was lost.'

Lost and blind, *perdido y ciego*. Blind to the truth of the Law of Moses, and lost to the Jewish fold. But to Francisca, a liminal woman shaped by two faiths, her brother seemed lost in the Christian sense too, which meant that when he died he would burn in hell.

Around the time that Francisca and the governor had their bitter late-night conversation, Isabel fulfilled the second part of the vow she had made to her aunt in Seville. She had promised to persuade the governor's adjutant, Felipe Nuñez, back to the Law of Moses. That Christmas of 1587 she tried, and in doing so she opened the door to disaster.

It happened one evening when Isabel found herself alone after dinner with Felipe. She asked him suddenly, 'In which law do you live?' The startled adjutant replied that he lived in the Law of Christ the Redeemer and intended to die in it, as his own parents had done.

Isabel told him that the Christian law was not a good law. She explained that her father had taught her something different, 'and all my brothers and sisters too, except the priest, who knows nothing of this'. She meant her elder brother Gaspar, the Dominican. She then proceeded to tell Felipe that Jesus Christ was not the Messiah, and that she and her family were awaiting the true Messiah.

'Be careful,' Felipe responded, 'because I believe in Jesus Christ Our Lord who came into the world, died and was resurrected in order to save us.' Isabel saw the danger she was in and quickly assured Felipe she had been joking in order to test his faith, but she urged him not to tell anyone else what she had said.

Felipe did what Isabel asked. He had no wish to denounce her and he kept her words to himself for as long as he could.

The rains came late in 1588. The maize crops failed, there was hunger in the capital, and *cocolitztli* returned to haunt the indigenous residents with its pain and unrelenting fever. But Luis had joined his family in Mexico City and his delight at being with them once again is evident in his book of miracles.

He recalled how one day he and Balthasar went to visit an elderly invalid they knew to be a secret Jew. The old man showed them a small notebook into which his doctor had copied verses from Deuteronomy. The invalid gave the precious book to Luis and Balthasar and from that day on they took to reading it with fervent devotion. But as they read they began to understand how far they had strayed from the true Law of Moses, and Luis said this realisation caused them to lament like a loving mother over the dead body of her beloved son. In response Balthasar decided that he too wanted to be circumcised.

They hired a razor from a barber. Balthasar fell to his knees and began to cut off his foreskin, and as he did he and Luis consecrated this act to the Lord, 'singing His praises and reciting the psalms of David'. Circumcision requires a steady hand however and the emotional Balthasar cut himself badly and began to bleed. He was in great pain but Luis didn't dare seek medical assistance. Instead he took Balthasar to an empty house belonging to their uncle, the governor, and tried to treat his brother's bleeding penis with salt and wine.

The salt intensified Balthasar's agony. In desperation Luis turned to a young friend 'who feared the Lord': a secret Jew like them, in other words. Luis was careful not to name this young man in his journal, but 'with God's help' the two of them managed to stop his brother's bleeding. Their uncle arrived, saw the bloodstained cloths, and asked what had happened. Luis said that he and Balthasar had disciplined themselves because this was the Lenten season and a time of penitence. He meant they had scourged themselves as many devoted Christians did at that time. The governor accepted their story. Whatever his suspicions, he had no wish to pursue this matter further.

•

After Balthasar recovered he and Luis began to talk intensely about the physician who had filled the invalid's little notebook with verses from Deuteronomy. His name was Dr Morales and they knew him because he had sailed with their family from Seville in 1580. He had settled in Mexico City but had felt unable to bear the counterfeit life he was obliged to live there. So a few years later he had returned to the Old World. Luis and Balthasar understood that he had settled in the Jewish ghetto in Venice, and they resolved that they too would leave for Italy and find a community where they could live their lives according to the Law of Moses.

They revealed their plan to Francisca. She gave them her blessing and they began preparing to sail in the first fleet leaving for Europe in the spring. But before setting out on their journey to the coast they decided they must talk to their brother Gaspar. They loved him in spite of what they saw as his spiritual blindness. Luis said they could not bear to leave him in that blindness, so they went to his monastery in the Plaza de Santo Domingo hoping to show him the error of his ways.

Luis recalled what happened in the journal he would eventually begin to write. He said they began by asking Gaspar whether it was true that Moses—'St Moses' they called him—had descended from Mount Sinai holding the tablets of the law on which the Lord had written his holy commandments. Gaspar said it was true and he took the Bible from among his books, found the relevant passage in Exodus and showed it to them. Luis read it in silence. When he had finished reading he looked up at Gaspar and exclaimed, 'So this is the law that we must keep!'

Gaspar understood all too well what Luis meant. He told his younger brothers angrily that while it was a good thing to read that law one should not observe it. 'It was once the Law of God,' Gaspar said, 'but it is finished now, superseded!' He was repeating the age-old Christian claim that the coming of Jesus had rendered Judaism obsolete, and tried to explain his case with a parable about a king who had a cape so threadbare that he eventually had to discard it and get another.

The three brothers fell silent. Luis said that through the window in Gaspar's cell they could see the orchard outside and the brilliant rays of the sun as it set below the horizon. It is strange to think that an orchard once lay at the heart of this great city, or that beyond it one could see the sun setting in the west. The sight was so enchanting that it inspired Balthasar to try once more to get through to his older brother.

'This cloak of the heavens and this shining sun that God created, have they changed, have they grown old?' he asked Gaspar.

'No,' Gaspar replied. Luis, who was watching him closely, believed that his older brother had seen the light in Balthasar's words, but Gaspar refused to give in, and who could blame him? To acknowledge the truth in Balthasar's beautiful analogy would have meant turning his world upside down, endangering the monastic career he had struggled so hard to achieve, and possibly even his life.

Gaspar tried to close the subject. 'Let us not talk about this anymore,' he said, adding, 'Blessed be the Lord for taking me out from among you.' Luis and Balthasar responded, 'May our Lord God be glorified for not leaving us in blindness and perdition like this miserable man.' And with that they left their 'sad and sightless brother'.

In the weeks that followed they returned to the monastery on several occasions in order to plead with Gaspar. But nothing they did or said could persuade him back to the Law of Moses.

Because we know that it will happen, and because we know about the risks that Isabel, Luis and Balthasar were taking throughout those years, their arrest seems inevitable. Yet it was not as certain then as it appears to be in hindsight. The Holy Office in New Spain was never very active in pursuit of secret Jews and the vast majority of its prosecutions were for blasphemy, bigamy and sexual misconduct by both laypeople and priests. The *Encyclopedia Judaica* notes that only around sixteen percent of inquisitorial trials in Mexico City were concerned with Judaising, that less than a hundred of those trials ended in executions, and that many of those 'executions' took place in effigy rather than in person.

So although in retrospect it can look as if the Holy Office deliberately pursued the Carvajal family, their trial transcripts tell a more frightening story: that there was no need to hunt them down, because people who live in fear and trepidation, as they did, will often incriminate themselves and others with little or no encouragement from the authorities. The transcripts also show that in the end it wasn't their reckless-ness or their profound religiosity that brought them to the attention of the Holy Office; it was the governor's political troubles that caused their downfall. If not for his quarrels with the vice-regal authorities the Carvajales' secret lives as Jews might never have been discovered.

The governor had been locked in battle with various viceroys for several years and should have known that this was one fight he could never win. The list of conquerors and explorers who flew too high and fell from grace in the eyes of the Spanish Crown was already strewn with far more famous names than his. Columbus, Balboa, Hernán Cortés, his son and heir Martín, and their kinsman in Peru, Gonzalo Pizarro, had all fared badly in the end. So it was with

Governor Carvajal. His difficulties began as a dispute over his jurisdiction in Nuevo León, and although it is sometimes presumed that his hidden Jewish ancestry must have caused his troubles, no firm evidence has come to light to prove that this was so. The evidence that does exist suggests a far more mundane explanation: that he did the wrong thing and the Spanish Crown punished him for it.

It was the question of slavery that brought things to a head. Almost fifty years earlier, when Spain had only just begun its conquests in the Americas, the Spanish Crown had proclaimed its New Laws forbidding the enslavement of Native Americans. Enforcing those laws had been a struggle from the first and Governor Carvajal was just one of many conquistadors who chose to flout them. He had arrived in the Americas with long experience in the slave trade. He had learned the business under the tutelage of his uncle and his father-in-law on the Guinea coast and saw no reason to stop this lucrative trade in humans now that he had reached the New World. The only difference was that he now bought and sold Native Americans instead of Africans.

The younger Luis never tried to hide his family's involvement in slavery, and although he often compared his own plight to that of the Hebrew slaves in Egypt, he does not appear to have felt any sympathy towards the Chichimeca he helped to capture and enslave. It is a common human trait, to be deeply attuned to our own sufferings yet blind to the sufferings of others. In any case, word of the governor's slaving activities reached the viceroy of New Spain some time in 1587. The Marqués de Villamanrique was the twelfth viceroy and whether he really cared about the Chichimeca or merely used their plight as an excuse for clipping the governor's wings is difficult to say. But his vice-regal role required him to maintain order in New Spain, and so on 8 August 1587 he sent a letter to the king, Felipe II, to report his concerns.

'Your Highness,' he wrote, 'I have been informed that Captain Luis de Carvajal, wanting to reduce some rebellious villages in the hills of Jalpa, being obliged to do so at his own cost and having no soldiers to go with him . . . gathered together forty men and promised them that they could make slaves of the Indians they defeated for a period of twelve or fourteen years.' It seems that the governor's ploy had worked. The men went with him to the rebellious villages, and when they got there over five hundred Chichimeca men, women and children had come out to meet them, requesting baptism.

These desperate villagers may have been hoping to avoid enslavement or slaughter, but if so their strategy failed. The governor had responded to their plea by executing eight of their leaders, and distributing the rest of the Chichimeca among his men. The viceroy told the king that in doing this the governor had separated fathers from their children, and husbands from their wives. He added that he had formally accused the governor of this criminal act and of provoking rebellion among otherwise peaceful natives. The governor claimed that he had now freed the Indians in question, but the viceroy did not believe him, so he requested the king's permission to punish Governor Carvajal, and liberate the people he had enslaved.

Communications were achingly slow in those times. The viceroy's letter was carried on the next fleet to Spain but a year passed before the royal permission he sought arrived. It came early in 1589, and when it did the viceroy dispatched his soldiers north to Nuevo León. They found the governor in the town of Almadén, near the present-day border with Texas. They brought him south to Mexico City and incarcerated him in the vice-regal prison on the great central plaza we now call the Zócalo.

Events move fast after that, like falling dominoes. The Carvajal documents in the Archivo General show that on the afternoon of 7 March 1589 the governor's adjutant Felipe Nuñez went to the Holy Office building in the Plaza de Santo Domingo. This was not the edifice that still stands beside the plaza today, but its predecessor, built from adobe and the rosy volcanic stone known as *tezontle* in the Aztec language.

'My name is Felipe Nuñez,' the adjutant told Inquisitor Santos García, who was in session that day. 'I am twenty-eight years old and a native of Lisbon, and I have come to report my concerns about a widow who is the niece of the governor of Nuevo León.'

Felipe explained what Isabel had said to him when she approached him at Christmas two years before. He said he did not know her name, and while that may sound odd to us, it is understandable given that the Díaz de Cáceres household was filled with relatives and servants, and Felipe was just a visitor there.

'How long have you known this woman's family?' Santos García asked.

'About ten years,' Felipe replied. 'I stayed with them in Medina del Campo but the woman was not with them at the time because she was living with her husband in Astorga. But I saw her later in Seville and in Pánuco and more recently in Mexico City.'

'Do you know the woman's brothers and sisters?'

'Yes,' Felipe said. 'They are Balthasar Rodríguez de Carvajal, who is single, Luis de Carvajal, single, and another younger boy of twelve or fourteen years. Also Fray Gaspar de Carvajal, the Dominican priest . . . and doña Leonor de

Carvajal, wife of Jorge de Almeida . . . and doña Catalina de León, who is married to Antonio Díaz de Cáceres . . . and doña Mariana, a young girl, and another little girl, Leonorica, or Anica, who is very young and lives with her mother, doña Francisca, which is where the widow is.'

'Where do the widow and her family come from?' Santos García asked. 'And what do you know about their caste and *generación*?' That word *'generación'* looks like a simple cognate for 'generation' and so it is in modern Spanish. But in the sixteenth century, in the context of an inquisitorial investigation, its meaning lay closer to English 'genus' and French 'genre', those terms for category and type that have come down to us from the Greek *'genos'*.

'I know that the widow's father came from somewhere near Benavente and had once served the Count of Benavente,' Felipe replied. 'I don't know where her mother was born, but they lived in Benavente for some years, and then in Medina del Campo. As for the family's caste and *generación*, I know nothing about it.'

'When the widow said the Law of our Redeemer Jesus Christ was not a good law, did she say which law was good?'

Felipe replied that she had not made any further comment about it, but some months later, when he was ill in Mexico City, she had sent him some chickens that seemed to have been slaughtered the way the Jews slaughter their birds.

'And during the time you have known this widow and her parents did you understand or hear it said that they had done or said anything against our Holy Catholic Faith?'

Felipe replied that he had heard nothing apart from what he had already declared.

In conclusion Santos García asked Felipe something he was obliged to ask every person who came before him to testify against another man or woman.

'Do you bear any hatred or malice against the widow, her parents or siblings?'

'In all my life I have never known anyone to whom I owe more, or for whom I have such love,' Felipe replied. He was thinking, no doubt, of Isabel's parents and the kindness they had shown him in Medina del Campo, and his response is perplexing, given that he had just betrayed them. 'I say these things in order to discharge my conscience, nothing more.'

Felipe signed the declaration he had made and Santos García instructed him to find out the widow's name. Felipe promised he would, but there was something else he wanted to say before he left.

'I have come from the kingdom of León to try to help Governor Carvajal who is a prisoner in the royal jail in this city, and whom I love very much and owe a great deal.' He went on, 'I have spent ten years in his company and have seen him live always like a good Christian.'

Felipe returned next day to report that he had learned the name of the widow in question.

'She is called doña Isabel,' he told inquisitor Santos García, 'and I think "de Carvajal" and her little brother's name is Miguel. And everything I have declared is the truth and I say it only in order to discharge my conscience.'

He said that he was leaving next day for the kingdom of Nuevo León but would return to Mexico City in two months.

Why did Felipe Nuñez denounce Isabel if he felt such deep affection for her family? He had clearly not been eager to report her, given the time that had elapsed since their conversation, and his reticence is understandable, not just because her parents had been kind to him in Medina del Campo, but because Felipe had no way of controlling what an inquisitorial investigation might reveal. What if it should emerge that his aunt in Seville had been a secret Jew? Isabel had no doubt told him this during their conversation. Silence had probably seemed the best response as far as Felipe was concerned. But then the governor was arrested, and his incarceration seems to have prompted Felipe to go to the Holy Office and report what Isabel had said to him.

Luis later provided an explanation for Felipe's conduct. In his book of miracles he wrote that Isabel was denounced by 'a heretic of our own nation to whom she tried to teach the divine truth'. So Luis believed that Felipe's ancestors had been Jews. If Felipe believed this too he may have considered it prudent, once the governor was arrested, to inform on Isabel in case word of their conversation should emerge from another source; from a servant perhaps, or even the governor himself, in whom Felipe had possibly confided. In any case, Felipe denounced Isabel, and went back to the northern plains and we never hear from him again. Whatever regret he might have felt is hidden from us. All we can do is read his testimony and try to infer from it what might have prompted him to act as he did.

Six days later the Holy Office issued a warrant for Isabel's arrest. It is still there in her trial transcript in the Archivo General: a yellowing parchment dated 13 March 1589, and signed by the prosecutor, Dr Bartolomé Lobo Guerrero. That same night the Holy Office notary took the warrant to the house by the canal gate where Isabel was living with her mother, her brothers and her unmarried sisters. He allowed her to gather a few belongings, and then he led her back to the Plaza de Santo Domingo and imprisoned her in one of the Holy Office cells.

Inquisitors Santos García and Alonso Fernández de Bonilla summoned Isabel to the audience chamber a few days later. They asked her if she knew why she had been imprisoned. She

ENTRANCE TO THE
FORMER HOLY OFFICE
BUILDING, MEXICO CITY,
JANUARY 2006.

replied that she believed her brother Fray Gaspar, her uncle
the governor and his adjutant Felipe Nuñez had denounced her
'because they understand very well that I observe the Law of
Moses'. She was mistaken; her brother and her uncle had not
denounced her, but they should have, given what they knew.
In her innocence Isabel had inadvertently incriminated them.

# 4

# CAPTIVITY

SPRING RETURNS TO MEXICO CITY AND IN THE HOUSE BY THE canal gate, in the street now known as Avenida 16 de Septiembre, Francisca and her family gather to talk in urgent tones about Isabel's imprisonment. There is nothing they can do to help her, but they must try to save themselves. Luis and Balthasar suggest they all flee together to the coast. It seems like a good plan but their friends warn that it will not work so Luis and Balthasar abandon it.

When Luis recalled this moment in his book of miracles he did not name those friends. He called them simply 'God fearers'. It was his code for secret Jews and, in this instance, he probably meant his brothers-in-law Antonio Díaz de Cáceres and Jorge de Almeida. They argued that the long and arduous journey through the mountains would be far too dangerous for Francisca and her daughters, and besides, they would attract the attention of the authorities if they tried to leave together. It was decided therefore that the young men of the family, Luis and Balthasar, would flee alone.

Luis said he did not know how to express the pain they felt as they prepared to leave their loved ones. But then he found the words. We parted, he said, 'with sorrowful cries and bitter tears and laments'. And like people everywhere who are torn apart by war and persecution, famine and poverty, they probably told each other that their separation would be brief, while fearing in their hearts that they might never meet again.

Luis and Balthasar rode out of the Valley of Mexico and up to the high, snowy pass between the volcanoes. From that elevated place beneath the clouds the instinctive thing to do is to turn and look down on the city far below. Perhaps the brothers did just that—took one last look—before beginning their journey east through the chain of high mountains that lies between Mexico City and the gulf coast. Luis left no description of their melancholy journey; but he later recalled that he and Balthasar reached the port of Veracruz in April, found a ship, and loaded their possessions on board. They were on the verge of escape, but once again they hesitated.

Earlier that year their love for their brother Gaspar had caused them to delay their departure. This time the thought of their mother, their sisters and their little brother Miguel alone and unprotected held them back. Luis wrote that although their ship was almost due to sail he decided to return to Mexico City to check on their welfare. Leaving Balthasar to wait for him on the coast, he saddled up his horse once more and rode back through the mountains.

Luis's instinctive sense that his family was in danger was correct. On 14 April, while he was making his way back along those steep mountain trails, Gaspar was taken into custody. The Holy Office constables led this eldest Carvajal brother from his cell in the Dominican monastery to a cell in the inquisitorial prison on the other side of the Plaza de Santo Domingo. That same night they arrested the governor too, and transferred him from the vice-regal prison on the central plaza, where he had been held since February, to the Holy Office jail.

Luis, who knew nothing of these latest arrests, entered Mexico City on 6 May. He waited three days before going to his mother's house in case the authorities might be watching it, but on the night of 9 May he took that risk and went to see her. She told him the terrible news about his brother and his uncle. Shattered by these latest blows Luis and Francisca sat down to take some supper and as they did they heard a loud knock at the front door. Luis ran to hide, while their Chichimeca maid opened the door. She found the Holy Office constables standing there. They had come for Francisca.

Luis, who listened from his hiding place, wrote later that at the moment of her arrest his mother 'donned the cloak of gentleness' and that even the constables were moved by her dignity and humility. He heard his sisters weeping and calling to their mother, 'Where are they taking you?' but Francisca did not or could not answer them. The drama was not yet over. The constables had brought a warrant for the arrest of Luis as well, which suggests they had indeed been watching Francisca's house. They searched the house, found him, and took him into custody too.

Luis tells us in his book of miracles that Balthasar returned to Mexico City that same night. He had not been able to bear the anxiety of waiting on the coast, so he had followed Luis through the mountains. When he learned about the arrests he found a room in the house of a friend and settled down to wait and pray and see what the Lord had in store for his mother and brothers.

Five members of the Carvajal family were now in prison—the governor, Gaspar, Isabel, Francisca and Luis. They made numerous appearances before the inquisitors during the months that followed, sometimes on the same day, but always alone, so that they could not hear each other's testimony.

The audience chamber was upstairs, above the jail. Inquisitors Francisco Santos García and Alonso Fernández de Bonilla sat behind a large desk of polished wood. Both were *hidalgos*: Spanish-born members of the lesser nobility, ambitious and well-educated. Men appointed as inquisitors in Mexico City never stayed long in their positions; the Holy Office usually served as a pathway to higher appointments within the Church, and so it was with these two. They would each move on and up to loftier positions as bishop of Guadalajara and archbishop of Mexico City respectively, but not for three years yet.

Their scribe sat at a small side table with his inks and quills, and as the governor, Francisca, Luis, Gaspar or Isabel spoke, he recorded what they said, filling the parchments on his desk with graceful loops and arcs that curl like ribbons across entire sentences. But, because he was diligent as well as stylish, we can read their replies and note the way their responses varied and changed over time.

Take for example that question about caste and *generación*. When the inquisitors put this routine query to the governor he declared without hesitation that his parents had been free of any stain of the race of Jews or Moors, 'or of any other newly converted sect', and he held to his story for the remainder of his imprisonment. At Francisca's first hearing she said, 'I am a Christian, whom God has raised, and I don't believe I have any Jewish or Moorish blood.' A few hearings later, however, she admitted that she did indeed bear that undesirable 'stain'. Luis said, 'From what I have heard, we are Old Christians, without descent from Jews or Moors, or any other sect.' Isabel said much the same.

Only Gaspar did not try to hide his Jewish ancestry. When asked about his caste and *generación* he replied that his father was a New Christian descended from Jews, and so was his mother; 'I think she is also from the same caste, of New Christians of Jewish ancestry. Or so I heard in Spain, and that is what I understand.' He added that he believed his Jewish ancestry had caused his expulsion from the Dominicans in Salamanca and the Franciscans in Medina del Campo.

Inquisitors Bonilla and Santos García summoned Luis to his first hearing on the afternoon of 12 May, three days after his arrest. 'My name is Luis de Carvajal,' he told them. 'I was born in Benavente in the kingdom of Castile. I am twenty-two years old and single . . . I live in Mexico City in my mother's house, from where they brought me to the cells on Tuesday night.'

They ordered him to relate his family history.

'My mother is Francisca de Carvajal,' he said, 'and my father was Francisco Rodríguez de Matos. I do not know the names of my paternal grandparents, but my mother's parents were Gaspar de Carvajal and Catalina de León and they died in Benavente.'

Luis did not mention that all four of his grandparents had been born in Portugal, perhaps because he feared the Portuguese connection would suggest a Jewish past. But he said he knew of two paternal uncles, one who had died 'in this New Spain', the other in Portugal. He added that his mother also had two brothers. One had lived in Guatemala, 'and they say he died in that land'. The other was the governor of Nuevo León. 'And I don't know any other uncles.' He did not name Domingo, the youthful Jesuit uncle he had never known. He told the inquisitors that he had three brothers—Fray Gaspar de Carvajal, 'a priest in the order of Santo Domingo', Balthasar Rodríguez de Carvajal and Miguel Rodríguez—and five sisters, whose names were Isabel de Carvajal, Catalina de León, Mariana de Carvajal, Leonor de Andrada and Anna, known as 'Anica', 'a little girl of nine years old'.

The inquisitors asked whether he was a baptised and confirmed Christian.

'I am,' Luis said. 'A bishop in Benavente confirmed me, although I do not remember his name.'

They told him to recite his prayers: another standard inquisitorial practice.

Luis went down on his knees and recited the Our Father, the Hail Mary and the Apostles' Creed in Latin. He followed them with the Articles of Faith and Commandments of God in Spanish. When he had finished the judges told him to relate the story of his life.

'I was born in Benavente,' he said, 'where I was raised in my parents' house. I learned to read, write and count there until the age of eleven when we went to live in the town of Medina del Campo, and I spent three years there in the Society of Jesus, studying Latin and rhetoric. And after that, my uncle the said Luis de Carvajal having come to this land, we came too, in his ship, along with the viceroy, the Count of Coruña. We disembarked—my parents and brothers and sisters—at the port of Tampico in the province of Pánuco and we lived there, in Tampico and Pánuco, for five or six years, and then my sisters doña Catalina and doña Leonor were married and came to live in this city.'

Luis said he had assisted his uncle in governing Nuevo León. After that he had spent some months in the silver mines of Taxco, in the Mixteca country, and in Oaxaca in the south. 'And I have been in no other part of New Spain except, in the past, in Zacatecas and Michoacán, while coming from the kingdom of León and I have not been in any other foreign kingdoms, nor studied more than I have said.'

'Do you know why you have been arrested?' the inquisitors asked.

'I don't,' Luis replied, 'but I presume it is because of the governor, my uncle, who is a capital enemy of my family because of the many arguments between him and my parents since the day he brought us here, deceived, from Spain, and because of which we are now poor and lost. And if my arrest is not due to my uncle, it must be because some enemy has given testimony against me.'

The inquisitors read Luis the first of three formal admonitions they gave to all their prisoners. They warned him that the Holy Office was not accustomed to arresting people without evidence that they had done or said things that were or seemed to be contrary to the Holy Catholic Faith, 'whether it be the rites and ceremonies of the Old Law of Moses, of the Jews, or of the sect of Mahoma or of Lutero,' meaning Mohammed or Luther. It followed that as Luis had been arrested, information of this sort had been given against him. Therefore, out of reverence for God, he should speak the truth and discharge his conscience. They assured him that if he did this he would be granted the mercy that the Holy Office was accustomed to grant to 'its good and true confidants . . .'

Their offer of mercy was not disingenuous. First offenders in the category of heresy had to be given a second chance, provided they confessed and promised to return to the Catholic faith.

'I understand very well what you have said,' Luis replied, 'but neither in speech nor in deed have I committed anything against the Holy Catholic Faith, nor do I have anything to confess, although it could be that because of my great sins someone has given testimony against me, perhaps my uncle, with his great hatred . . . and I don't have anything else to declare.'

His hearing was drawing to a close but certain practical matters required attention. The inquisitors asked Luis what security he could give to cover the costs of meals and other essentials during his imprisonment. He explained that he had nothing to offer because the goods that he and his brother traded belonged to their mother. The inquisitors told him to return to his cell, search his memory and speak the truth the next time he appeared before them. They ordered him to keep silent in the jail, and not shout to other prisoners. Luis promised to obey. He read and signed the transcript the scribe had made. Then the guards returned him to his cell.

•

Next morning Luis appeared again before the inquisitors. They asked about his movements in recent months.

He told them that in April he had been passing through Xalatlalco, seven leagues from Mexico City, when he learned that the viceroy's men had arrested his uncle, the governor, who had then been transferred from the royal prison to the Holy Office cells. When he heard this he had galloped straight to his mother's house in Mexico City to find his brother Balthasar. They had discussed their concern that their uncle might give some kind of testimony against them and had resolved to flee to the gulf coast. From there they would sail to Havana, and find passage back to Spain.

He described their journey to Veracruz and the fears for their mother and sisters that had prompted him to return to Mexico City. He added that he had not received any letters from Balthasar since then. 'And neither I, nor my mother, have written to him.'

The inquisitors asked if anyone in Veracruz could verify that he had been there in April.

'You could speak with the mulatta,' Luis suggested, 'the widow called Isabel de la Cruz, in whose house we lodged.'

And to help prompt the widow's memory, he provided a description of himself and Balthasar.

'Balthasar is twenty-six years old,' Luis said, 'with a good build, a white face, and a thin, blond beard. He wears a wide-brimmed hat, a blue cape, green and blue clothes, rides a tall, dappled horse and carries a sword.

'And I am twenty-two years old. I have a white face, a sparse beard, and I wear the same clothes. I am of medium build.'

White faces, sparse beards, blue and green clothes. It is the only description we have of them.

After Luis had returned to his cell the inquisitors wrote to their colleagues in Veracruz. Search all the inns for Balthasar de Carvajal, they told them, and when you find him, arrest him and convey him to our cells in Mexico City.

The scribe took their letter down to the dispatch rider waiting in the courtyard below. The courier saddled his horse and set out for the coast along the same precipitous and icy trails Luis and Balthasar had taken in March.

Luis, in his cell, knew none of this. The following Monday he was summoned for a third time. The inquisitors asked him whether he had recalled anything more.

'I have not remembered anything,' he said, 'and there is nothing I can say.'

They cautioned him a second time, repeating their warning about the forbidden rites and ceremonies of the Law of Moses, of 'Mahoma' and 'Lutero'.

He replied that from the beginning he had said all that he could say, 'and I have neither done nor said anything, nor seen anything done against the faith . . . and I believe this misfortune, this *mal*—' he meant his imprisonment '—has been caused by my uncle out of the enmity he bears towards me.'

With that they returned him to his cell with the usual warning to scour his memory and speak the truth when he appeared again before the tribunal.

June came, and with it early summer, but no more deadly *cocolitztli* for the moment. Hummingbirds and butterflies returned to the Valley of Mexico and the breezes blowing off the snow-capped volcanoes to the east of the city refreshed those residents who were free to walk through the streets and plazas. But Luis de Carvajal was not free. He lingered on in his cell and as far as we can tell he was alone throughout that time.

His conditions were probably not as bad as they would have been in a European prison. One former inmate of the Holy Office cells in Mexico City told her sister that they were like bread and honey compared with those in Portugal. The Holy Office in Mexico City was only twenty years old. Its adobe prison was damp and its floors were made of earth, but some cells had windows, and during a subsequent imprisonment Luis would tell his sisters that he could see out into the patio. The cell walls were so soft and porous that prisoners could poke holes in them, pass notes and whisper to each other.

The Mexican historian Solange Alberro, who has made a careful study of life in the cells beneath the audience chamber in Mexico City, notes that the ration sheets in the Archivo General de la Nación show that prisoners were reasonably well fed. Chocolate, still a curiosity in Europe, was a common beverage in its homeland of Mexico, and prisoners were served hot chocolate mixed with sugar, cinnamon and chilli. They ate quince paste prepared by the nuns of the city, bread, cheese, raisins, eggs and fruits of the New World like zapotes and avocados. There was a catch; on their release the prisoners were billed for the rations they had consumed. But, if one had the money and wanted to survive, the expense was worth it.

Nevertheless, the prisoners' world was 'agitado', to use Solange Alberro's term: a noisy, anxious space in which inmates spent their days and nights in clandestine communications, trying to decide what to say during their hearings. The uncertainty and angst about whether to confess and ask for mercy or stand firm and deny everything could consume a prisoner's every waking moment. And if, as in the case of Luis de Carvajal, you were not the only member of your family to be imprisoned, you had to try to imagine what your mother or your sister, your uncle or your brother might be saying each time they went upstairs to the audience chamber.

A month passed. On the afternoon of 19 June the inquisitors summoned Luis once more.

'What kind of injurious information did you and your brother fear your uncle might give about you?' they asked.

'About nothing in particular,' Luis told them, 'just out of enmity.'

They said they could not see why there was such enmity between him and his uncle, and why he feared false testimony.

Luis said he had replied as best he could in order to prove his innocence.

'And he did not say anything more,' the scribe noted.

The inquisitors asked what Luis had heard about his uncle's arrest.

'I heard it said to Balthasar, my brother, that my uncle had been arrested by the Inquisition, and taken out of the hands of the viceroy.'

They asked, 'And why did you fear that while imprisoned in the Inquisition he would give false testimony against you?'

'I feared his enmity,' Luis responded.

Speak the truth, they cautioned him.

'We imagined it all,' he said, 'as we didn't know for certain, and we suspected that if perhaps he was arrested it might have been for something against the faith, or for having done or said something to other persons, and being imprisoned and afflicted he might want to take vengeance against me and my brother.'

'Well, why would he want to take vengeance in matters that affect the Holy Office, rather than others?'

'Because he was brought to the Inquisition; for no other reason,' Luis replied.

'Why did you and your brother flee Mexico City when you saw your uncle arrested?' they asked him yet again.

'Because of the fear I described,' Luis said, 'and because we feared his malice at that time and not before.'

They asked, 'Do you know of any other people who have been arrested by the Holy Office?'

'I know about my mother doña Francisca de Carvajal who was arrested the same night I was,' Luis replied, 'and my sister Isabel de Carvajal who was arrested two and a half months ago; and I don't know of any other persons.' He knew very well about his brother Gaspar, but for some reason he pretended he did not.

They asked what he and Balthasar had talked about in Veracruz, and why Balthasar felt so much more fearful of their uncle than Luis did.

'Because the hatred was greater and went back further, with my brother,' he replied.

'And why did Balthasar, your brother, not return to Mexico City with you?' they asked.

'Because he was to wait until I advised him about the imprisonment of the said governor. But I didn't advise him because then I was arrested.'

They issued a third warning about the forbidden rites of the Law of Moses, of Luther and Mohammed.

When they had finished Luis declared that he had not seen or heard anything and that God would reveal his innocence and openness, because he feared nobody except the governor. With that the guard returned him to his cell.

He remained there for the next two weeks, until 4 July when they summoned him again.

'Have you remembered anything?'

'No, I have nothing more to say.'

They explained that as he was less than twenty-four years old they had appointed a guardian for him from among the Holy Office lawyers. Luis watched as his guardian swore to defend him well, faithfully and diligently. Then the judges returned him to his cell.

Three weeks later he appeared again before the inquisitors. It was 27 July, his sixth hearing, and he noticed an unfamiliar figure in the audience chamber. The Holy Office prosecutor had come to present his indictment against Luis.

There may have been a shuffling of parchments, a clearing of throats, as Dr Lobo Guerrero stood to read his accusation. The scribe recorded only that when he spoke it was to announce his belief that Luis de Carvajal was a baptised and confirmed Christian who had committed apostasy against the Catholic faith by returning to the rites and ceremonies of the Old Law of Moses.

Dr Lobo Guerrero told the judges he had evidence that Luis had washed the body of someone close to him who had died, and that such washing was a ceremony of the Law of Moses. He said Luis was well read in the Old Testament, and cited its prophets 'whenever occasion presents itself, particularly Isaias'. He added that Luis's pious enthusiasm for those prophets had led him to believe that Jesus Christ was not the promised Messiah. Nor did he believe in the Holy Trinity.

The prosecutor submitted that Luis had fled with his brother to Veracruz because the Holy Office had arrested his sister Isabel, and he feared that he too would be arrested. Furthermore, Luis had perjured himself, 'keeping quiet about other crimes and about others whom he knows are Judaisers and live in the faith and observe the said Law of Moses'.

Dr Lobo Guerrero concluded on an ominous note. He asked that if the case he was preparing against Luis was not well proven then Luis should be tortured 'until he confesses the truth'. He also recommended that if Luis were found guilty as charged, he should be released—*relaxado*—to the secular authorities so that they might punish him as an example to others.

We know from Luis's later writings that he doubted his capacity to withstand pain. As for 'release to the secular arm', it meant he would be executed. Ecclesiastical authorities throughout Western Christendom were careful never to associate themselves directly with death sentences, on the basis that the Church should not be seen to have blood on its hands. Whether in Spain or England, France or Portugal, men and women found guilty of heresy were released to the secular authorities for execution. In England, for example, the heretic hunter and eventual saint Sir Thomas More deplored the number of heretics granted leniency when, in his opinion, they should have been 'left to the secular arm'.

It is an expression that Cervantes used to comic effect when he had the priest in *Don Quixote* turn three of the sad knight's chivalric novels over 'to the secular arm of the housekeeper'. But there was nothing funny about Luis's predicament, and he would have understood the menace in that mundane-sounding phrase. Yet all was not lost. The offer of clemency remained and he could have chosen this moment to confess and ask for mercy. The transcript shows that he kept his nerve, however, and when he spoke it was to repeat his protestations of innocence.

'It is true that I am a baptised and confirmed Christian,' he declared, 'but I deny the rest because I have not done or imagined any such things; and on the question of caste and *generación*, I believe I come from Old Christian stock, although it is possible I have been deceived in this.'

He denied there had ever been heresy in his actions. He told the inquisitors that although it was true he had washed his father's body after death, he had no idea it was a Jewish ceremony. He had done it simply in order to get rid of the stench.

He rejected the claim that he was well read in any prophet, and said that although it was true he had questioned his elder brother Gaspar about the mysteries of the Holy Trinity, he did this in order to enrich his devotion to the Law of Our Lord Jesus Christ, not because he doubted its truth.

Luis insisted that his story of the journey to the coast was just as he had told it; he and Balthasar had not fled because they feared the Holy Office, but because they feared their uncle's enmity. As for ceremonies of the Law of Moses, he was adamant that there had been none.

'Nor have I done anything to anyone,' he concluded, 'and I trust in Our Lord Jesus Christ.'

'With this,' the scribe wrote, 'having been warned to scour his memory about the prosecutor's accusations and speak the truth, he was ordered to be taken to his cell.'

Five days later the inquisitors sent for Luis again. They told him he should have a learned lawyer to help him respond to the accusation, and asked him to choose between two advocates. He chose the lawyer who had been appointed as his guardian three weeks earlier.

When Luis returned to the audience chamber two days later his lawyer was present. Holy Office lawyers did not function as defence lawyers do in Western courtrooms today. Their role was not to defend prisoners against allegations against them, but to encourage them to repent and ask for mercy. So Luis's lawyer and guardian counselled him to speak the truth for the sake of his conscience, as well as for the defence of his case.

Luis responded as he had done at every hearing since his arrest in May.

'I am a baptised Christian,' he said, 'and I don't have anything more to say apart from what I have declared in my confessions, because although I have scoured my memory I don't recall anything more . . .'

The scribe recorded that at this point the prosecutor entered the audience chamber to announce that he would soon present the testimonies of several witnesses to support his case against Luis. Luis would have guessed that his imprisoned family members were among those witnesses. He had no way of knowing what they had said about him, however. It was something he would have to think about as he prepared himself for the next hearing.

'And with this,' the scribe wrote, 'the prisoner was warned and ordered to be taken to his cell.'

# 5

# ACTS OF FAITH

LUIS WAS NO LONGER ALONE. IN JULY ANOTHER PRISONER—
a defrocked Franciscan—was placed in his cell. The inquisitors
told Luis that as he looked so sad and emaciated the Franciscan
would provide him with company. In reality they probably
hoped the disgraced monk would spy on Luis and encourage
him to confess, but if this was their plan it did not work. Luis
wrote later, in his book of miracles, that he and the Franciscan
quickly became close friends.

Luis never named the Franciscan in his journal. He
called him simply 'a Franciscan' or 'the monk' or 'this good
foreigner'—'este buen estrangero'. Why foreigner? He and the
monk had both been born in Spain, but Luis, who considered
himself a Jew, probably meant 'gentile'. The monk's name was

in fact Francisco Ruíz de Luna, and although his trial records are missing from the archives in Mexico City fragments of information about him have survived in other sources. Prisoners had to be fed, for example, and the money spent on their rations had to be recorded in order to be recovered later. The ledger sheet for Francisco Ruíz de Luna is still in the archives in Mexico City and it shows that he was arrested on 27 June 1589 and received two hundred and forty-five days' worth of ordinary rations.

The Chilean historian José Toribio Medina unearthed a few more details about the Franciscan when he was preparing his *Historia del Santo Oficio de la Inquisición en México*. Medina learned that the Franciscan had served in the Spanish province of Valencia and later in Nicaragua. However he was using false ordination papers obtained in Italy and when his superiors discovered this early in 1589 they expelled him from the order. Investigations into priestly misconduct formed a major part of the work of the Holy Office, so in June he was arrested, and a month later he was placed in Luis's cell. It was a happy encounter for both men. Luis had been longing for a book of psalms, and the monk brought just such a book with him. It was a breviary, the little book of daily prayers carried by every monk and priest and nun in Catholic Europe. The Franciscan lent it to Luis, and Luis gave thanks to God for this profound kindness.

Luis wrote in his book of miracles that they spent the next eight nights in long and impassioned conversation about religion, and that on one of those nights, after he had been fasting all day, Luis had a dream that stayed with him for the rest of his life. He described it like this: a vial of sweetest liquid appeared to him in his cell and in his dreaming state he understood that the liquid was divine wisdom. He sensed that Solomon, 'the wise king', was also present in the cell and he heard the Lord tell Solomon to take a spoon, fill it with the liquid, 'and give it to this boy to drink'. Solomon had then put a spoonful of the sweet liquid into Luis's mouth. Luis drank it and felt so filled with consolation that he forgot about his imprisonment and the danger he was in.

The inquisitors knew nothing about Luis's dream, or his deepening friendship with the Franciscan. But on the morning of 7 August the jailer told them that Luis had requested a hearing. Such requests from prisoners often meant they had decided to repent and make a full confession. The inquisitors ordered Luis to be brought before them. He climbed the stairs behind the jailer and as he entered the room he fell to his knees, beating his breast, kissing the floor and weeping. The scribe recorded that he cried out, 'I have sinned, mercy, mercy.' The inquisitors ordered him to get up off his knees and sit down. He did what he was told, and when he had composed himself he began to speak.

'God has inspired me,' he said, 'although I deserve to be condemned for my guilt and have battled all these days with the Demon who would not let me confess or say or declare the truth which is . . . that here in Mexico City, six or eight months before he died, my father Francisco Rodríguez de Matos spoke to me about the Law of Moses of the Jews, telling me that this was the path to follow if I wished to be saved, because that Law had been given by God's hand, and if I want to find salvation I would achieve it that way . . . and I, as a young person, was frightened of this new idea and replied that it seemed like a hard thing to do because all the wise men of the world observe the Law of Jesus Christ. So I asked my father what he would say if I followed both Laws and he responded, "No, you can only follow the Law of Moses," and I, having respect for my father, said to him that I would do this; and so from that time on I have been in this error, although with great remorse to my conscience that kept speaking to me and telling me to confess, of which I have repented well and truly.'

In the book of miracles Luis would later write he said that it was his mother, his sister, his brother and his cousin who introduced him to the Law of Moses, and that they did this in Medina del Campo when he was eleven or twelve. So why did he attribute his conversion to his father when he described it to the inquisitors? No doubt in order to protect the living members of his family.

He continued, saying that after his father's death he had returned to Pánuco in the northern kingdom of Nuevo León to see his mother and siblings, and when he told Francisca, Isabel and Balthasar what his dying father had revealed to him they admitted that he had taught them the Law of Moses too. From that day on, Luis said, the four of them often talked together about the Law of Moses and about the true Messiah they were awaiting who would gather together the dispersed people of Israel.

Luis described the day when he and Balthasar had visited Gaspar in his monastery and tried to convince their elder brother that if God had given the Law to Moses then that was the Law they should all now be following. He described how Gaspar had leapt from his seat insisting that the rites of the Law of Moses were the rites of the devil, and they should pray for divine forgiveness. Finally, Luis admitted that when he and Balthasar fled to Veracruz it was because of Isabel's arrest, not the governor's.

'That is the truth,' he concluded, 'and with this I have nothing more to say except that I acknowledge that my guilt and my sins are grave, and that they do not deserve pardon.'

'And he said this with many tears and sighs,' the scribe added, 'asking, while kneeling, to be given penance with mercy.'

Luis continued his confession on Wednesday and Friday that week. He told the inquisitors about the Bible he had purchased after his father's death, and how within its pages he had read all the prophets, especially Ezekiel and Esaias, 'and all the prophecies relating to the promised Messiah, because I believed he had not yet come and that Jesus Christ was not him'.

He recalled the way his mother and his sister Isabel had observed the Sabbath each week from Friday evening until Saturday night by wearing clean, festive clothes and placing clean linen on their beds. He said they tried to avoid eating bacon and pork products, although this was not possible when they were guests in Christian households. And he described the feast days he had learned to observe, such as Passover, 'the Day of Penance' and the fast of Queen Esther, which he never called 'Purim', probably because he did not know that word.

He said his father had told him that their family belonged to the people of Israel. 'And that I and those who observe the Law of Moses are the Chosen People of God and descendants of the Israelites, and that all of us are descended from

Abraham, Isaac and Jacob.' His father had explained also that his own parents and grandparents had been Jews.

'My father did not say their names,' Luis continued, 'because he was a reticent man; only that they were born in the town of Mogadouro, in Portugal, close to Benavente. And he also told me that my mother, Francisca Nuñez de Carvajal, is descended from the same Jews of Israel.'

Luis told them about how his uncle the governor had asked him years earlier whether he knew that his father lived in the Law of Moses, to which Luis had replied that it was a great wickedness. He admitted that when he and his brother fled to Veracruz it was not just because Isabel had been arrested, for they felt certain she would not reveal them as Jews. They had indeed feared their uncle, because some years earlier Balthasar had confided certain doubts about the Holy Catholic Faith to him, and the governor, in anger, had threatened to denounce him to the Holy Office.

Luis said that after his father died Gaspar had asked him whether Francisco had requested and received the sacraments, and whether a cross had been placed above his bed. 'And he asked these questions with such curiosity,' Luis explained, 'that I thought it possible Fray Gaspar knew or suspected that our father observed the Law of Moses.'

He added that he didn't know for certain because Gaspar had never really declared his suspicions. 'Nor do I know whether he knew, the way the governor did.' Luis was doing his best to protect his eldest brother.


Luis returned to the audience chamber that Saturday. They asked him whether any other people were present in the house when he, his mother, his sister Isabel and brother Balthasar celebrated the Jewish feasts he had described.

He said his other sisters and his younger brother Miguel had been there along with his brothers-in-law, two black women and some Indian slaves, but none of them knew anything about the Jewish observances taking place.

'We were very guarded and cautious,' he said, 'and stopped when other people entered.'

His answer was almost certainly untrue. Catalina, Leonor and Mariana would later say they did take part in those observances and they would describe them in careful detail. But in August, when Luis made this statement, he was trying to protect them too.

'How long have you been in the keeping, belief and observance of the Law of Moses?' the inquisitors asked.

'It has been five years, more or less,' Luis replied, 'since the day my father began to teach me, until the Day of Transfiguration of Jesus Christ just passed, when the Lord enlightened me and converted me to the Evangelical Law, as if all my heart burned with fire. And I left my belief in the Law of Moses and determined to confess the truth, as I did the following Monday. Until then I couldn't rest without feeling that live flames were coming from my heart.'

The afternoon was drawing to a close. They asked Luis which law he now believed in. He fell to his knees, pressed his hands together and replied that he had now abandoned his belief in and observance of the Law of Moses.

'With the grace of God,' he told them, 'I want to believe in Our Holy Catholic Faith . . . and to live and die as a good and faithful Christian.'

Inquisitors Santos García and Fernández de Bonilla listened to this emotional declaration. When Luis had finished they assured him that although his sin had been great and he deserved to be condemned for it, he could have confidence in the mercy of God. But they wanted him to search his memory further for any information about persons 'present, absent, alive or dead' who had strayed to the forbidden Law of Moses.

'In tears,' the scribe wrote, 'he said that he has done so and will search his memory and speak the truth of what he remembers.'

Two days later they sent for Luis again.

'Have you recalled anything relating to your cause?'

'No,' he replied.

They showed him the transcript of the statements he had made throughout the previous week. He read it and declared that it was accurate. The inquisitors returned him to his cell. It was Monday 14 August 1589, and the prosecutor, who had been present throughout this hearing, announced that he accepted Luis's confession.

A trial could not be concluded unless a prisoner formally ratified his or her confession. So twelve days later the inquisitors summoned Luis to the audience chamber for that purpose. They had invited a panel of 'honest and religious persons' in the form of two Dominicans to act as witnesses as they asked Luis whether he agreed with what he had declared and deposed about other people in his confessions to the Holy Office.

'I do,' he said, 'because it is the truth.'

The prosecutor, Dr Lobo Guerrero, was there. He announced that he would use Luis's testimony to prove that Francisca and Isabel had been Judaising, and that Gaspar and the governor had failed to denounce them. But the inquisitors had one more formality to complete before the ratification could be accepted. Just as with Felipe Nuñez back in March, they asked Luis whether he had spoken out of hatred or enmity. It was a question they put to all witnesses and confessants. But this was Luis's first inquisitorial trial and he sounds puzzled, even hurt, by the suggestion that he could act with malice towards his own family.

'How could this be, Señor,' he asked, 'when they are my mother and my sister and brother? I don't say it for any reason other than to tell the truth.'

On 20 October, a Friday, the prosecutor presented the testimonies he had gathered against Luis during the preceding months. Gaspar, Francisca and Isabel had all testified that he was secretly devoted to the Law of Moses. Luis wept as their words were read to him, knowing as he listened that like him they had chosen to confess rather than die. Or perhaps he wept to think that he lived in a world where mothers could be made to testify against their sons, and sons against their mothers and beloved sisters. Whatever the reason, he assured the inquisitors that he had told the truth and had nothing more to say.

'And I ask that you use mercy with me,' he implored them, 'taking into consideration that as a boy of a young age I was led astray by my parents who impressed that bad Law of Moses on me as a tender person . . . and I believed them readily, an error I now understand and I know for certain that it was an error and that the true Law in which I must save myself is the Evangelical Law of Jesus Christ in which

I wish to live the rest of my life, and die in, as a good and faithful Christian, after first doing serious penance for the great sin I have committed against Our Lord Jesus Christ and his Divine Law.'

The scribe wrote, 'And with this the prisoner was warned and returned to his cell.'

Was Luis's transformation genuine? The inquisitors thought so. In November they met with their advisers on the Council of the Inquisition to determine his fate, and all five members voted for mercy. They would offer Luis reconciliation to the Church in a ritual act of faith: an auto-de-fe. But he must forfeit his goods to the Holy Office and spend the next four years in a monastery to receive instruction in the Holy Catholic Faith. Throughout that time he would have to wear a penitential habit over his clothes—the shameful and conspicuous 'blessed sack', or sanbenito, of yellow wool with two St Andrew's crosses embroidered on it in red—so that everywhere he went people would know he had committed an act of heresy and apostasy.

Luis's ordeal was almost over, but his mother's was not. Francisca had confessed soon after her arrest in May that she observed the Law of Moses. But she had refused to admit that her children observed it too, and on 10 November her denials

FIRE & SONG

led her to the torture chamber. Luis, who had gouged a small hole in his cell door with a mutton bone, watched her pass by in the corridor and wept when he saw where she was going.

Francisca was stripped to her undergarments, fastened to the rack, and made to endure six wrenching turns of the cords. At the final turn she told her tormentors, 'I don't know what to say except that I am sad to have been born from my mother's womb. My fate is misery and my old age is wretched.' The inquisitors told the guard to loosen the ropes and take her from the rack to recover a little. When she had rested for a few minutes they ordered him to take her close to it again. She stood beside the apparatus. They warned her to speak the truth and this time she broke down.

'I am not the only member of my family to observe the Law of Moses,' she admitted. 'My husband kept this law, and all my sons and daughters observe it too, except Gaspar.'

Later, when Luis described his mother's ordeal in his journal, he said that he had heard it all, and her cries caused him greater suffering and bitterness than anything he had endured to that point. Suffering, bitterness and possibly something else that he did not articulate; shame and remorse, perhaps, to think that while he had confessed in August, she had held out longer and had tried so hard to protect her family.

His sister Isabel endured a similar fate three weeks after Francisca. During her second hearing in March Isabel had confessed that her husband, her aunt in Seville and her father had taught her the Law of Moses: all of them were conveniently deceased. She had refused to implicate any living members of her family. On the morning of 27 November inquisitors Santos García and Bonilla took her to the torture chamber too.

The torturer gave one turn of the ropes. The scribe wrote that Isabel uttered great cries, and after that she began to speak. She kept on talking, as if trying to hold them at bay with her long answers. If so her strategy worked. She suffered one more turn of the ropes, but no more after that. Fear had produced the desired effect, as it usually did. She admitted that her mother Francisca and her brothers Balthasar and Luis had also taught her the Law of Moses. After that the guard returned her to her cell.

In December, as winter returned to Mexico City, Luis's brother-in-law Antonio Díaz de Cáceres left the house he shared with Catalina and headed for Acapulco on the Pacific coast. From there he set sail for Manila.

Eight years later he admitted fleeing because he knew Catalina and her sisters were about to be arrested. How he knew is unclear. It is possible that he had a paid informant in the Holy Office. In any case, the day after his departure

Catalina and her sisters Leonor and Mariana were duly taken into custody. Anna, who was only nine, was removed to the house of the Holy Office scribe, Pedro de los Rios, to be cared for while her family was in prison. As for ten-year-old Miguel, his whereabouts at this stage is uncertain.

During their hearings Catalina, Leonor and Mariana said that they knew nothing about their caste and *generación*, but admitted having observed the Law of Moses for many years. Catalina, who was twenty-four, said that her aunt in Benavente had introduced her to it by teaching her a psalm of David. This may have been true. Or she may have been naming a dead person as her teacher in order to protect her living relatives.

The sisters described the feasts and fasts they were accustomed to observing, such as Passover and 'the feast of Queen Esther'. They meant Purim but never used that term. Seventeen-year-old Mariana said that during Passover, 'which falls in Holy Week', they gave thanks to God for freeing the people of Israel from captivity in Egypt. She recalled how in Tampico her brother Luis had bought a Bible, translated passages from it into Spanish and read them aloud to her and her sisters.

Leonor, who was just sixteen, described the foods she had been taught to avoid, such as pork and bacon, and the feasts and fasts her family had observed. Like her sisters she expressed a keen desire to live as a Christian from now on, and follow the teachings of the Holy Mother Church. Like them she was given a second chance.

Winter mornings in the Valley of Mexico are cold and shim-meringly bright. But sometimes fog obscures the sun, and on mornings like these the temperature plunges and the chocolate sellers, flower vendors, street sweepers, even the police officers, huddle together at braziers to warm their hands and talk about their hopes and their uncertainties.

We do not know whether the residents of Mexico City awoke to fog or sunlight on 24 February 1590, the day chosen for the auto-de-fe, but the weather would not have troubled the Holy Office. The historian Miguel Avilés, who has made a careful study of autos-de-fe, tells us that the inquisitors could always interpret the weather conditions as propitious. If the day turned out sunny, he writes, they might comment that heaven and earth conspired to its brilliance. If rain fell they would say the abundant water accentuated the gravity of the procession. Or they might observe that the crowds, 'their eyes flooded with fervent tears', were so moved by the occasion that heaven joined them with its own unceasing deluges.

At first light that morning—St Matthew's Day according to the Catholic ritual calendar—the members of the Carvajal family were given the prescribed breakfast of wine, bread and honey to sustain them during the long day ahead. Then they were led from their cells to the patio of the Holy Office building. Luis had glimpsed his mother's and sisters' shoes from time to time through the hole in his cell door as they passed by in the corridor—or thought he had—but this was the first time he had seen their faces since May the previous year. They stood together dressed in conical hats and penitential habits. They could not touch or embrace, but may have cast furtive glances at each other.

Gaspar did not join them on the patio. Although monks and priests accounted for a substantial proportion of inquisitorial investigations they were excused from public acts of repentance on the grounds that their appearance might bring the Church into disrepute. But the governor was there, a fallen conquistador in his ignominious yellow sanbenito, and so was the defrocked Franciscan who had shared Luis's cell. When all was ready they were led out with the other penitents into the Plaza de Santo Domingo.

This pretty square has altered little since that morning in 1590. Stone pillars line its western side, and the monastery where Gaspar lived, and where he and Luis had buried their father's body in 1584, still occupies the plaza's northern edge. Francisco's body was no longer in its grave; the Holy Office constables had dug up his remains and placed his bones in a casket to be carried in procession to the auto-de-fe along with an effigy in his likeness. It was essential that unrepentant heretics be publicly condemned and their bodies obliterated, even if they were deceased. Later that day the secular authorities would burn Francisco's effigy and his remains in a public place, for all to see.

The Carvajal family members began their slow march—the so-called 'procession of infamy'—to the Plaza Mayor, carrying long green candles in their hands. Green was everywhere that day: in the Holy Office banner fluttering at the head of the procession, and in the tall, painted cross that had been erected inside the cathedral where the auto-de-fe would take place. Green was the emblematic hue of the Holy Office because it signified hope, ironic as that might seem to us now.

Nothing in the physical space and setting of an auto-de-fe was left to chance. It was intended as an enactment, almost a rehearsal for the Last Judgement, and its purpose was to inspire awe and terror in the hearts and minds of all who witnessed and took part in it. A high wooden platform divided into right and left sections had been constructed inside the cathedral. The inquisitors, the prosecutor, the secular authorities and the city's dignitaries, including two kinsmen of Hernán Cortés, the city's conqueror, sat on the right. The sinners, as we would expect, sat on the left.

The ritual began with a celebration of the mass. After that the notary called each penitent, one by one, to the special pulpit that had been erected at the front of the platform. 'Is Francisca Nuñez de Carvajal here?' he called. Francisca made her way to the front and stood listening as her crime of Judaising was made known to the congregation. Then she swore an oath of abjuration. 'I, Francisca de Carvajal, abjure, detest, renounce and withdraw from all and any heresy . . .' Isabel, Catalina, Mariana, Leonor and the governor did the same. So did the disgraced Franciscan. They were all *reconciliados* now.

When Luis's turn came he rose to his feet, a thin pale figure in his yellow sanbenito. He walked down the passageway between the left and right sections and, with the help of his lawyer and guardian, he began to speak.

'I, Luis de Carvajal, abjure, detest, renounce and withdraw from all and any heresy, especially that for which I am notorious and to which I have confessed: the Old Law of Moses, its rites and ceremonies.' He told the congregation that he spoke with a pure and truthful heart, and now desired to live and die in the Law of Jesus Christ. 'And I swear to Our Lord God and the four sainted evangelists, and by the sign of the cross, to be obedient to the blessed St Peter, Prince of the Apostles and Vicar of Our Lord Jesus Christ, and to our very saintly father Sixtus the Fifth, who today governs the

Church, and his successors after him.' Luis asked everyone assembled there to be his witnesses that if at any time he should relapse into his former heresy, he would be cursed and excommunicated. He signed his name to his oath of abjuration.

'And with this,' the scribe wrote, 'the said Luis de Carvajal was absolved in form.'

The Carvajal family's imprisonment in the Holy Office cells was finally over. Four days later the warden led Luis out into the Plaza de Santo Domingo once again. They walked west for several blocks until they reached the hospital and convent of San Hipólito. It had been constructed thirteen years earlier from stone retrieved from fallen Aztec temples, and this elegant building still stands beside the busy Hidalgo metro station, across from the Alameda gardens. These days couples like to sit in the cloisters around its patio and listen while musicians serenade them with guitars and mandolins.

But San Hipólito held no charm for Luis de Carvajal in March 1590. He had been told he must spend the next four years there, performing the duties of a sacristan and receiving daily instruction in the Catholic faith. His mother and sisters, meanwhile, had been consigned to house arrest in the parish of Santiago Tlatelolco. He felt the pain of separation from

FORMER HOSPITAL DE
SAN HIPÓLITO, MEXICO
CITY, JANUARY 2006.

them very deeply and, later, when he recalled his time at San Hipólito, he said that he had washed its floors with his tears.

Luis never saw his uncle again, nor his brothers Balthasar and Miguel. The governor had denied his Jewish ancestry throughout his trial and insisted that he came from Old Christian stock. When the inquisitors told him that his sister had admitted observing the Law of Moses he said that in that case someone other than their parents must have taught her, because he knew his mother and father had been good Christians. At the auto-de-fe the governor had been sentenced to perpetual exile from this land he had helped to conquer.

Two days later the vice-regal soldiers returned him to the royal jail, and he died there a few months later while waiting for the ship meant to carry him into exile.

Balthasar disappeared once the auto-de-fe was over. He knew now that his family had survived and would eventually be released, but he was still a wanted man, and it was time to leave New Spain. So one night when it seemed safe to do so—perhaps when there was no moon and the streets were especially dark—he left his hiding place in Mexico City. Luis received a message through one of their friends to say that Balthasar and Miguel had left the city and were heading for the coast.

A few days later he learned that they had been captured and he wept at this terrible news. But then word came that 'the good cargo' had arrived at a safe port after all. Balthasar and Miguel had reached the Gulf of Honduras. They had found a ship whose captain was an 'Israelite', and were on their way to Spain, from where they hoped to journey onwards to a Jewish community in Italy. When Luis recalled all this in his journal he did not say who had brought this happy news to him, only that he was overcome with joy and gave praise to God, 'for He is good and supreme . . . and His mercy is infinite'.

•

Luis continued to feel God's mercy. A few months after he began his penitential term at the Hospital de San Hipólito, the Holy Office notary came to tell him that he was to be transferred to the house in Santiago Tlatelolco where his mother and sisters were living. It seems that Luis's brother-in-law Jorge de Almeida, young Leonor's husband, had persuaded the inquisitors that while he was away on business Luis should join Francisca and her daughters temporarily, in order to protect them.

We do not know how Almeida managed this. He was a rich man who enjoyed the power and influence rich men enjoy in most societies and it is possible some money changed hands. The inquisitors would not have called it a bribe. They might have called it a 'redemption fee', like the one that penitents had to pay in order to be freed from their sanbenitos—except that in Almeida's case no fee would be recorded.

Whatever it took, whether persuasive words, money or both, Almeida arranged for Luis to join his mother and sisters, for a while at least. And Luis, who sensed God's hand in every joy and sorrow he experienced, set out for Santiago Tlatelolco, giving thanks to the Lord for this new and unexpected blessing.

# 6

# THE BOOK OF
# MIRACLES

WHEN LUIS ARRIVED IN SANTIAGO TLATELOLCO HE ENTERED THE Indian part of the city, but he never called it by its Nahuatl name, not in writing anyway, perhaps because 'Tlatelolco' was too difficult for his European tongue. He called it simply 'Santiago'. It was a name he had known since childhood: Santiago the Apostle, Santiago the Moor-Slayer, Santiago the patron saint of Spain.

Luis and his family were free to leave their house. They had no guards to restrict their movements because the penitential habits they were obliged to wear in public encased them in a portable prison. They wore them when they attended mass to take communion. They wore them when they walked beneath the stone columns that lined Tlatelolco's plaza at that time, and whenever they crossed the square to buy oil and bread, fruits and vegetables at its famous marketplace.

The conquistador-chronicler Bernal Díaz del Castillo, who had been one of the first Europeans to see it seventy years earlier, had described the market like this: 'And when we arrived in the great plaza which is called "Tlatelulco" we admired the great multitude of people and merchandise there and the great sense of harmony and order in everything.' Bernal described the gold and silver, the jade and turquoise, the feathers and plumes, the woven blankets, the skins of deer and otters and 'lions and tigers'—he meant jaguars and pumas—that he saw for sale in Tlatelolco's plaza.

Bernal also noticed stalls piled with curious foods he had never seen before: chocolate, tomatoes, avocados, pumpkins, chillis, beans of all kinds, pineapples. He saw strange birds he called *'gallos de papada'*—roosters with jowls, or turkeys—and slaves the Aztecs had captured in the distant realms beyond their city. 'I tell you that they bring so many of them to that great plaza to sell,' he wrote, 'the way the Portuguese bring black people from Guinea.'

Tlatelolco had changed by the time the Carvajal family went to live there in 1590. The city's indigenous inhabitants still bought and sold their wares at its marketplace, but plague and eruptive fevers had decimated their communities. The burning sickness they called *tlatlacistli*, possibly influenza, broke out the year Luis arrived. They perished in their thousands, but he, like most Spaniards, remained untouched.

The house where his mother and sisters lived is gone now, but Luis said it stood close to the Church of Santiago that still dominates Tlatelolco's great plaza. The house had a high brick chamber where they kept statues of Jesus Christ, the Virgin Mary, Mary Magdalene and other saints to demonstrate that they were faithful Christians. And downstairs, at ground level, there was a passageway lined with large earthenware

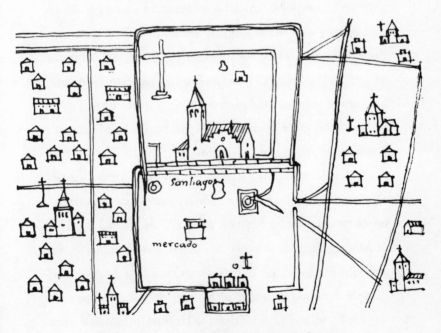

SIXTEENTH-CENTURY SKETCH OF PLAZA IN SANTIAGO TLATELOLCO. ATTRIBUTED TO CARTOGRAPHER, ALONSO DE SANTA CRUZ.

jars where Francisca and her daughters used to sit to do their needlework.

In Tlatelolco Luis began to write. It was a dangerous thing to do, but like others before and since—Emanuel Ringelblum in the Warsaw ghetto or Primo Levi after Auschwitz—he felt an urgent need to record his experiences. Luis did not date the entries in his narrative, so we do not know the hour or day or night when he began. But sometime after his release from the Hospital de San Hipólito he took a pot of ink, a quill and a small black notebook measuring nine by fifteen centimetres, and writing in tiny letters in order to conserve paper he wrote, 'From Mexico City in New Spain, in grave danger, by the liberated José Lumbroso of the Hebrew nation, among the pilgrims and captives in Occidental India.'

It is a resonant beginning. We hear an echo of Europe's dream that the Americas might be India in that expression 'Occidental India'. And when Luis describes himself as a captive member of the Hebrew nation we understand immediately that he has not, after all, abandoned the Law of Moses. Then there is the name. He was Joseph now, for although he called himself 'José' in that first line he used 'Joseph' for the remainder of his text, as if he had paused, quill in hand, and realised that the Hebraic form would draw him closer to his ancestors. As for 'Lumbroso', it had been a familiar surname among the Sephardim in the days when it was possible to live openly as a Jew in Spain. It may even have been one of his family's ancestral names. Luis, however, does not mention any such familial association. He would later explain 'Lumbroso' purely in terms of its semantic relationship to light—'lumbre'—and enlightenment.

Within the sanctuary of his notebook Joseph the Enlightened would tell his story in his own way, with a freedom he did not have when he spoke before the inquisitors, with his life and the lives of his mother and his sisters in his hands. He would later describe this autobiographical work as a book of miracles. He wrote it, he said, in order to acknowledge the many gifts and mercies he had received from the hand of the Most High, 'so that they may be known to all those who believe in the Holiest of Holies'. He hoped to send it to his brothers Balthasar and Miguel one day, or take it to them himself, once he had completed his four years of penance and was free again.

He took great care to keep his journal secret. Each time he finished writing in it he went downstairs to the passageway where his mother and sisters liked to sit and sew. He had found a loose board in the wall there. He lifted the board and slipped his notebook inside for safe-keeping. That way, even if the house were to be searched, no-one would find it.

●

Luis wrote over fourteen thousand words in his book of miracles. He used little punctuation and no paragraphs. He understood those conventions, but paper was a scarce commodity and besides, he had to work furtively and fast. There is something else about his story: he told it in the third person with only one or two lapses into first. 'Joseph did this,' he wrote, or, 'Joseph did that.' It was a protective strategy, no doubt, in case his notebook should be discovered, but it is possible that Luis also wanted to give his account a legal formality, like that of the Holy Office scribes who recorded what they heard in the third person. Or perhaps as a Jesuit pupil in Medina del Campo he had seen Ignatius Loyola's third-person autobiography and wished to emulate its style.

In any case, Luis said he would relate his story 'until the twenty-fifth year of his wandering'. He promised to recount it truthfully and from the beginning, and as far as we can tell that is what he did. He confirmed that he was born and raised in Benavente, a *'villa de la Europa'*, until the age of twelve or thirteen when he moved with his family to Medina del Campo where he received the light of God's holy knowledge from his mother, his brother, his sister and his cousin. Luis recalled his voyage to the New World when he was fourteen. He said his parents had wanted to go to Italy to live in one of its Jewish communities, 'where the true God could be better served', but instead they had come to New Spain at the urging of his uncle.

The change of plan had brought his family such suffering that Luis believed it must have been a punishment from God for their sins. He does not say what sins he had in mind, but when David Gitlitz was preparing his study of secret Jews in Spain and Portugal he found that they lived in a state of constant shame, lamenting their double lives and failure to follow the Law of Moses correctly. It was this deep and nagging guilt that lent the Day of Atonement such profound significance in the fragmentary ritual calendar they tried to follow.

Luis described his family's 'inconsolable exile' in Tampico and the miraculous day when he managed to buy a Bible in that place of sweltering heat and vicious mosquitoes. He recalled the moment when he made his commitment to the Law of Moses by circumcising himself down by the Pánuco River, and the day some years later when Balthasar did the same, and endured such agony. In a circuitous reference to his mother Luis wrote that a sister of their uncle who knew and loved the Lord learned later what had happened. He said that Francisca asked with great tenderness why he and Balthasar had not come to her in their time of need. Luis does not tell us how he responded to her question. Presumably they had kept away so as not to incriminate her.

•

For a time during 1590 relations between Luis and his mother were not so tender however. When Luis arrived at Francisca's house in Santiago Tlatelolco he was horrified by what he found there. 'Having come to the company of his mother and sisters,' he wrote, 'Joseph found them buying and eating gentile foods.' They were attending mass, too, and praying Christian prayers. Luis knew what had driven them to this. 'Their enemies had filled them with fear,' he wrote, meaning the inquisitors. But he added that the evil counsel of some friends had also influenced his mother and sisters. Luis did not name those friends but his brother-in-law Jorge de Almeida, Leonor's husband, was almost certainly among them.

Almeida was very different from Luis. He considered himself a Jew but fasted only when it suited him. He refrained from eating pork in his own house, but ate it with an easy conscience when he dined with gentiles. He felt no need to risk his life for his religious beliefs, and was prepared to kill in order to protect himself. One of his friends would later tell the Holy Office that Almeida had murdered his African slave when he suspected she had learned his secret.

But Luis did not possess Almeida's pragmatic approach to their ancestral faith, and so he set out to bring his family back to the Law of Moses. 'With divine help,' he wrote, 'Joseph laid before his mother and sisters the example of the saints who were willing to be torn to pieces rather than eat or even pretend to eat forbidden foods.' Luis, who did not know that sainthood is a Christian idea, often called the heroic men and women of the Bible saints. In this case he was referring to the holy scribe and martyr Eleazar, in the Book of Maccabees, who chose death at the hands of his persecutors, even when they offered him the option of merely pretending to eat pork.

We do not know how long Luis spent beseeching his mother and sisters. He wrote that 'because their hearts were with God it took little effort to persuade them back to the Law of Moses', and his words imply that they submitted very quickly. However long it took, he wrote that they soon abandoned the unclean foods they had been eating, 'and with many tears and trepidation they returned to their God and their Lord'. No wonder they felt such trepidation. They had much to fear, not just from their God, and Luis, but from the Holy Office. Francisca and Isabel had been tortured during their imprisonment and bore the marks on their wrists to remind them of the pain and humiliation they had suffered. They knew the consequences of breaking the oaths of abjuration they had sworn in the cathedral. There would be no second chances if they were caught and by returning to the Law of Moses they placed their lives in peril.

How could Luis have urged them to pursue this dangerous path if he really loved them? He was a young man from that foreign country we call the past, and it is often difficult to understand his way of thinking. Although he was only twenty-two he was now the head of his family and it is clear from the letters he would later write to his mother and sisters that he saw it as his moral duty to guide and protect them in both worldly and spiritual matters. It is equally clear from those letters that he feared eternal suffering after death more than death itself, and wanted to save himself and them from that fate. That was the mental world in which he lived. He saw himself as a Jew but he accepted the Christian belief in a punitive afterlife. Since childhood he had seen that afterlife depicted in the chapel murals of Castile: scenes of hideous and never-ending torture, of lost souls hanging by their tongues, impaled and burned and boiled and cut into a thousand pieces, not just once but over and over again.

Those images of brutal and eternal torment cannot have been easy to ignore. They are hard to look at even now when few of us would take them seriously as harbingers of what awaits us after death. But sixteenth-century Christians, and Christianised Jews like Luis, had no way of reasoning away the eschatological fear those paintings evoked. And so he implored his mother and his sisters until they returned to their thrice-weekly fasts, their avoidance of pork and bacon and pork fat, and their cautious observance of the Jewish holy days.

It is difficult to read Luis's account of their capitulation without a deepening sense of dismay. If they had kept the promises they had made at the auto-de-fe they could have left New Spain once their period of house arrest was over. They might have made their way to refuge in a Jewish community in one of the Italian states or in the Ottoman Empire and lived long and fruitful lives with children and grandchildren around them. But they did not. Instead, at Luis's insistence, they resumed the double lives they had to lead in order to survive in this world, and be saved in the next.

Jorge de Almeida fled New Spain around the middle of 1590. He left because he suspected that the Holy Office had decided to arrest him, but before leaving he promised Leonor that in Madrid he would do his best to work for her freedom and that of her family. And so he did, for the next four years. Meanwhile little Anna, who had been living in the house of the Holy Office notary since her family's arrests the previous year, was returned to Francisca amid great rejoicing.

In December 1590 the warden of the Holy Office came to visit Luis. It was his duty to see how this young penitent was getting on, and he brought startling news concerning Luis's former cellmate, the Franciscan. At the auto-de-fe in February the monk had been sentenced to six years in the galleys off Havana, but he had now been brought back to Mexico City in chains. The warden told Luis that the monk had smashed a statue of Jesus, or the Virgin Mary, or one of the saints. Luis did not know or care which. The commandments given to Moses on Mount Sinai forbade the worship of false gods, so to Luis the statues were just empty idols anyway. But the news of the Franciscan's return filled him with fear.

He explained why in his book of miracles: he wrote that there had been a wooden crucifix in the cell he had shared with the Franciscan, and one night when the two of them were sitting in darkness together with just one candle to provide a fragile light, the monk had taken the crucifix in his hands and said, 'If I were to place this in the flame it would burn like any other wood.' It was a strangely suggestive comment to which Luis had replied, 'So now you see in what you place your faith.'

A silence, perhaps, as his words hung in the darkness.

Luis wrote that this brief exchange had altered every-thing between them. That night they had begun to talk about religion, and once they had broached this dangerous subject—absurdly dangerous in their circumstances—they spoke of nothing else for eight days. At the end of that time, Luis wrote, the Franciscan came to understand and accept that the Law of Moses was God's truth. He had praised the Lord for allowing him to receive this sacred knowledge and had danced around their narrow cell, singing, 'Great is the Lord and worthy of praise, for choosing to enlighten a sinner like me.' When Luis recalled all this in his book of miracles he wrote that this good gentile's soul had been as filled with God's truth as if he had been raised on it all his life.

But now the Franciscan had been brought back in chains to Mexico City, and Luis feared that his friend would reveal the part he had played in converting him to the Law of Moses. We do not know how many anxious weeks Luis endured as he waited to see what would happen. He tells us only that the warden—who sounds like a surprisingly candid man—eventually returned to say that during questioning the Franciscan had indeed named Luis as his teacher. He had insisted, however, that Luis had converted him before, rather than after making his confession in August 1589.

We know from the transcript of Luis's second trial that this was not the case: that the Franciscan's conversion took place after Luis repented and was granted mercy, not before. So the Franciscan had lied to save Luis's life, in other words, but Luis, as always, attributed his deliverance to God. 'In this way,' he wrote, 'the Lord saved Joseph from that harsh and dark prison.'

It sounds as if his friend's courage and compassion meant nothing to him, but Luis understood what Ruíz de Luna had done for him. In his last allusion to the Franciscan he wrote that that monk had earned the crown of martyrdom through his virtuous conduct.

But Luis's comment is curious because the Franciscan received the customary reprieve for a first heretical offence, and there is no evidence to suggest that he was executed. He suffered for his new faith, however. The inquisitors devised a far harsher penalty for him than they had for Luis, perhaps because he had once been a monk. They sentenced the Franciscan to endure two hundred lashes, and if he survived that punishment he was to be returned to the galleys for ten years.

Luis would have known, as every European knew, that few men could survive ten years as a galley slave. The Franciscan's demise might be slower and less public than other deaths, and only those who toiled beside him on the rowing benches, and those who eventually threw his body into the sea, would know when it came. But he would be no less a martyr than a man or woman who died at the stake.


It is difficult, in our secular age, to understand why anyone would take the mortal risk of embracing a forbidden faith while imprisoned in the cells of an institution like the Holy Office whose mission was to enforce the strictest religious orthodoxy. Why did the Franciscan take that risk? Perhaps like so many Europeans at that time he felt anxious and uncertain about how best to save his soul. It is also possible that his ancestors had once been Jews, that he knew this and saw his conversion to the Law of Moses as a return to the true faith. But we should not discount Luis's personal influence in this matter. The passionate voice that still speaks to us through his book of miracles and in the letters he would later write, even the beautiful handwriting in which he gave visual form to his beliefs, suggests what a powerful advocate he must have been for his faith. If we were sixteenth-century Europeans caught up in those tumultuous times of faith and doubt, we too might be persuaded by his assurances that the only way to find salvation was through the Law of Moses.

7

# EYES FILLED
# WITH LIGHT

IN MAY 1592 INQUISITORS SANTOS GARCÍA AND FERNÁNDEZ
Bonilla were elevated to the status of bishops. They would not
be free to leave the Holy Office until their replacements were
appointed, but it was a great step forward in their ecclesiastical
careers. Meanwhile, in Santiago Tlatelolco, the members of the
Carvajal family went to mass in their penitential habits, and
prayed aloud with the Christian congregation. But at night,
in the upstairs chamber of their house, when they were sure
no-one could hear, they danced and sang a song that began,
'Blessed be those who await the God of Israel.'

Every Friday morning they told their Chichimeca servant-
girl to put clean linen on their beds, and every Friday evening

they gathered to listen as Luis sang a special canticle to begin the observance of the Sabbath. His song recalled the anguish of Jewish exiles since ancient times and his own family's sorrows. We do not know what tune he followed, only his words have survived:

> If with great care each day
> We sang praises to the Lord
> He would give us happiness
> And aid us in everything,
> Our misfortunes would not be so constant,
> Our great adversity would not last,
> We would make ourselves worthy of his goodness,
> And of peopling his holy city,
> Where our years would be long,
> Free from danger and harm.
>
> I confess that for being disobedient,
> We left our land rejected,
> We live among uncircumcised peoples,
> Affronted with hunger and war,
> All with different cruelties
> We left our land rejected.
> We returned to the Lord, who is compassionate,
> So that he will make our spirits happy.

On Saturdays Luis read the psalms of David to his mother and sisters. His friend Manuel de Lucena sometimes brought his harp to the house in Santiago and played it as they sang, and a young girl known as Justa Méndez came too. Luis seems to have liked Justa and might have married her, if circumstances had been different. But he had other friends outside his family circle, and one of them was a curious mystical hermit known as Gregorio López.

Gregorio López lived several kilometres from Santiago, in the utopian community of Santa Fe. It had been founded soon after the Conquest as a refuge for indigenous families—a place where they could be protected from the vices of Europeans and educated in Christian ways—and the mysterious López had been living there for some years by the time Luis encountered him. Some residents of Mexico City thought López might be Crown Prince Carlos, the supposedly deceased son of Felipe II, because of his resemblance to the king. Others suspected López of being a heretic because his religious beliefs and practices seemed quite unorthodox. He had, in fact, been examined by the city's first inquisitor but found innocent of all charges. How Luis came to know López is uncertain, but they had a great deal in common. López, like Luis, was devoted to the Old Testament and spent his days translating it into Spanish. And like Luis he considered the cult of Catholic saints to be nothing but the worship of false idols.

We know little about their friendship, only that it blossomed while Luis was living in Santiago Tlatelolco, and that one day when Luis went to Santa Fe, wearing his sanbenito, as he was obliged to do whenever he went out in public, López remarked that he deserved to wear this penitential garment more than Luis did. His comment convinced Luis that his new friend secretly observed the Law of Moses, and although we do not know whether they ever spoke openly about this, Luis continued to visit Gregorio López at Santa Fe as often as he could.

Meanwhile the time drew near for Luis to return to his original place of confinement in the Hospital de San Hipólito and he dreaded the thought of leaving his mother and sisters. He would miss them, and it is possible that he feared they would return to Christian ways once he was gone. Yet once again he won an unexpected reprieve. In his book of miracles he explained what happened: 'As the time approached for Joseph to return to the hospital, an old monk, a man of great virtue, came to see his mother.' It seems that Francisca begged the monk to let Luis stay with her. Her pleas touched the old man's heart and he decided to do what he could to help.

He went to the Holy Office to discuss her request with the inquisitors and returned with a solution. It so happened that the monk was director of the Franciscan College of Santa Cruz Tlatelolco, beside the Church of Santiago, and he needed an assistant to copy out his letters and sermons. He also needed another Latin tutor for the Aztec boys who studied at the college. Luis knew Latin and his handwriting was very fine. Therefore the inquisitors had agreed to let Luis complete his penance at the college, beneath the old Franciscan's supervision. That way he could stay on in his mother's house.

The Franciscan's name was Fray Pedro de Oroz and Luis was fortunate to have met him. Fray Pedro had been born in what was then the kingdom of Navarre, so he had spoken his own Basque tongue before acquiring Spanish, a fact that probably explains his later ease with the indigenous languages of Mexico. As a young man he had come to Mexico City in search of riches, but once there he had abandoned his worldly dreams and joined the order of Saint Francis. He studied Latin and theology, mastered Nahuatl, the Aztec tongue, and he also knew the language of the Otomí people of central Mexico.

Fray Pedro's Franciscan colleagues described him as a meek and peaceful man, never given to impatience, a learned man who delighted in mental prayer and the precious moments when he could leave the duties of his directorial post and spend time in quiet meditation. A portrait miniature of him has survived that seems to bear out that description. In the portrait Fray Pedro's head is bowed. His beard and tonsured hair are white, and his eyes look out at us with a calm and contemplative intelligence.

Luis wrote in his book of miracles that Fray Pedro and his people loved him. So who were Fray Pedro's people? They were Franciscans like him: learned men, philologists, ethnographers and prolific writers. Bernardino de Sahagún, who compiled the great compendium of Aztec life we call the *Florentine Codex*, was one of them. He had died a few months before Luis arrived at the college, but his distinguished indigenous colleague, Antonio de Valeriano, was still there when Luis arrived. So was the historian Gerónimo de Mendieta, who was busy writing his renowned attack on Spanish policy in the New World, *Historia Eclésiastic Indiana*.

The former college still stands beside the Church of Santiago in Tlatelolco square and it is as famous in the history of colonial Mexico as the scholarly men who once lived there. It had been established soon after the Conquest for the purpose of educating the sons of Aztec nobles in Latin, Romance (as Spanish was known at that time), arts and theology. It had a printing press, tools for binding books and a fine library. The Franciscans had dreamed that their college would be the cornerstone of a new and virtuous Indian church in the New World. By the time Luis arrived there, however, their messianic dream was over, and Gerónimo de Mendieta had taken to comparing his sorrow with that of the prophet Jeremiah lamenting the fall of ancient Jerusalem.

Yet the college was still a profoundly erudite and studious community to which Luis, with his searching intellect, was well suited. The spiritual path along which he was travelling was very different from that of the Franciscans, however. They were busy learning what they could about this New World their compatriots had conquered. They wanted to master its languages and understand its cultural and religious traditions in order to bring its people to the Christian faith. They did not oppose the Conquest. They saw it as a divinely

FORMER COLLEGE
OF SANTA CRUZ
TLATELOLCO,
JANUARY 2006.

inspired act essential to the eradication of pagan religion and the introduction of Christianity. But they wanted to protect their new indigenous proselytes from corruption by Spain's conquistadors and settlers.

Luis, on the other hand, appears to have felt little interest in the indigenous people around him, and the rare allusions he makes to them are contemptuous and brief. His passion was for the Jewish faith and culture that had been torn from his family in 1492, and he seems hardly to have noticed the young Aztec boys who now became his pupils.

At night those boys slept in a lamp-lit dormitory. By day they walked through the college cloisters dressed in blue habits. On Sundays and holy days they sang hymns in Latin and Nahuatl in the Church of Santiago. Luis, with his pale face and yellow sanbenito, would have stood out among those copper-skinned, blue-robed boys and the Franciscans in their sandals and brown robes. Luis tells us nothing about them, however, and little about the college—except to say that within its walls God filled his hands with treasure. He didn't mean gold or silver, turquoise or quetzal feathers; Luis's treasures were the books and manuscripts he found in the college library.

Luis had heard about monastic libraries like the one at the college of Santa Cruz Tlatelolco. His Franciscan cellmate had told him about them one night, saying, 'They keep the books out so that anyone may consult them and read them.' After hearing that Luis had yearned to visit such a place and soon after entering the college his wish was granted when Fray Pedro gave him a key to its library.

In retrospect Fray Pedro's trust in Luis seems rather surprising. Luis was a reconciled heretic and, in any case, as a layman he was forbidden to approach the scriptures and other theological tracts without the mediation of clergy. Perhaps Fray Pedro sympathised with his young protégé's desire for learning, or thought he saw signs of a religious vocation in Luis and wanted to encourage it. But we might be reading too much into this incident if we interpret it like this. After all, one of Luis's tasks was to copy out Fray Pedro's letters and sermons, and the library with its desks, its parchments, its quills and pots of ink was the obvious place to do this.

But libraries are dangerous places in societies that seek to restrict their citizens' knowledge, and the library at the Franciscan college in Santiago was no different. In 1590 its collection included ninety or so calfskin volumes filled with the works of Aristotle, Plato, Virgil, Juvenal, Pliny, Plutarch and Josephus Flavius. The massive Spanish/Nahuatl dictionary that Fray Alonso de Medina had completed during the years when he was teaching at the college was there, along with many other dictionaries and grammars of indigenous languages. But the works that meant the most to Luis as he sought to recover his ancestral faith were those of the early Christian theologians, St Augustine and St Jerome, because they contained so many rich allusions to the Jewish Bible.

A century earlier a young Sephardic exile known as Judah ben Jacob Hayyat had described the moment when he first began to taste 'the sweet joy of learning', and his words seem to capture something of Luis's experience in the college library. In the evenings when the Franciscans went to supper, Luis stayed on among the calfskin volumes, and within its walls he, like Judah before him, 'entered the realm of knowledge', and his eyes 'filled with light'.

Another parallel comes to mind: the literary critic Stephen Greenblatt has described the way the great sixteenth-century Bible translators William Tyndale and Thomas Cranmer transformed 'the deepest things, the things upon which the fate of the soul depended' into ordinary and familiar English. In Mexico City in 1590, Luis de Carvajal embarked on a similar task. While the Franciscans ate their frugal evening meal in the college refectory, he read the Bible furtively by candlelight, and translated what he read from Latin into Spanish.

He did not realise that the faith he was constructing for himself in the college library was an antiquated, biblical version of Judaism. In his innocence and isolation he had no experience of rabbinic Judaism, and did not know that it permitted and even encouraged learned commentaries on the subtleties of divine law. Had he known he would probably have been shocked, just as many secret Jews were shocked when they reached a city like Amsterdam or Salonika and encountered rabbinic teaching for the first time in their lives. Luis had never known that privilege, and he never would. Most of the ideas that he derived in the college library in Santiago Tlatelolco were based firmly on the Five Books of Moses, and it was the revelatory words of those ancient books that he took to his family and friends each night.

Fray Pedro continued to enrich Luis's mind. One day he told him, 'Look what precious things we are bringing to our college.' The precious things were four volumes of Latin commentaries or 'glosses' on the Bible. A great Franciscan scholar had prepared them two centuries earlier. Luis had never heard of this scholar, but as soon as he opened the first volume of Nicholas of Lyra's work he saw that it offered great insights into the Hebrew Bible. Lyra, who had died in 1349, had been a fine Hebraist and had intended his commentaries for Christian theologians. But for Luis they opened a door to forbidden learning as he tried to recover the lost threads of his

Jewish past. So after Lyra's glosses were added to the college library Luis went there every night and spent many hours bent over his desk with his candle and his quill, translating them into Spanish.

He described Lyra's writings as food for his soul and, as if they were not nourishment enough, one day Fray Pedro showed him yet another collection of Latin commentaries. Their author was a Dominican known as Gerónimo de Oleastro, and his subject was the Five Books of Moses. Fray Pedro wanted Oleastro's commentaries arranged in alphabetical order, and the task brought Luis the most profound pleasure. 'It suited Joseph's desires and inclinations so perfectly,' he wrote in his journal, 'that without God's help he could never have experienced such joyous work, even if he had offered to pay for it with his blood.'

There is poignancy and paradox in Luis's response to Oleastro, for Oleastro had once been an inquisitor in Évora. He had presided over the Holy Office tribunal in that city just a few years after Luis's Portuguese relatives were released from its cells, and they were lucky to have avoided him. He had pursued New Christians with such savage zeal that his superiors had thought it best to transfer him to the tribunal of Lisbon. Luis probably did not know about Oleastro's inquisitorial career, or understand that Oleastro—yet another skilled Hebraist—had based much of his work on that of the great

Sephardic philosopher Moses Maimonides. All Luis knew was
that he loved Oleastro's commentaries. He gave thanks to God
for revealing through them 'things not previously known or
heard in the lands of captivity', and it is gratifying to think
how horrified this former inquisitor would have been if he
had known that a young Judaising heretic was using his work
to recover his Jewish faith.

The years passed. Catalina's husband, Antonio Díaz de
Cáceres, returned to Mexico City in March 1592 but kept
his distance for fear of being tarred with the brush of her
Judaising. Finally, at the urging of the Holy Office, Fray
Pedro de Oroz talked with Díaz de Cáceres and persuaded
him to resume his role as Catalina's husband and protector
of her mother and sisters.

In April the following year Catalina, Mariana and Leonor
were permitted to remove their penitential habits. Those
stiff, yellow garments were hung on the interior walls of
the cathedral, along with those of their father, Francisco, and
their brother, Balthasar, who had been tried in absentia, to
remind the congregation what would happen to them if they
strayed into the arms of another faith. After that the sisters
continued to spend their days sewing beside the window in
the downstairs passage, while every morning Luis crossed the

plaza to the college. Those who watched him go knew from his penitential garb that he was a reconciled heretic. Everyone also knew that the authorities had burned an effigy of his father for the religious crime of Judaising.

A woman called Susana Galbán took a particular interest in the Carvajal household. Susana, who often called on Francisca, noticed that whenever Luis referred to his deceased father he called him 'my father, who is in glory'. This troubled Susana because she knew that Francisco Rodríguez de Matos had been burned in effigy for being a secret Jew, so how could he possibly be in glory? Susana sometimes took her needlework along when she visited Francisca and her daughters. She sat sewing and chatting with them by the window in the passageway, and from time to time she would invoke the name of Jesus Christ and his mother Mary. But she observed that they never joined her in this, and only ever referred to one sole God.

Susana noticed other things. She saw that Francisca and her daughters bled their meat and placed it in water, and that on Saturdays they dressed in their finest clothes, while on Catholic feast days they wore clothes that were old and worn. Susana also noticed that one of Francisca's younger daughters—sixteen-year-old Mariana—had begun to suffer episodes of madness and had taken to hurling holy statues into the street to smash them while her desperate family did their best to stop her. An African slave called Anna de la Cruz was passing by the Carvajal house one day and she said later that she saw the statues lying broken in the street, heard Mariana's mother and sisters remonstrating with her and Mariana shrieking abuse at them.

One day Susana Galbán went to visit Francisca and found Mariana talking to herself and saying, 'Yes, I believe, no I don't believe. Which is better? To believe or say that one does not believe? Or say I believe as I did when I was a Jew before the inquisitors?' Another time Susana heard Mariana call herself the anti-Christ and declare to no-one in particular, 'Because I say these things they say I am Morales, and that because of me they will be burned.' She was referring to the physician who had prepared the little notebook filled with verses from Deuteronomy and later escaped to Italy. Susana also heard Mariana muttering, 'Many Jews eat bacon because they say they are Christians and are not . . . be quiet, be quiet . . . that faith will leave you . . . I also want to eat bacon because they say I am a Christian.'

This glimpse of Mariana's confusion and mental turmoil is pitiful. Years later, during a more lucid period in her life, she would remember those years of madness when she did not know who she was, or which faith she should be following. 'I suffered great melancholy brought about by the troubles I had, and by my sins,' she would say. Luis described her troubles too, in his book of miracles. He wrote that after enduring severe depressions for some time she had gone mad. 'And in her madness she takes up the idols in the homes of her heathen neighbours, and before their eyes she throws them from their windows to be shattered below.

'The madness of this poor young girl is such,' Luis wrote, 'that by day and by night she babbles without cease; but in the course of her ravings she sometimes speaks bald truths to the monks and idolatrous women who visit her to try to cure her of her illness.' He added that during her bouts of insanity she did and said such dangerous things that they feared she would accidentally reveal their secret adherence to the Law of Moses.

Mariana posed a terrifying risk to her family. But Luis endangered them too. Each time he opened his little black journal to record his story he placed his life and theirs in jeopardy, and it was not the only incriminating notebook he possessed. He had another, covered in green velvet, in which he had copied out translations he had made of the psalms. Mariana loved this book. One day she went with Luis to visit a friend, possibly young Justa Méndez, and she took the green notebook with her, secreted in her bodice. It slipped out as they walked through the streets but Mariana didn't notice for some time that it was missing. When she did finally notice she and Luis retraced their steps, searching frantically for the little green book, but they never found it. Mariana was inconsolable. Luis had spent months, perhaps years, preparing those translations. She and her sisters had considered the little notebook 'a precious jewel' and its loss terrified them because they had no idea where it was, or who had found it.

From that day on they bought only the smallest quantities of oil and other household necessities because they felt sure they would soon be arrested. Luis wrote that whenever someone knocked at the door they feared the Holy Office constables had come for them, and one night they heard precisely the sort of loud, official knock they had been dreading. Their Chichimeca maid came to tell them that the authorities were at the door. In a state of panic Luis and Francisca went down to face them. It was a false alarm. The inspector of bakeries stood waiting on the threshold with two baskets full of bread in his arms. He explained that as the loaves did not meet the minimum weight required of the city's bakeries the magistrate had told him to bring the bread to doña Francisca and her children, because he knew they lived in constant need.

In his book of miracles Luis mentions further acts of kindness on the part of gentiles in Mexico City. His comments suggest that, at least during the period following his family's release from the Holy Office cells, those gentiles regarded them with sympathy rather than hostility; as fellow Christians who had fallen by the wayside, rather than detestable Jews. In any case, he gave thanks in his usual manner when he recalled the gift of bread. 'In this way,' he wrote, 'the Lord filled the house with His blessing.' But nothing could assuage his fears and so he took to scraping and gouging gaps in the wall of his mother's house so that he could escape if the Holy Office constables came for him.

One day around this anxious time a stranger entered the college cloister and asked for Luis. He was a visiting commissary of the Holy Office and Luis, in fear, went forward to meet him. What else could he do? There was nowhere he could run. The commissary told Luis to follow him to his room. Luis went with him and once inside the room the commissary gave him a sheet of paper and asked him to copy some verses onto it. Luis, in his heightened state of fear, believed this must mean that the Holy Office had his little green notebook and wanted to compare his handwriting with the handwriting in its pages. He took up the quill and ink and with a beating heart he copied out the verses.

Later that day he returned to his mother's house expecting arrest at any time. It was another false alarm however. It turned out that the commissary had a brother, a Dominican, who had heard that Luis's handwriting was particularly fine and hoped Luis might transcribe a book of prayers for him. To that end he had asked the commissary to obtain a sample of Luis's hand. That was all there was to this episode. 'When Joseph understood that his fears had been unfounded,' Luis wrote, 'he gave thanks to the Lord.'

But Luis' difficulties were not yet over. The Dominican liked his handwriting so much that he forwarded a blank notebook to the college and asked that Luis begin copying the prayers into it. Luis could not refuse, but he feared this task would leave him little time for his translation work and his devotions to the Lord, and this troubled him deeply.

In 1594, as the Carvajal family's term of penitence was finally drawing to an end, the youngest daughter, Anna, fell ill with quinsy. Quinsy is an abscess between the tonsils and the wall of the throat, which is rarely seen in the developed world these days. Anna, who was fourteen at the time, suffered it for more than eight months and her misery was such that the surgeon attending her decided to lance her throat in several places. This brutal treatment left Anna barely able to speak.

Only Leonor could understand her and Luis says that the physician, the surgeon and the entire family came to depend on her to interpret for them.

Around the same time Mariana endured an agonising treatment for her mental illness. Luis said that two physicians applied ten 'cauteries of fire' to her abdomen—he meant they burned her with hot irons in accordance with the conventional medical treatment of the day—and that the burning caused her such pain that she attacked her mother and sisters and would have killed them if not for the grace of God. He added that even complete strangers were moved to pity and compassion for Mariana and her family. 'Those strangers wept as many tears,' he wrote, 'as if they were close relatives.' It was clearly a time of great suffering for the Carvajal family, but Luis wrote that the Lord had inflicted these trials on them as a merciful punishment; merciful because they offered an opportunity for atonement. 'For like sinning monks,' he wrote, 'we need both bread and the rod for this life.'

In the midst of all these troubles two visitors arrived at Francisca's house in Santiago. They were a father and son known as Ruy and Diego Díaz Nieto and they had come from Spain with two letters for Luis: one was from Balthasar, the other from Jorge de Almeida. Balthasar sent good tidings tinged with sadness. He wrote that he had settled in Ferrara's Jewish quarter and married a beautiful Jewish woman called Esther. She had borne him a son, but unfortunately the child had died. Esther was pregnant again, however, and she and Balthasar prayed that this time their infant would live. Balthasar added that he was attending a school of wise men who were very learned in the Law of Moses. As for young Miguel, he had taken the name 'Jacob Lumbroso' and gone to live in Salonika. He too was becoming very learned in the Law of Moses.

Jorge de Almeida's letter brought more good news. He had promised when he fled to Madrid four years earlier that he would do everything he could to expedite the release of Leonor and her family from their penitential obligations. He wrote to announce that he had at last been able to arrange the requisite documents but needed to pay a fee before he could send them on to New Spain. Luis does not explain in his account of Almeida's letter whether the funds were an official fee or a bribe to a Crown or Holy Office official. Perhaps he did not know. In any case he thought about how best to raise those funds and decided that collecting alms was one way.

Collecting alms was a familiar activity in Luis's world. People of all kinds, even high-born men and women, walked the streets of Spanish cities gathering ransoms for the release of their relatives who had been captured by corsairs. But in order to do this Luis would need permission to leave the house in Santiago, so he decided to ask his new Dominican patron for help. The Dominican obliged. He persuaded the Holy Office to allow Luis to leave for a while and Luis, as always, described this as another miracle. 'By order of the omnipotent Lord God,' he wrote, 'Joseph was given leave for six months.'

He set out in June 1594, carrying letters of introduction from the provincials of the Franciscan and Augustinian orders, and those official letters won him a kindly reception wherever he went. He wrote that whenever he called at a Franciscan or Augustinian monastery the monks gave him lodging and offered him meals. 'But Joseph did not forget the law and the commands of his Lord God, and did not accept their offerings of food, so as not to defile himself, and told them he had already eaten . . .' 'There were many times,' he wrote in his book of miracles, 'when he left these detestable men and went to eat his bread among the beasts, thinking it was better to eat with cleanliness among the horses than in uncleanliness at the tables of his pampered enemies.'

Luis spent two months away from Mexico City and in that time he collected eight hundred and fifty pesos from the 'barbarous gentiles' with whom he lodged. 'May the Lord God of Israel enlighten them,' he wrote, 'and bring them to

His holy recognition so that all His creatures will adore and serve Him.'

In 1590, when Luis began to record his story, he said he would describe his life until the twenty-fifth year of his wandering. In the end he wrote for four years more than he intended, and as he drew his narrative to a close he suddenly began to give explicit dates for the events he described. He wrote, for example, that the decrees of liberty his brother-in-law had obtained in Madrid arrived with the first fleet in September 1594, and that on the afternoon of Thursday 6 October a constable knocked at the door of the Carvajal house and told the family they were required at the Holy Office.

Trembling, they followed the constable through the streets of Mexico City, but all the inquisitors wanted was for them to ratify certain declarations they had made in 1589, to the effect that young Miguel observed the Law of Moses. This was necessary so that Miguel's effigy could be burned in the next auto-de-fe. The Carvajales knew the real Miguel was safe in Salonika now so they did not hesitate to ratify their statements. Then they returned to their house in Santiago and sang songs of praise to glorify God's holy name.

Soon after Luis learned that the brother of their close friend Manuel Gómez Navarro was gravely ill and in danger of dying. The brother's name was Domingo, and Luis and Manuel de Lucena decided that in order to save his soul they should try to persuade him back to the Law of Moses before he died. Their efforts failed. Luis wrote that Domingo 'closed his ears' to them. But he did not die, as they had expected, and as he recovered from his illness Luis and Manuel began to fear that he would denounce them to the authorities. Their fear was so great that they talked of killing Domingo in order to save themselves. Manuel de Lucena's wife, Catalina Enríquez, suggested giving him a cup of chocolate containing poison and Luis thought this prudent at first. But he was not as ruthless as his brother-in-law Jorge de Almeida, who had murdered his African slave to prevent her from denouncing him. 'God says do not kill,' Luis told his friends, 'therefore it would not be good to do this.'

The dates come fast from this point on. On Monday 10 October the release documents arrived and Luis wrote that his family's joy was such that their gentile friends rejoiced with them. Two weeks later, on 24 October, he, Francisca and Isabel were finally permitted to take off their sanbenitos. They had completed their penance and were free to leave their house in Santiago, and New Spain, if that was what they wished.

But on the very day of their release Domingo Gómez Navarro did as Luis and Manuel de Lucena had feared he would. He went to the Holy Office and denounced them as

Judaisers. Six days later Manuel was arrested and Luis wrote that he too was expecting to be arrested at any moment. Yet the constables did not come for him, and he understood this to mean that the Lord had decided to deliver him with an extraordinary miracle.

He was wrong: a new misfortune now befell his family. He was writing with great urgency and caution now, but he said it was the gravest they had so far suffered. 'What it was, and how it came about is not being written because the writer is still in the lands of captivity, although with the help and blessing of the Highest and Most Powerful Adonay, God of Israel, he is on the verge of leaving one of the greatest and most dangerous captivities that people of our nation have suffered.' Luis was practical as well as devout. He sounds as if he was expecting a miraculous rescue on the wings of an angel, but we will later learn that in fact he and his family were on the point of leaving for Spain.

Luis opened his book of miracles for the last time on 30 October 1594, the same day Manuel de Lucena was arrested.

'Joseph and his family, through the singular kindness of the Lord our God, live in no less danger than Saint Daniel in the lions' den,' he wrote, 'where the All Powerful, with a great miracle, closed their cruel mouths with which, if He had not intervened, they would have torn Daniel to pieces.' He concluded with a rare shift into first person. 'Therefore

I humble my heart, I adore and glorify His holy name and declare that He is good and very great, and that His mercy is eternal. May He support us, and all Israel. Amen.'

After writing those final words he lifted the board beside the window in the downstairs passageway, slipped his notebook inside, and left the house in Santiago forever.

## 8

# BETRAYAL

Mexico City, December 1594. Icicles hang beneath the balconies and there is snow, as always, on the slopes of the volcanoes. In the marketplace at Santiago Tlatelolco men and women come and go carrying baskets of tomatoes, corn, chocolate and avocados, while across the square at the Franciscan college the Aztec boys in their blue tunics study and pray beneath their tutors' watchful eyes.

In the Holy Office building on the Plaza de Santo Domingo two new inquisitors are in session. The younger of the two is Licenciado Alonso de Peralta. His age at this time is uncertain, but we know that he was born in Arequipa, Peru, of Spanish parents, and had come to Mexico City only recently from Spain. He would later be appointed archbishop of La Plata in what is now Bolivia, and as archbishops always had their portraits painted we have some idea of what he looked like at that time: thin, with a long nose, elongated eyes, a rather dainty mouth and a balding head. His colleague at the Holy Office was the former prosecutor Dr Bartolomé Lobo Guerrero, who had now been promoted to the post of inquisitor. He too would eventually be made an archbishop, and his portrait, now in the cathedral museum of Lima, shows a man of around fifty years of age, with a broad face, dark eyes, a moustache and tight, black curly hair.

Luis's friend Manuel de Lucena was downstairs in the cells; he had been there since October. They had questioned him three times and on each occasion he had denied that he observed the Law of Moses or knew anyone else who did. But on 20 December he appeared before the inquisitors for a fourth time and on that winter's afternoon he admitted that he was indeed a follower of that forbidden faith. He still denied knowing any other offenders, but his admission was a breakthrough for the inquisitors. They told him to think hard about what he could recall and speak the truth next time he appeared before them.

They summoned Manuel again two days later.

'Have you remembered anything?'

*Don Bartolomé de Lobo Guerrero.*

PORTRAIT OF BARTOLOMÉ LOBO GUERRERO. COURTESY OF
FERNANDO LÓPEZ, ARCHIVO HISTÓRICO Y MUSEO DE LA
CATEDRAL DE LIMA.

PORTRAIT OF ALONSO DE PERALTA. COURTESY OF LA CATEDRAL
DE SUCRE, BOLIVIA. *PHOTOGRAPHER: MARÍA POMPEYA PATZY
AVILÉS, DIRECTORA DEL MUSEO ECLESIÁSTICO DE SUCRE.*

'Yes,' he replied. 'When Luis de Carvajal was in Santiago, placed there by the Holy Office, I went there sometimes and on some of those occasions I found him with a Bible and other books and saw that he was extracting ethics from the scriptures and I understood that Fray Pedro de Oroz had ordered him to do so.'

'Why did you visit the said Luis de Carvajal, given that you are a Jew who observes the Law of Moses while Luis has been converted to the Law of Jesus Christ?'

'Because we had been friends before; and because I had given Luis three hundred pesos and wanted to reclaim it.'

They asked whether he had ever gone abroad with the said Luis de Carvajal and, if so, whether Luis had ever done this without his penitential habit.

Manuel thought about this for a moment. He admitted that four months earlier he and Luis had visited Pachuca together and Luis had worn a cloak to cover his habit.

That was all for the day. The inquisitors warned Manuel to consult his memory and the guard returned him to his cell.

Christmas came and went, and Hanukkah, the Festival of Lights, for those who remembered and dared to observe it. They were probably very few. The Carvajal family never mention Hanukkah in their trial transcripts and David Gitlitz believes it was of little importance to the secret Jews of Spain and Portugal. It seems to have slipped from their memory, unlike Passover, Yom Kippur and 'the feast of Queen Esther', which they never forgot.

Luis's whereabouts at this time are unclear but on 19 January the wife of Manuel de Lucena appeared before the inquisitors. Catalina Enríquez was heavily pregnant at the time of her arrest, and she admitted celebrating Passover and other Jewish feasts with Manuel and Luis. A few weeks later young Justa Méndez, friend to Luis and his sisters, was arrested and she made the same admission. Manuel, Catalina and Justa were prisoners and in grave danger when they gave their testimonies, but there were others who came forward to testify against Luis of their own volition.

Susana Galbán, the woman who had often visited Francisca in Santiago, was one of those voluntary witnesses. On 21 January she went to the Holy Office and asked to see the inquisitors. She described herself as the wife of a knife-maker named Martin Pérez. She said she was fifty years old, more or less, came from Braga in northern Portugal, and in order to discharge her conscience she had come to reveal certain things she had seen and heard while visiting the Carvajal household.

She told the inquisitors she had heard Luis describe his father as 'being in glory' even though Francisco had been burned in effigy as a heretic. She said she had seen meat bled and placed in water in Francisca's kitchen and had noticed that Francisca and her daughters never mentioned Jesus Christ or Our Lady. She reported what she had heard Mariana babbling in her madness. 'And what I have said is the truth,' Susana swore, 'and I declare it by way of discharging my conscience and in accordance with the oath I have sworn.' The scribe noted that as she could not read Inquisitor Peralta signed the transcript on her behalf.

Nine days later, on the morning of 30 January, Manuel de Lucena asked to see the inquisitors. The jailer escorted him upstairs to the audience chamber.

'Why did you request this hearing?' they asked Manuel.

'Because I want to speak the truth and discharge my conscience,' he replied, 'because I understand I must do this for the sake of my salvation. And if until now I have denied everything and not spoken the truth it was because of my concern for flesh and blood and friendship . . .'

Manuel went on to describe a day a year and a half earlier when he had visited Luis at the Indian college in Santiago.

'I found him extracting ethics from the Bible, and I said to him these are beautiful things that you are writing and he replied that they were and said that he regretted that all creatures did not open their eyes. He added that those who break the word of God will be broken, therefore the Christians will be broken for breaking the Law of Moses which is the Law of God, and I responded, blessed be the Lord for not making me one of those who break the Law.

'And from that point on we went on discovering about each other, Luis de Carvajal and I, talking and declaring many things about the Law and its strength. And I put some doubts to Luis de Carvajal, as a man who observes the Law of Moses and is well read in the Bible, so that he could talk about them and satisfy them. And the said Luis de Carvajal told me that he saw that I also observed the Law of Moses and the authorities of the Old Testament, and so from that day on we would be like brothers, and although unworthy of doing so he would commend me to God in his prayers . . .'

'Did the said Luis de Carvajal tell you that his mother and sisters observed the Law of Moses?' the inquisitors asked.

'He didn't say so in particular,' Manuel replied, 'and I didn't ask for certain because Luis de Carvajal being a Jew, and knowing so much about the Law of Moses, and being so well read in it, it was clear that they observed it and that

Luis taught them, so I kept the suspicion in my heart, as something I must keep secret.'

Manuel added that one night when he had slept at the Carvajal house Luis had arisen between ten and eleven to pray psalms and his mother and sisters had prayed with him.

Manuel's sixth hearing ended at that point. Throughout the three months since his arrest he had said nothing to incriminate Luis, his mother and sisters. So why did he suddenly begin to speak on 30 January? Probably because he thought that by then they were on their way to safety.


The following day Susana Galbán knocked once more at the doors of the Holy Office. 'I come in order to discharge my conscience,' she told Dr Lobo Guerrero, 'and to say and reveal what I understand of the people of Luis de Carvajal, against whom I deposed the other day.'

She had taken great care since her last appearance to find out whether the members of the Carvajal family put clean linen on their beds on Fridays, and whether they kept the Sabbath on Saturdays. 'And so, last Friday, I watched the Chichimeca maid who serves them, called Lucia, carrying in her arms a sheet that she had washed that day, and a basket of wet clothes on her head.'

Susana had asked the maid about the sheet and Lucia explained that she had been told to place it on the bed of doña Isabel. After that Susana had gone upstairs in the Carvajal house and found Isabel in bed although it was ten or eleven in the morning. Isabel had said she was indisposed, but Susana noticed clean sheets on her bed, 'and also on the bed that doña Francisca shares with her daughter Leonor, and on that of Luis de Carvajal'. Susana seems to have inspected the entire house after that. She had entered the sitting room where she saw the table set for a meal and young doña Leonor dressed in rich black velvet, as if for a festival. She noticed a pot on the fire full of meat, and when she peeked inside it looked like chicken.

The following day Susana had returned to the house with a tonic for Isabel. The grateful Francisca had invited her to eat supper with them and while they were eating Luis had approached his mother and murmured something to her. Susana, who was listening as hard as she could, heard Francisca reply, 'With fat, with fat.' Susana had looked at her plate and realised that although her eggs had been fried in pork fat, the others' had been cooked in oil.

'All this has led me to suspect that the Carvajal family must observe the Law of Moses,' she told Dr Lobo Guerrero. 'And this I have said in order to discharge my conscience, and having been read my testimony I approve and sign it, and I do not make it through hatred or enmity, and I swear to keep it secret.'

So ends the testimony of Susana Galbán, a woman who spied on her friends, crept around their house, inspected their bedchambers and their cooking pots, listened to their conversations, questioned their servant and took the information she had gleaned to the Holy Office. Why did she betray them? We will probably never know whether she acted out of malice or genuinely felt it was her civic duty to report her suspicions. Her birthplace might go some way towards explaining her actions. Susana came from Braga, in that remote and mountainous part of northern Portugal where so many Sephardic exiles had settled in 1492. It is a small detail but possibly significant; because if Susana knew or suspected that her own ancestors had been Jews she may have acted out of fear in order to protect herself, just as Felipe Nuñez had done six years earlier.

Luis would have known what prompted her to act as she did. His cautious words to his mother during the meal they shared with Susana suggest he did not trust this constant visitor. But he never mentioned Susana, or if he did his words were not recorded.

Luis had not escaped, no matter what Manuel de Lucena may have hoped. The constables captured him near Taxco the day after Susana completed her testimony. They took him to the cells on the night of 1 February, and the jailer noted that he was carrying a leather bag containing three small notebooks filled with 'good handwriting in Latin'. One was a book of psalms, the second was entitled *Prophete* and the third *Génesis*. The jailer confiscated them.

When morning came he placed Luis in a cell with another prisoner, a priest called Díaz. The priest watched Luis closely and noticed that a little after midday he faced towards the east, knelt and began to pray. Luis kept on praying until five in the afternoon. Throughout that time he uttered just one word—*Adonay*—and kissed the floor each time he said it.

When he had finished praying Díaz asked him who he was.

'My name is Luis de Carvajal,' Luis replied. He added, 'Did you see me when I went out dressed in a sanbenito during the auto-de-fe in February five years ago, on the day of San Mathias?'

'No,' Díaz replied.

'Well, I was imprisoned here for being a Jew,' Luis told him, 'and before I took part in the auto I taught the Law of Moses to a Franciscan called Francisco Ruíz de Luna who was also a prisoner here because he held mass without being ordained to do so.'

Luis told Díaz what had happened after he was reconciled in 1590, explaining how he had been sent to the Hospital de San Hipólito, where they made him sweep the floors and where he couldn't eat from the pots of food because they contained bacon.

'After that they placed me in Santiago Tlatelolco,' he continued, 'and there God filled my hands with treasure because Fray Pedro de Oroz entrusted me with the key to the library, and I was able to complete my confirmation in the Law of Moses, because in that library was a Bible and an Oleastro from which I drew ethics ... And now I want to die in the observance of the Law of Moses!'

With that Luis danced around their tiny cell, saying that God would bring him to the sacrifice, just as Abraham had brought his son, Isaac, to the sacrifice on the mountain. It was the first of many parallels Luis would draw between the binding of Isaac and the death he knew he must now face.

He told Díaz, 'The day of the dog San Mathias is a good day to die because that was the day on which I was reconciled five years ago, and so I want to burn and suffer for God on the same day, particularly because this year the feast of San Mathias will fall on Saturday, the Sabbath day of the Jews.' Luis said he had danced for joy like this on the day he was arrested too, because he knew he would be burned.

'How is it that you don't fear death,' Díaz asked, 'given that you know you are going to be burned?'

'I don't fear it,' Luis replied, 'because I am circumcised.'

He told Díaz that he had circumcised himself at the age of eighteen with a pair of scissors. He recalled how in October the inquisitor had asked whether he was firm in the Law of Jesus Christ and believed that Jesus Christ was the true Messiah promised in that Law.

'I told him "yes" in order to be freed from my penitential habit,' Luis said, 'but this time when they call me to a hearing with the inquisitor dog, if the Messiah has come and is in earthly paradise with the prophets Elias and Enoch, and was not engendered as you Christians say'—as Jesus, in other words—'then I will go to Him and you, dog, will go to the inferno, where I think I will see you burning.'

Díaz sat listening to all this and when Luis paused for breath Díaz announced that he would like to learn about the Law of Moses.

Luis fell to his knees in joy.

'Now I want to die for the Law of God because I have found someone to teach and to whom I can declare it,' he cried.

He took off his hat and extracted a tiny notebook from the taffeta around the brim. Díaz saw that someone had copied out the Ten Commandments in its pages and that the first letters were large and illuminated. Luis explained that he had copied the text from the Bible. They had taken the Bible from him when they brought him to the 'House of the

Abomination'—he meant the House of the Inquisition—but they had not found this little notebook hidden inside his hat.

Luis then told Díaz about his friends who also observed the Law of Moses. He said he had taught the Law to Manuel de Lucena, and to Manuel's brother-in-law, a man who would not reveal anybody to the Holy Office, 'even if they break him to pieces'. Luis named his brother-in-law, too, Antonio Díaz de Cáceres, 'who lives in the street of San Agustín'.

As the sun went down Luis ate some bread and two plantains and bathed himself with his drinking water. He told Díaz he intended to fast next day because it was Friday, and he would observe the Jewish Sabbath on Saturday by singing psalms and giving praise to God and reciting couplets that Dr Morales—who was now living in a Jewish community somewhere in Italy and was called Abraham—had taught him. As for teaching Díaz about the Law of Moses, Luis suggested they begin at half-past six that evening. Luis would pray before going to sleep and he would show Díaz how to pray like him.

It is painful to hear Luis like this. He sounds crazed and feverish as he dances in his cell, boasting that he will soon be burned and talking with wild indiscretion to a man he does not know.

What made him trust Díaz so readily? It is difficult to say. We know almost nothing about Díaz, only that he was a Holy Office spy and cunning enough to deceive an emotional and frightened Luis. The fact that he was a priest may have helped him to win Luis's trust, however, because Luis's experiences with men of the Church had been surprisingly benign until this point. His Franciscan cellmate had embraced the Law of Moses and protected him from the inquisitors. Fray Pedro de Oroz and his colleagues had shown him great kindness at the college in Santiago Tlatelolco, and as Luis's trial unfolds we will learn that he had another clerical friendship, with an unnamed monk in nearby Texcoco. Presumably the memory of those friendships inclined Luis to bare his soul to Díaz. It was a terrible mistake on Luis's part. Next day Díaz went to the inquisitors to tell them everything that he had said, and it is clear that Díaz was not inventing the things he told the inquisitors. He reported information that only Luis could have known, and that would later be corroborated by Luis himself and other members of the Carvajal family.

Luis continued to speak far too freely during the days that followed. He told Díaz that Manuel de Lucena kept the Law of Moses 'with perfection' and he talked about his family, too, recalling how his mother, Francisca, and his sisters, Leonor and Mariana, used to dance with joy in Santiago and sing 'Blessed be those who await the God of Israel'. He told

Díaz about his brothers Miguel and Balthasar, saying they were now in Italy and had adopted the names David and Jacob Lumbroso, and he showed Díaz a fragment of paper on which he had written the commandments in Latin in letters of gold. Díaz noted all this, and on the morning of Thursday 9 February he went upstairs again to divulge the latest bits of information he had gleaned.

That same afternoon the guileless Luis appeared before the inquisitors for the first time. They began with the usual questions designed to establish his name and place of birth.

'I am called Luis de Carvajal,' he replied. 'I was born in the town of Benavente in the kingdom of Castile. I am the son of Francisco Rodríguez de Matos who was burned in effigy by this Holy Office and of doña Francisca de Carvajal, his wife, who was reconciled for observance of the Law of Moses. I am thirty years old and today it is nine days since I was arrested and placed in the secret cells of this Holy Office.'

They asked whether he had been a prisoner of the Holy Office before and had been punished by it. They knew he had, but this too was a standard question.

'Yes, I have been a prisoner of this Holy Office,' he responded, 'and was reconciled by it for having observed the Law that God gave to Moses, and it will be five years,

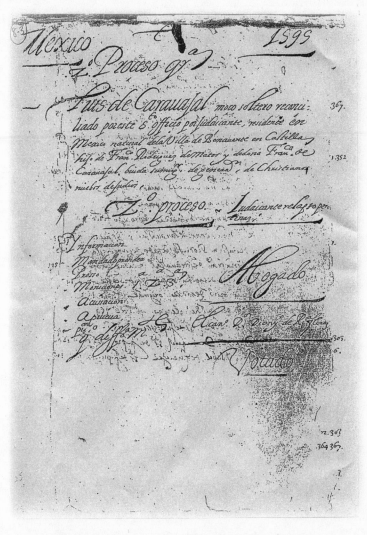

FRONT SHEET OF LUIS DE CARVAJAL'S TRIAL TRANSCRIPT,
1595–1596. INQUISICIÓN VOL. 14, COLECCIÓN RIVA PALACIO.
COURTESY OF THE ARCHIVO GENERAL DE LA NACIÓN,
MEXICO CITY.

more or less, from this present month, on the twenty-fifth, that I went out in the *auto público* that was celebrated on the day of San Mathias, wearing a penitential garment, and was sentenced to perpetual incarceration.'

'When the *auto* finished,' they asked, 'did you abjure your apostasy and observance of the Law of Moses and swear not to reoffend? And did you sign the abjuration document?'

Luis replied, 'I swore and promised never more to return to offend in this way or in any other type of heresy, but I do not remember whether I signed my name.'

The inquisitors showed him the abjuration document. He acknowledged the signature at the bottom as his.

They asked whether he knew, presumed or suspected why he had been brought as a prisoner to the Holy Office.

He replied that he did not.

They read him the same obligatory admonition he had heard in 1589: that the Holy Office of the Inquisition was not accustomed to arresting people without sufficient evidence, and as Luis had been arrested it followed that evidence had been given against him. Therefore, out of reverence for God, he should speak the truth and discharge his conscience.

Luis replied that he had not done anything against the Holy Catholic Faith. 'Nor have I seen anyone else do anything.'

The inquisitors turned to the subject of the three little books he had been carrying when he was brought to the Holy Office cells. 'Why were you carrying those volumes?'

'Because since childhood I have been devoted to reading the Holy Bible,' he replied.

'But what did you do with the fourth volume that contains the New Testament of Our Redeemer, Jesus Christ? Where did you keep it?'

The absence of the New Testament, dedicated to the story of Jesus, had aroused their suspicions.

'I kept the fourth volume in my saddlebag,' he responded, 'because I was on my way to speak with the provincial of Santo Domingo, to request permission for my brother Fray Gaspar de Carvajal to go to Spain with my mother and sisters. The fourth volume did not fit in the leather bag,' he added, 'so I placed it in my saddlebag.'

They asked him what other books or papers he possessed that related to the Old Testament. 'None,' Luis replied, 'except some books in Romance like *El Símbolo de la Fe* by Fray Luis de Granada, *El Espejo de Consolación*, *Guia de Pecadores* and *Diálogos del Amor de Dios*.' Luis apparently did not know that the writings of this great Catholic mystic were considered heretical by the Holy Office, or surely he would not have mentioned them.

With that the inquisitors brought the hearing to a close and returned him to his cell. They already knew that Luis had returned to the Law of Moses or, worse, had never really abandoned it. But Luis did not know that they knew. He admitted nothing and his silence suggests that despite his rapturous bravado about wanting to be burned, he still clung to some hope of survival. The fact that he had been planning to escape New Spain suggests that he had not been seeking martyrdom. Now that he had been arrested he was trying to be brave and accept and embrace the death that awaited him, as a martyr should—but he was scared.

That night Luis told Díaz about a Franciscan in Texcoco who secretly observed the Law of Moses. He also talked about Gregorio López who resided at the Hospital de Santa Fe, 'three leagues from this city', saying that López kept the Law of Moses with even greater perfection than he did.

Luis urged Díaz to visit Gregorio López once he was released from prison. 'Tell him you have been my cell companion,' he said, 'and he will advise you about the path you should take, because he believes that one should go singing and preaching the Law of Moses . . . And tell Gregorio López also of the happiness I felt in my cell. Tell him that I sang and danced with great rejoicing because I knew that I was going to die for my God and Lord.'

Luis had further instructions for Díaz. He wanted Díaz, once he was released, to go to the house in Santiago and retrieve the notebooks he had hidden there.

'Go to the upper room of the building,' Luis told Díaz, 'and there you will see some statues of Jesus, the Holy Virgin and Mary Magdalene that I intended to burn because we were on the verge of leaving for Spain . . . In the ceiling of that room you will find a loose board where I hid my notebook. Take the little book, and guard it as if it were precious pearls, because it will help you with your doctrine.

'Then go downstairs to the corridor. There are some earthenware jars there and beside them is a window. Move a chair beside the window, climb onto it and you will touch a false board. Behind it you will find another little book that I made to send to my brothers in Pisa, where they are living as Jews, so that they will have the pleasure of keeping it.' It seems that Balthasar and Miguel were in Pisa now. In any case, Luis told Díaz to wrap the notebooks as if they were a parcel of letters, then take it to a friend of his who would ensure it reached his brothers, wherever they happened to be.

Next day Díaz told the inquisitors about the notebooks. They sent their constable to the house in Santiago Tlatelolco.

He found the statues Luis had described, and the little book of miracles hidden nearby. 'But the other one the witness here refers to was not found,' he told the inquisitors.

Where had it gone? Someone, a friend perhaps, or one of Luis's sisters, had taken it in order to keep it safe.

# 9

# JOSEPH

LUIS'S TRUST IN DÍAZ LASTED JUST LONG ENOUGH TO CAUSE irreparable harm, but it ended on the afternoon of 10 February. Díaz went upstairs once more and while he was gone the jailer placed another prisoner with Luis. There is nothing in the records to explain why the jailer did this, but the prisoner, whose name was Franco, took the opportunity to warn Luis that Díaz was a spy and an informer.

'And look, Luis de Carvajal,' Franco told him, 'if you have said anything there is no remedy now, for you will be uncovered.'

When Díaz returned to the cell Franco had gone and Luis was sitting in wretched silence. He did not speak for an hour, but finally he turned and said, 'That little book I gave you was a good flower.' He meant the book of commandments he had given Díaz on their first day together. 'I want it back,' he said.

Díaz handed it to him and Luis tried to erase a name on one of its pages.

'Oh, don't tamper with the name,' Díaz told him.

Luis looked up. 'I have uncovered you,' he said, 'and know who you are.'

'I am your brother!' Díaz protested, but Luis knew better now.

'For the sake of the One God,' Luis implored his betrayer, 'I ask that you reveal only me and not my mother and sisters because they will burn them.'

Luis begged him not to reveal the friends he had spoken about either. But it was too late and he knew it.

'Where was my judgement,' he wept, 'when I poured out my heart to you, telling you about everyone who keeps the Law of Moses? May those unfortunate people stay safe.'

Luis added that it was a blessed thing for him because his death would give pleasure to God. But he was inconsolable to think that he had inadvertently condemned the people he loved. He had to find a way to save them, if he could.


Next morning, 11 February, Luis requested a hearing. Dr Lobo Guerrero, who had been prosecutor in his trial five years earlier, received him alone.

'Why have you asked for this hearing?'

'Because yesterday I did not speak the truth or conduct myself with the openness required of me,' Luis replied.

With that he began to confess. He told Dr Lobo Guerrero almost everything he had confided to his memoir. He described his induction into the Law of Moses in Medina del Campo, and his spiritual life since then. He talked about the Jewish holy days he had observed since childhood such as Passover and the festival of Queen Esther. He explained that he refrained from eating pork and the meat of animals that did not chew their cud or had cleft hooves, or who crawled along the earth. He said he did not eat fish without scales, and consumed only meat that had been bled. He told Dr Lobo Guerrero about the day when he had circumcised himself with scissors beside the River Pánuco. He described the little book filled with verses from Deuteronomy and recalled how he and his brother, Balthasar, had wept when they read about the curses that would come upon those who do not observe the Law of God. But they had also read that God offered mercy to true penitents, and so, kneeling down, they had promised to put right their conduct from that day on.

It was about this time, Luis said, that Balthasar decided that he too wanted to be circumcised, and after he had recovered from this surgery they had continued their observance of the Law of Moses until, on the eve of their departure for Castile,

Luis had been arrested by the Holy Office. Luis explained that while in prison he had taught the Law of Moses to his cellmate Francisco Ruíz de Luna.

'And during that time I confessed to observing the Law of Moses, and for fear of my life and so I would not be burned, I falsely declared that I was converted to the Law of Our Lord Jesus Christ. I would have been a traitor if I had abandoned belief in the Law that God gave to Moses, as a man who never parted from that Law, and always held it in my heart, although I showed myself to have parted from it in this tribunal and outside of it, even in front of my mother and sisters.'

'Even in front of my mother and sisters . . .' His confession sounds so heartfelt and sincere, yet every time he mentioned his mother and his sisters he cast them as innocents who had no idea that he had continued to observe the Law of Moses after his reconciliation in 1590.

As for himself, 'Today I believe the Law of Moses and always have believed it since learning about it in the town of Medina del Campo. And I think I will be saved through this belief and not through the Law of Our Redeemer, Jesus Christ, whom I do not accept to have been the Messiah promised in the Law. Nor do I believe that the Messiah has come, and so I await him. And the commandments I believe and obey are those given in Exodus chapter nineteen, and Deuteronomy chapters six and seven.'

Dr Lobo Guerrero told Luis to recite those commandments.

'I would like to kneel,' Luis replied, 'because in saying them I will have to utter the Holy Name of God, Our Lord, who created the sky and the earth.'

'Stay as you are,' Lobo Guerrero said, and so, still standing, Luis began.

'The first says *Oye Israel!*' he declared in Spanish. 'Hear Israel!' Then shifting suddenly into Hebrew he began to recite the beautiful prayer that Jews say before they die. The scribe did his best to record what he heard but his transcription is imperfect, whether due to his lack of Hebrew or the quality of Luis's recitation we do not know.

'*Semha Israel, Adonay Alhieno,*' the scribe wrote, instead of '*Shema Israel, Adonay Eloheinu*'. He omitted the next phrase—'*Adonay Echad*'—perhaps Luis himself omitted it—but managed to approximate the liturgical response, writing '*Varocsem*' for '*Baruch Shem*', '*que voz*' for '*Kevod*', '*malcuto*' for '*Malchuto*' and '*leolamvaet*' for '*Leolam Vaed*'.

'Which means,' Luis concluded, 'Hear, O Israel, the Lord Our God is One. Blessed be the name of His glorious kingdom, forever and ever.'

The *Shema* is the only Hebrew prayer Luis appears to have known in its entirety. We have no idea how he learned it, but when David Gitlitz was preparing his study of clandestine Jewish life in the Iberian world he found that it was often the only Hebrew prayer to survive in the memories of Iberian Jews after 1492. The *Shema* reflects the essence of the first commandment, but it is not part of that commandment. Luis understood this distinction. He would later tell his sister Leonor that the idea of linking it to the first commandment had come to him in prison. He was using it now to demonstrate that the Christian notion of a Trinitarian divinity—Father, Son and Holy Spirit—contravened the law that God gave to Moses on Mount Sinai.

Luis moved on to the other nine commandments, as familiar to Christians as to Jews with their instructions to worship no gods other than He who gave the law to Moses, to never take His name in vain, to keep the Sabbath, to obey one's parents, to refrain from killing, committing adultery, bearing false witness and coveting one's neighbour's wife and belongings.

'And I have kept these commandments,' he said, 'in observance of the Law of Moses . . . and I believe in the Law of Moses and believe that I will be saved through it and not through that of Jesus Christ Our Lord . . . And, as I have said, I await the Messiah promised in the Law, who will redeem Israel and take it out of captivity and the ills it suffers and confound all the idols of the world like the figures of Christ and Our

Lady the Virgin Mary and of the saints and other figures and statues of gods of the people and barbarous nations, bringing them all to the true knowledge of God Our Lord, as contained in the prophecies . . .'

He said he wanted to recite the thirteen articles of the law that God gave to Moses, 'that are the fundamentals of the holy religion of the Jews, not all of which articles are against the articles of faith of the Christians . . .' But the scribe noted that 'being given the hour' the señor inquisitor brought the hearing to a close.

Luis's confession runs to over fifteen hundred words in Spanish and is in essence a version of his memoir with that one critical difference: the assertion that his mother and sisters had stayed true to the vows they had taken in the cathedral five years earlier and did not know that he had returned to the Law of Moses.

It takes at least an hour to read the confession aloud, but Luis may have needed longer when he made it that Saturday morning in 1595. He had no written text to guide him, as we do, and may well have hesitated over certain phrases while considering what to say. The scribal record does not capture any of those natural pauses. Nor does it tell us how Dr Lobo Guerrero responded to what he heard.

Mexico City was his first and last appointment as inquisitor and his theological training at the University of Salamanca had probably not prepared him for a heretic as erudite as Luis de Carvajal. He had arrived in New Spain in 1580, the same year as Luis, but the majority of cases in which he had been involved since then concerned the usual mundane offences of blasphemy, bigamy and clerical misconduct. Only thirteen instances of Judaising had been brought before the Holy Office since his arrival and those had all concerned the Carvajal family and their circle.

Luis had been twenty-three and blessed with youthful innocence when Lobo Guerrero first encountered him in 1589. Luis was twenty-nine now, resolute and learned. We cannot hear his voice as the inquisitor did that Saturday morning, but his words convey the expressive power of an Old Testament prophet. When he insists that the Lord God is One and the figures of Jesus, Mary and the saints are idols of barbarous nations, he could be Moses himself, or Isaiah or Jeremiah railing against idolatry. Like those ancient prophets, Luis insists on saying what must be said, no matter the consequences. And there is something else about his words: they sound like the kind of admonition the judges of the Holy Office were accustomed to giving rather than receiving.

Did Dr Lobo Guerrero shake his head and sigh, or sit impassive and composed? Did he conclude the hearing because the hour was late, or because he could not bear to hear any more from this young man he had once believed to be a genuine penitent? We cannot know the inquisitor's inner thoughts. All we know is that he told Luis to check the transcript to see that his words had been correctly recorded. Then he instructed the guard to take Luis to his cell.

Luis returned to the audience chamber on Tuesday afternoon. This time both inquisitors were present and they began by asking whether he had remembered anything, and warning him that if he had he should declare it in accordance with the oath he had taken.

'The articles of the Law of Moses are thirteen in number,' Luis replied. It was not what they had asked him, but they listened as Luis recited the articles he had gleaned from the work of their colleague Oleastro in the college library in Santiago Tlatelolco. When Luis had finished the inquisitors asked him what other aspects of the Law of Moses he had observed since being reconciled by the Holy Office.

'When I had a nocturnal pollution while asleep,' he replied, 'I used to bathe myself at night near Ezcapuzalco, in the channel of water that comes to Santiago. And I used to fast in the middle of the week, eating at midday so that I would not be seen to observe the Law of Moses. And when I was imprisoned in these cells last time I fasted every day in observance of the Law of Moses, apart from Saturday which I observed as a festival day in memory of the fact that God rested from creating the world on the seventh day. And I haven't eaten bacon or meat that is cooked with it because God has forbidden us to eat pork, and also things that come from it; and I didn't drink all day either because it is a tradition of the Jews that the day we fast we don't drink . . .

'And while travelling I tried to observe the Sabbaths,' he continued, 'and I recall that last September, while passing from Zimapan I paused in a little Indian village close to Pachuca to observe and fast the Great Day of the Lord and I bathed in a nearby creek, and stayed three days in that village in order to observe the Great Day of the Lord; and because I wasn't certain on which two of the three days it fell I fasted from Wednesday night until Friday night, not eating or drinking, and I sent to the house of Manuel de Lucena for some candles and Lucena sent them and some cakes fried in oil, and although I didn't speak about the fast with Manuel de Lucena he understood that I had stayed in the village in order to observe it.'

They asked, 'When you celebrated Passover were there lamb and bitter herbs on the table, as laid down in the Law of Moses?'

'No,' Luis replied, 'I celebrated only with tortillas, and as for the lamb's blood to be spread on the doors of the house, I didn't dare do that.'

'Apart from teaching the Law of Moses to Francisco Ruíz de Luna in the cells of the Holy Office, have you taught any other persons outside?'

'No.'

They questioned him about the old invalid who had given him the notebook filled with verses from Deuteronomy.

'When you talked with him about the things of the Law of Moses,' they asked, 'what other persons were present?'

'Only Balthasar Rodríguez, my brother,' Luis replied, knowing that Balthasar was far away and safe from prosecution.

'What other people do you know in this city and outside of it who observe the Law of Moses?'

Luis told them he knew that Manuel de Lucena and Manuel Gómez Navarro observed it, 'but no other persons'. He added that he knew about these two because once while travelling from Mexico City to Pachuca they had admitted to each other that they observed the Law of Moses.

Manuel had testified a few weeks earlier that he and Luis had declared themselves as secret Jews in the Indian college at Santiago. The inquisitors would have noted that discrepancy, as we do. They concluded the hearing at that point, however, warned Luis to think carefully before his next appearance, and then returned him to his cell.

They sent for him again next morning.

'Have you remembered anything relating to your cause?'

'No,' he replied, 'but I have been contemplating in my cell the value of circumcision, and have found that since I circumcised myself I have been given a strong weapon against lust, and with the help of God I can resist it, because before I took the sacrament of circumcision I was torpid, dishonest, carnal and lustful.'

They showed no interest in his circumcision.

'Do your mother and sisters observe the Law of Moses?'

He must have feared this question above all others.

'They have not observed it since being reconciled by the Holy Office,' he replied.

'What law do they observe?' the inquisitors asked.

'The Law of Jesus Christ.'

'How do you know they observe the Law of Jesus Christ?'

'I know because in words and deeds my mother and sisters do what the Law of Jesus Christ commands.'

'How is it that you observe the Law of Moses, persevere in its belief, feel convinced that you will be saved through it and that no-one can be saved through the Law of Jesus

Christ, and yet you have not taught the Law of Moses to your mother and sisters, even though you understand that by keeping the Law of Jesus Christ they will be condemned?'

'I didn't dare because of my great fear that the Holy Office would arrest us and we would denounce each other.'

'This is not to be believed,' they told him, 'because you have taught the Law of Moses to strangers—and we have abundant information about that—and you did so out of your zeal to spread the Law of Moses and extend its belief, and because you felt a need to save those persons you taught. It is clear you trusted those strangers, so who could you trust better than your mother and sisters who, for the love of son and brother and blood, would not have denounced you to the Holy Office? And for the same reason you must surely have felt an obligation to care for their salvation and wellbeing, rather than that of strangers.'

'What I have said is true,' Luis replied, 'because when I taught the Law to Francisco Ruíz de Luna I was already a prisoner and in the danger I feared.' He'd had no reason to fear denunciation, in other words.

'But you have said and declared that you taught the Law of Moses to Francisco Ruíz de Luna after having falsely confessed to the Holy Office,' they countered, 'and that you feigned conversion while continuing to believe in the Law of Moses. So Francisco Ruíz de Luna could have denounced you to the Holy Office and you would have been in the same danger as if you had taught him the Law of Moses while free and outside the cells of the Holy Office.'

There was an undeniable logic in their question, but Luis replied that as he had taught his mother and sisters before their arrest by the Holy Office, there was no need to teach them again after they were reconciled.

'Because if they did observe the Law of Moses then God, who is judge of all that goes on inside us, would know. But on the outside I have not seen them do anything in the Law of Moses.'

The inquisitors asked, 'In your heart, what do you believe and suspect of your mother and sisters with regard to belief in the Law of Moses?'

Luis replied that he believed fear of the Holy Office had obliged them to refrain from observing the Law of Moses.

The inquisitors put the question another way.

'Do you understand,' they asked, 'that this fear obliged your mother and sisters to not believe the Law of Moses in their hearts?'

Luis replied by paraphrasing their words. It was the safest thing to do. 'I understand that the said fear obliged them to *not* believe the Law of Moses.'

But they persisted. 'In which of the two things are you better informed: that your mother and sisters observe the Law of Jesus Christ, or observe the Law of Moses?'

'The Law of Jesus Christ,' he replied.

'Then if you observe the Law of Moses and are so perfect in observing it, and your mother and sisters keep the Law of Jesus Christ, which is so contrary to the Law of Moses, how have you lived with them and dealt with them, given that the Law of Moses makes a prohibition that the Jew must not live with the gentile nor any other person of another religion, nor deal with them, but must draw away from them?'

'I had nowhere else to go,' Luis said, 'and I confess that I sinned mortally in dealing with my mother and sisters because I knew they observed the Law of Jesus Christ, and I will be accused of this by God, although until now I didn't know it was a sin.'

Luis sounds startled to think he might have broken a tenet of Mosaic Law. But had he? A passage in the New Testament Book of Acts suggests that in the ancient world Jewish law prohibited Jews from associating with anyone 'of another nation'. But the inquisitors would have known very well that in Europe, ever since the fourth Lateran Council in 1215, it was Christians, not Jews, who had insisted on segregation between the two faiths. Venetian and Roman authorities had confined their Jewish residents to ghettos; the city of Arles had made them wear yellow cloth badges over their hearts. The king of England had expelled them from his kingdom and the king of France had followed suit.

Later, throughout the fifteenth century, Spanish Christians had restricted and controlled the lives of Spanish Jews until they too had expelled them. But the inquisitors did not pursue this theme any further. They had something more important to discuss with Luis.

'Now that you believe in the Law of Moses and believe you will be saved through it, do you call yourself by any name other than Luis de Carvajal?'

Hearing this he would have known that they had found his book of miracles. There was no point him denying anything he had written in it.

'I call myself Joseph Lumbroso,' he said, 'and I took "Lumbroso" because of a dream I had while imprisoned in this jail five years ago, which was that a vial of precious liquid came to me, covered with a cloth, and that God said to Solomon, Take a spoonful of this liquid and place it in this boy's mouth; and Solomon placed a spoonful of that liquid in my mouth and I awoke and felt so consoled that I no longer felt oppressed by my imprisonment, and understood that the dream was a light, *una lumbre*, from God, who wanted me to observe the Law of Moses and understand the meaning of the Holy Scriptures.'

With that the hearing ended. The inquisitors warned Luis to be ready to declare everything he recalled at his next hearing. He examined that morning's transcript to confirm that it was a good and true record, and despite what he'd said about his adopted name he signed it 'Luis de Carvajal'.

The inquisitors reconvened that afternoon. They began, as always, by asking whether Luis had remembered anything.

'No,' he replied.

'Have your brothers Balthasar and Miguel taken Jewish names?' they asked.

'Balthasar Rodríguez is called David Lumbroso,' Luis responded. 'As for Miguel, I do not know whether he has taken a Jewish name.'

'Do you still believe in and observe the Law of Moses and do you think you will believe in it and observe it from this time on, and persevere in it?'

'I still believe in and observe the Law of Moses,' Luis replied, 'and I want to live and die in it.'

They asked on what basis he had withdrawn from belief in the Law of Jesus Christ and passed to belief in the Law that he said God had given to Moses.

'For many reasons,' Luis replied, 'and because of the fundamentals I have drawn from Holy Scripture.' He went on to recite the thirteen principles of Maimonides that he had read in Oleastro. 'And I have been inspired by all these fundamentals,' Luis concluded, 'since I was taught the Law that God gave to Moses: to have it, believe it and persevere in it until death, and perform the rites and ceremonies that I have performed in its observance, and await the Messiah promised in the Law.'

Dr Lobo Guerrero and Licenciado Peralta had listened as Luis revealed the principles that guided him. 'Would you be prepared to submit yourself to religious Catholic men who might help you and take you out of the error and blindness in which you are living,' they asked him, 'and convert you to the Law of Our Lord Jesus Christ?'

'I am not living in error or blindness but in the truth,' Luis replied. 'But I do wish to hear those Catholic and religious learned men, in order to speak with them about the said fundamentals . . . so that they can satisfy me in the doubts I will put to them. And if they satisfy and convince me,' he added, 'I will convert to the Law of Our Lord, Jesus Christ, and if not I will die in the Law of Moses, because I desire nothing more than to save my soul.'

The inquisitors read him the second of the three admonitions they were required to give all prisoners. They reminded him that he was obliged to tell what he and others had done, and asked him to open his eyes to understanding and see how blind he was in drawing apart from the Law of Our Redeemer, Jesus Christ, and persevering in the Law of Moses with such obstinacy and pertinacity. 'Because in abandoning the error in which you are living you will redeem your soul and put yourself on the path to salvation, because there is no other path but to believe in Our Redeemer, Jesus Christ, and in his blessed Law of Grace.'

Luis replied that he had told them all he knew about himself and others. 'And as for the rest, I will think well about it and consider whether I walk in error or not, and I will not pray to God for anything other than to be given the grace to be saved. But at this point I understand because of my knowledge that I do not walk in error, but on the path of truth.'

With that they gave him the usual warning to consult his memory. Then they returned him to his cell.

Luis remained there until the morning of Saturday 25 February, when Dr Lobo Guerrero sent for him.

'Have you remembered anything?'

'No,' Luis replied.

The inquisitor showed him the book of miracles he had hidden in the house in Santiago Tlatelolco. Luis would have known this moment was coming ever since that question ten days earlier about whether he now went by a different name.

'I recognise the book,' he said, 'and the handwriting is mine.'

'What does it contain,' the inquisitor asked, 'and why did you write it?'

'It contains the story of my life,' Luis replied, 'and I wrote it as a record of the miracles and mercies that God has shown me, with the intention of sending it to my brothers, Balthasar Rodríguez de Carvajal and Miguel Rodríguez, so that they would know about those miracles and mercies.

'Everything in the book is true,' he added, 'and I affirm and ratify everything I have said in it.'

Dr Lobo Guerrero had read the book with care.

'What did you mean when you said that fear of carnivorous wolves caused your mother and sisters to turn away from the Law of Moses? Who were those carnivorous wolves?'

Luis explained that he had been referring to the administrators of royal justice.

'Did your mother and sisters say they had not confessed to observing the Law of Moses because they would be burned?'

Luis replied, 'I swear by the Lord of Hosts in whom I believe and whom I adore that they did not say that.'

The inquisitor asked, 'What was the mercy that God showed Joseph, as described in this book, when he took him from the convalescent hospital to live with his mother and sisters? And are you the Joseph referred to in this book?'

'I am that Joseph,' Luis replied, 'and the mercy God showed me was in reuniting me with my mother and sisters.'

•

That afternoon both inquisitors were waiting for Luis.

'Have you remembered anything in relation to your cause?'

'No,' he replied.

They asked him to identify the person he had referred to in his notebook who had escaped from their constable and fled to Spain in order to procure Luis's freedom and that of his mother and sisters.

'It was my brother-in-law Jorge de Almeida,' he replied, 'because he feared the inquisition wanted to confiscate the dowry of his wife, my sister doña Leonor, who was reconciled by the Holy Office.'

'What is the captivity endured by your mother and sisters that you refer to in your book?' they asked.

'I was referring to our sentence of perpetual imprisonment and the wearing of penitential garments,' he replied.

They told him to name the young girl who had been arrested by the Holy Office after the imprisonment of her mother and sisters.

'It was my sister doña Anica,' Luis replied.

They asked him whether doña Anica knew something that she had failed to confess so as not to cause harm to others.

Luis answered, 'No.'

They reminded him that the Law of God does not permit lies, and as he was observant of the Law of God he should answer truly.

Which of your sisters was 'the enemy of the idols and idolaters and of these blind, ill-fated people'?

'My sister doña Mariana, who had always observed the Law of Moses and had believed it in her heart and knew as much of the Bible as I did, so we used to talk about it together. And she lost a little book of mine covered in green velvet in which I had translated many things of Holy Scripture and she lost her reason for fear of the damage she could cause me, because the said book was in my handwriting and signed with my name.'

'Why did you say in your book that you, your mother and sisters were in danger because of the madness of doña Mariana?' they asked him.

'It was a mistake to write that,' Luis replied. 'We didn't have anything to fear because of doña Mariana being mad.'

The inquisitors said that his answer still did not satisfy them because in his book he had said they were in danger because doña Mariana had thrown their household idols through the windows and had uttered many truths; so what were the truths that placed them in such grave danger?

'Well, although doña Mariana was mad, and therefore we had nothing to fear, she uttered many prophecies and blasphemies about the sacramental altar, and this couldn't help but engender fear in us.'

They pointed out that according to this answer Luis had not spoken truly when he said he had made an error in his writing.

'I made an error in everything I wrote about our feelings of fear and danger, because it was clear that in reality there was no reason to fear what a madwoman said or did.'

They asked him about the idols doña Mariana had thrown through the windows, and about the 'idolaters' he had mentioned.

'The images were of Our Lady and of La Magdalena,' Luis replied, 'and others that I don't recall. And the idolaters were the Christians.'

'What did you mean,' they asked, 'when you said that in all your difficulties your mother and sisters hoped that the Most High would bring you relief and take you to a place where, in acknowledgement of all these mercies and charities, you could sing praises to glorify His holy name among the servants of God?'

'I meant the travails and illnesses of my mother and sisters,' Luis replied, 'especially of doña Mariana and doña Anica, and we wanted to give praise to the Lord for having freed us from those travails and troubles.'

They asked, 'Where did you want God to take you in order to give praise, as you say in this book?'

'We intended, my mother and sisters and I, to go to a big city in Spain where we were not known and leave the Indies and the infamy in which we lived. And there we would give praise to God for having freed us from the said toils and troubles.'

They told him this did not make sense because they could give praise to God in Mexico City.

'Didn't you really mean in your book that you hoped God would take you to a place where you would have the liberty to observe the Law that God gave to Moses?'

'This was not our intention.'

'Who were the servants of God among whom your mother and sisters hoped to offer praise?' they asked.

He said that speaking for himself he believed that those who observed the Law of Moses were servants of God.

They asked him whether his mother and sisters were among those servants.

'No,' he replied.

'Well then why did you say in your book that your mother and sisters were among those servants of God who gave praise to Him?'

'I made an error,' he replied, 'because *hominis est errare*, to err is human.'

With that the hearing ceased. The inquisitors warned Luis to recall as much as he could. Then they returned him to his cell.

Winter drew to a close. On 2 March, as the air outside the Holy Office jail began to warm, Dr Lobo Guerrero sent for Luis again.

'Have you remembered anything in relation to your cause?'

'No.'

Dr Lobo Guerrero had been reading Luis's book of miracles.

'Why do you say in your book that after being called to the Holy Office and returning free to your house, you sang songs of praise to the Lord and celebrated the joy of this mercy and your liberty with hymns?' He was referring to the day when the family were called to ratify their statements about Miguel.

'Because of the fear and trepidation we had felt,' Luis responded.

'What mercy could God show your mother and sisters, if they had no reason to fear?' Dr Lobo Guerrero asked.

'Santa Susana had nothing to fear either,' Luis countered, 'yet she went tearful and weeping, and then returned to her house in joy.' He was alluding to the story in the Book of

Daniel in which the virtuous Susana is wrongly accused of adultery, sentenced to death, but saved at the last moment.

The inquisitor showed Luis the three small notebooks he had been carrying when he was brought to the cells on the night of 1 February. Two were covered with white paper, a third with tawny calfskin. One of the white books contained the commandments and articles of the Law of Moses, the second contained prayers to the Lord, and the third was a psalter with illuminated letters in silvery ink.

Luis admitted they were his. 'The two covered in white paper contain my handwriting,' he said, 'and the calfskin-covered book is in the hand of a Jew called Agustín Juarez who lives in Santiago, and to whom I taught Latin.'

Dr Lobo Guerrero had something else to show Luis. The constable had found a letter from Balthasar when he searched the house in Santiago for Luis's notebooks.

'This is the hand of my brother Balthasar Rodríguez,' Luis said, 'although it is signed Francisco Rodríguez.' He had accidentally said his father's name. 'I mean Francisco Ramírez.'

The inquisitor asked about the 'Diego' in Balthasar's letter.

'That is my brother Miguel,' Luis answered.

'And does he observe the Law of Moses?'

Luis admitted that he did. 'And in another letter that I have destroyed Balthasar told us that Miguel had gone to Salonika, a Turkish city close to Constantinople, where he has become very learned in the Law of Moses. 'He is a saint,' Luis added, with what sounds like quiet pride.

'Where is your brother Balthasar Rodríguez at present?'

Luis said that he believed Balthasar was now in Rome because he had received more recent letters sent from there.

'Who was Balthasar Rodríguez referring to in his letter when he said that they had heard that "he" was dead?'

'He was referring to me,' Luis explained, 'because they had heard over there that I had died.'

'To whom did Balthasar Rodríguez write this letter?' Dr Lobo Guerrero asked.

'He wrote it to my mother and sisters, and to me, although he addressed it on the outside to me alone.'

'What did your brother mean when he suggested that you, your mother and sisters should give praise to Our Lord, because other prisoners had received sentences of six or seven years for fewer sins . . . ?'

'He meant,' Luis replied, 'that other Jews who observe the Law of Moses with greater perfection than us were prisoners for longer than us.'

'Didn't your brother Balthasar Rodríguez say this because he understood that your mother and sisters observed the Law of Moses, and as they didn't observe it perfectly, they had sinned more than other Jews who observed it with greater perfection, and therefore they suffered a longer time in prison?'

Luis took great care with his answer. He said that the letter had been written before his mother and sisters were reconciled, but as Balthasar had not known about their reconciliation he thought they still observed the Law of Moses. That was why he exhorted them to have patience and faith in the Lord.

With that Dr Lobo Guerrero warned Luis to consult his memory and returned him to his cell. The Holy Office prosecutor, Dr Martos de Bohorques, who had been present at this hearing, announced that he accepted what Luis de Carvajal had said.

# 10

# DAYS OF
# CONSOLATION

WINTER GAVE WAY TO SPRING IN MEXICO CITY. IT WAS A TIME OF
soft breezes and sky-flowers, of hummingbirds and butterflies
and the young trees in the Alameda gardens coming into leaf.
But the warmer weather brought the much feared *cocolitzli*
once again, and as usual the city's indigenous residents began
to perish in great numbers.

In February Luis had danced in his cell, saying he wanted
to die on the anniversary of his false reconciliation. That day
had passed and he had no idea how long he must wait for
the death he said he desired. Prisoners sentenced to be killed
during this violent age of faith often found the waiting hard
to bear. In 1564 an Anabaptist martyr in what is now Belgium
told her family, 'I hope that shortly it will be done with me,

for I want nothing more than to please the Lord and die a holy death.' Twenty years later a Catholic priest awaiting execution in Protestant England confided to his friends that he too wished that what must be done could be quickly done because the waiting had 'somewhat dulled' him.

This man and woman echoing the words of Jesus in Gethsemane were willing to relinquish their earthly lives. They did not fear what lay beyond death because they felt certain of their welcome into paradise. They feared, however, that their human frailties might rob them of the strength to die a good death, a holy death, a martyr's death. Luis de Carvajal would have understood their fear, if not their Christian faith. He had confessed and knew he would be killed, but he would not have wanted to be 'dulled' any more than the Anabaptist woman or the Catholic priest.

After his hearing on 2 March he spent the next eleven days in his cell and he was alone throughout that time. What did he do to sustain his spirits and his courage? No doubt he reflected on the questions he had fielded so far and searched his memory for scriptural passages to use in hearings to come. And we know from the series of letters he would soon begin to write that he thought constantly about his mother and his sisters and prayed that they were safe. Meanwhile he listened carefully to the sounds of the Holy Office prison, to the footsteps in the corridors, and the voices of other prisoners calling to each other and to him.

The inquisitors insisted on silence in the cells, but the Holy Office jail in Mexico City was not a silent place; one later inmate would say it was as raucous as a marketplace or a blacksmith's forge. Men and women called and whispered to each other in Portuguese and Spanish. Some spoke in fragments of Nahuatl, Mayan or Otomi languages they had learned from indigenous Mexicans, while those who had worked in the transatlantic slave trade communicated in a patois derived from the languages of Guinea and Angola. Luis took part in these acts of defiance. Early in 1596 the jailer would complain to the inquisitors that Luis had been singing a little rhyme to the man who brought his meals. According to the jailer, Luis's song went like this:

> Five names of Manuel, two Pedros, two Sebastianes,
> Two Tomases, Héctores, Gabrieles,
> Jorges, Andrés and Danieles,
> Two Antonios; but there are no Juanes,
> *Que es cosa y cosa, galanes.*

Luis's little song was an expression of resistance. He was using it to show that despite the rule of silence he knew very well who his fellow prisoners were and had been communicating with them.

•

Dr Lobo Guerrero sent for him on the morning of 13 March.

'Have you remembered anything?'

'No.'

'Do you still wish to persevere in your belief in the Law of Moses and await the Messiah promised in the said Law?'

'I do,' Luis replied. 'It is my wish to be confirmed in the Law that God gave to Moses, and await the Messiah in confirmation of that which God Our Lord promised through his prophets, and to imitate the saintly zeal of Matathias who, in the hour of his death, said to his sons: "Sons, be zealous in the Law of God and give your lives for the holy testament of our fathers." I wish to await that life that St Tobias said God will give to those who keep faith in Him,' Luis continued, 'remembering what God said through Jeremiah: "Lord, Hope of Israel, all of those who forsake thee will be confounded and thrown into the inferno and all those who depart from thee will be written in the earth because they have forsaken the Lord, the fountain of living waters."' Luis was quoting Jeremiah 17:13 but that verse contains no mention of the faithless being thrown into the inferno; whether by accident or on purpose Luis had introduced that phrase into the prophet's words.

Dr Lobo Guerrero ignored Luis's rendition of Jeremiah's dire warning and responded with his own. He recommended that Luis should ease his conscience by telling the truth about himself and other persons who had done or said things against the Holy Catholic Faith. And he repeated that if Luis did so, his case would be handled with brevity; only brevity, not mercy this time.

'I have told you everything I know about myself,' Luis replied, and the guard returned him to his cell.

Luis remained there for the next ten weeks. No more hearings, no more transcripts. Yet despite the silence in the official records we know a little about his life at this time from the series of letters he began to write in May. In those letters he said that for a while after his arrest he had been kept in one of the dark cells in the depths of the building: terrible places reserved for the most recalcitrant prisoners, where mosquitoes flourished in the humid air. But after three weeks in that darkness he was moved to a cell at ground level where, although still shackled, he had a window and could see the sky by night and by day.

The jailers had confiscated the notebooks he had filled with psalms and scriptural passages, but as far as we can tell they made no attempt to stop him following the rituals his cellmate Díaz had witnessed: fasting, cleansing his body with his drinking water, spending hours each day on his knees in prayer, facing east towards the ruined temple in Jerusalem. And as the Lenten prelude to Easter began, and fish from Lake Texcoco replaced the mutton in the prisoners' rations, Luis would have sensed that it was time to prepare for Passover.

In Spanish the word for Easter is *Pascua*. It is also the word for Passover, and this semantic duplication is no accident; it reflects the origins of the Christian feast in the Jewish tradition, for *Pascua* is derived from the Hebrew *Pesach*, and the same concurrence occurs in other European languages. The Portuguese have their *Páscoa*, the Italians their *Pasqua*, the Greeks and Russians have *Pascha*, the French *Pâques*. These great liturgical occasions, Passover and Easter, fall within weeks, sometimes days, of each other. But the secret Jews of Spain and Portugal, marooned in a hostile Christian world, found it hard to determine the fourteenth day of the Jewish month of Nisan when Passover begins, and their confusion must have deepened in 1582 when the Christian calendar changed from the Julian to the Gregorian count.

Some secret Jews dealt with their dilemma by beginning Passover on the first day of April each year. Others observed it during Christian Holy Week, which moves between March and April, according to the cycles of the moon. Luis had told the judges that his family always celebrated Passover during the fourteenth moon of March, so presumably he observed it around that time in 1595, alone in his cell, watching the night sky through his little window. He had no wine or salt water, no bitter herbs or unleavened bread for the Seder meal, but wheat and corn tortillas formed part of his daily rations and presumably he made do with these, as he had made do with cakes fried in oil when he celebrated Yom Kippur alone on the plains near Pachuca.

On the last day of March Dr Lobo Guerrero and Licenciado Peralta wrote to the Supreme Council in Madrid to report that they were holding twenty or so 'Portuguese' prisoners in Mexico City. Among them, they said, was a man named Luis de Carvajal who had recently been released from the penitential garment he had worn for five years. They knew now, however, that his reconciliation to the Church had not been genuine. 'He has confessed and says he wants to die in the Law of Moses,' they wrote, 'and he awaits the Messiah promised in that Law whom he says has not come . . . He is so pertinacious and unshakeable in his belief in the said Law that it is a pitiful thing, *"una cossa de compassión"*.'

'He has been a great teacher,' they continued—it was a description that would have pleased Luis—'and because of what he told his cellmate who pretended he wanted to be taught the Law of Moses, we have learned a great deal about those in this city who observe it.' They added that until now

Luis had not wanted to confess about anyone other than himself and one of his sisters who was insane. 'With regard to his mother and sisters, however, information has come to light that they observe the said law and are *relapsas*, although we have not yet arrested them.'

So when the inquisitors wrote that letter at the end of March 1595 Francisca and her daughters were still free. But they could not escape Mexico City. Mariana and Anna were still gravely ill and the journey through the mountains to the gulf coast was even less feasible than it had been six years earlier. There was little they could do except pray, and wait for the knock on their door that they knew would come eventually.

In May Luis heard that they had been arrested. He would later say that when he received the news he fell to his knees, wept bitter tears and cried to God for help. What could he do to console them? He could not lead them in songs of praise, or comfort them with psalms, as he had during their years in Santiago Tlatelolco. In the end he dried his tears and did what he had always done when he wanted to guide and comfort those he loved. He began to write.

Prisoners of the Mexican Inquisition were endlessly inventive when it came to communication. They tapped out words on the adobe walls of their cells in an alphabetical code not unlike the one the novelist Arthur Koestler would invent four centuries later for his fictional prisoner Rubashov. The inmates of the Holy Office jail in Mexico City found ways of writing too. They extracted straws from the brooms they used to sweep their cells; they dipped the straws in soot from their candles, in mixtures of soot and honey, or in lemon and orange juice, and they used these rudimentary tools to write on scraps of cloth and paper. Luis was no less ingenious than his fellow prisoners. He had no quill or ink or paper, but he did have a pin and knew he could write with it if only he could find a suitable surface.

We do not know how many minutes or hours or days it took him to discover such a surface, but eventually he found what he wanted inside one of the New World fruits he received in his daily rations: the avocado. Concealed within its buttery flesh is a stone, in reality a giant seed, as smooth as polished wood once its fragile outer membrane is removed. Like wood it can be scratched and marked with a sharp object, so some time around 13 May Luis used his pin to carve some words into an avocado stone. When he had finished he wrapped the stone in a fragment of purple taffeta, concealed it inside a melon, and asked the jailer to take the melon to his sister Leonor.

Five days later, on 17 May, the jailer, whose name was Reyes, took it to the inquisitors. He told them that the previous Saturday evening, 'the thirteenth of this present month', the prisoner Luis de Carvajal had asked him to take the melon to his sister doña Leonor. Reyes explained that Luis understood that his sister and his mother were imprisoned in the Holy Office cells and had been sending gifts to them. 'Understood'—*entendia*—not 'knew'—*sabia*. The difference will turn out to be significant.

'I looked inside the melon,' Reyes said, 'and found among the pips an avocado stone wrapped in a piece of purple taffeta.' The scribe noted that Reyes cupped his hands to demonstrate the way the taffeta had been wrapped around the avocado stone. 'And when I looked closely at the stone I noticed writing on it that said, *"Paciencia como Job".*' Patience like Job. Reyes could not make out the next words but then he saw, 'Souls of my heart, Adonay N. Sr. visits you.'

'And it seems these letters mean *"Adonay Nuestro Señor*: Adonay Our Lord,"* Reyes said. 'And on this stone are other letters that say, "I have it. Glory be to God. I am in shackles for my God."'

Reyes produced another avocado stone. Luis had hidden this one inside a plantain. 'Felicitations!' he had scratched on it. 'May the angels and saints of Adonay in Paradise await us, my martyrs, blessed of Adonay. I thought I would go alone, my blessed one. Send me signs if you are on your own or not. May Adonay remember our saintly mother. I have you and her and everyone in my heart . . .'

'I cannot read the next letters,' the jailer told the inquisitors, 'but they seem to say "*atravesadas*".' *Atravesado* means 'crossed' but the plural, feminine ending -*das* suggests that Luis was using it to refer to his mother and sisters in an adjectival sense. The context of this isolated word is lost to us, but Reyes could make out further writing that said: 'I have confessed the truth of A. about myself alone.'

Reyes had something else to report.

'And last night, Tuesday 16 May, Luis de Carvajal gave me another plantain for doña Leonor, his sister, and in the middle of the said plantain was another avocado stone wrapped in a piece of black fabric that seemed to have been cut from his hat.' Reyes held the avocado stone up to show the inquisitors. Like the others it must have come from one of the large avocados so common in Mexico, where they can grow to more than twenty centimetres. On it Luis had scratched in tiny writing, 'My angel, felicitations, for the journey to Paradise is better than the journey to Castile. Blessed is the bread you ate and the water you drank and the earth you trod and the womb from which we came forth, for in a little while we shall go to profess the sacred religion of the angels and saints and see the land of Adonay. Oh, what beautiful gardens, music and festivals await us there. Wonderful tournaments will be held in heaven when Adonay crowns us for our unyielding faith. Let none of us lose heart, for with the help of Adonay, my Lord God, beyond the crest of this hill is glory. Who could tell all that the Lord has shown me? But with his help we will be together soon. Three weeks I spent in a dungeon, then Adonay, my Lord, took me out and put me where I can see the sky by night and by day. By a miracle I have had a Bible here for eight days. Blessed ones of Adonay, I commend you to Him. When I remember you I forget myself. He has revealed great mysteries to me so do not fear those worms. What a good Lord and God we have, and a good and holy Law we believe in. God showed me one night in secret some tortillas made of wheat flour . . .'

'I cannot read the next letters,' the jailer said, 'but they seem to say something about Paradise, and then, "Listen, my angel, don't let them confuse you. Adonay Our Lord is God and there is no other."

'And I recall,' the jailer continued, 'that on Sunday when Luis de Carvajal gave me the plantain I have mentioned to give to doña Leonor his sister, he also gave me a paper with some raisins in it to give to his mother; and when I looked at the paper I found among the raisins a piece of lime—that's what it seemed to be—and across it a toothpick, or piece of thin stick, fastened like a spit, and a piece of tawny linen. And when Luis de Carvajal gave me the plantain to give to his sister doña Leonor he gave me another piece of peel that went in the bowl beneath the plantain, and in that piece of peel was another little stick, like a spit, to fasten it.' Reyes held up the three avocado stones, the purple taffeta and black fabric, the pieces of lime peel and the toothpicks like little spits. The Holy Office scribe noted them as evidence in the transcript, and the inquisitors sent the jailer on his way.

We never learn the significance of those little sticks, the lime peel, or the piece of tawny linen. They may have been a preordained message the family had devised in case one of them was arrested, or a rudimentary set of symbols Luis had invented in his cell in the hope his sister would understand their meaning. Nor do we know how he obtained a Bible, or what he was referring to when he wrote, 'I have it.' The mysterious object may have been the pin with which he carved his messages. Prisoners were permitted to receive clothing and foodstuffs from their relatives on the outside and his sisters could have concealed a pin in just such a gift or, for that matter, simply paid the jailer to take it to Luis. Reyes was notoriously eager to accept bribes from prisoners and their families; so much so that six years later his conduct would become the subject of a formal investigation.

What is clear from Luis's messages is that he was trying with all his heart to prepare Leonor for martyrdom. 'Dearest martyr, beloved of Adonay,' he called her, and urged her not to fear 'those worms'. And when he described the blessed bread she had eaten and the earth on which she had walked, he did so in the preterit past tense, with a terrible finality, as if she would never do them again. 'Blessed is the bread you ate, *el pan que comistes* . . . the earth you trod, *la tierra que pisastes.*' It is a blessing still current in the Castilian village where his great-great-grandparents had been baptised in 1492. And in the gentlest tones, as if whispering, he told Leonor, 'I thought I would go alone, my blessed one.' Go where? He meant to Paradise, in the presence of Adonay.

Leonor never read her brother's tender words. The warrant for her arrest, still secure within her trial transcript, shows that she was not yet in custody when he carved them into avocado stones for her. So Luis was mistaken to think she was already a prisoner in the Holy Office cells, and the fact that the jailer, Reyes, did not rectify his error suggests it may have been he who planted the idea in Luis's head in the first place to see what would happen. Or perhaps he simply saw Luis's error and took advantage of it.

Whatever the truth behind this tragic muddle, Luis waited in vain for a response from his sister, and while he waited he continued to send her messages, not knowing that his loving and consoling words were endangering her. His assurance that he had confessed the truth of Adonay about himself alone was not especially incriminating. But his allusions to martyrdom, to 'blessed ones of Adonay', to the 'good Lord and God we have' and 'the good and holy Law we believe in' implied without doubt that she and her mother and sisters shared Luis's heretical beliefs.

It was enough for the prosecutor. On 17 May he made out warrants for the arrest of Leonor and Francisca and sent the notary to take the two of them into custody. They were no longer in Santiago Tlatelolco. After Luis's arrest they had fled to the house of Catalina's husband, Antonio Díaz de Cáceres, but the notary found them there. He probably went around midnight when the streets were empty—it was the usual time for such arrests. But anyone still abroad at that hour would have noticed the forlorn sight of this mother and daughter being led by lantern light towards the Plaza de Santo Domingo.

Next morning the jailer reported to the inquisitors that Leonor and Francisca had been placed in the cells. Isabel would remain free for another four weeks; Anna, Mariana and Catalina for quite a bit longer.

There is nothing in Luis's trial records or in his prison letters to suggest that he ever understood the error he had made. He went on writing messages and two days after Leonor's arrest he asked the jailer to take another plantain to her. When Reyes looked inside he found four tiny scraps of blank paper. The transcript does not say how Luis might have come by those fragments, but prisoners received quince paste and raisins wrapped in paper in their daily rations, so Luis may have torn that paper into pieces in the hope that Leonor would use it to write to him.

Later that day he sent her another plantain. When the jailer looked inside he found half an avocado stone. On it, in tiny letters, Luis recalled a dream he'd had the night before: an empowering dream full of hope and optimism, like the one about Solomon that he had experienced during his first imprisonment. Like Joseph in Genesis, who had been a gifted interpreter of dreams, Luis explained it for her. He told Leonor that in his dream he had seen armed men with harquebuses stalking a flock of ducks. He said the stalkers represented the 'tonsured ones'—he meant the inquisitors—while the flock had symbolised their family, but he assured Leonor that the ducks had escaped by flying on wings of holy prayer towards 'the powerful God who defends us'. He finished by asking her to send this message on to the sisters of his heart and soul, by night, if she could.

The jailer took the avocado stone to the inquisitors. They examined it and devised a plan. The avocado stones had been useful so far but they were perishable. The words inscribed on them were tiny and sometimes indecipherable, and their size restricted how much Luis could write. 'Leave ink and a quill in Luis de Carvajal's cell with the greatest dissimulation,' they told Reyes. 'And leave some paper too, wrapped around raisins or some other gift.' It seems they hoped to entice Luis to write more freely and incriminate himself and his family even further.

The jailer did as he was told. He left some raisins wrapped in paper in Luis's cell, along with ink and a sheet of extra paper, and he asked Luis to use the ink and paper to write down some medicinal remedies they had been discussing. But Luis did not immediately abandon his messages on fruit. That evening he gave the jailer two pears, one for Leonor, the other for his mother and his other sisters whom he mistakenly assumed were in prison. Reyes took the pears to the inquisitors.

'Dearest Rachel,' Luis had scratched on the one for Leonor. It was an allusion to his namesake Joseph's wife in Genesis. 'Adonay, my Lord, has taught me so I could comfort you and has given me paper and ink. Send me news, my angel, on another pear. Write with a needle and send it by night, telling me about your spirits and your health and who is with you, or if you are alone . . .'

On the pear intended for his mother and his other sisters he had scratched, 'My loves, blessed ones of Adonay, my God visits you and comforts you in your tribulation.'

He invoked the names of the heroic women of the Hebrew Bible in a bid to raise their spirits. 'Courage, courage like Deborah, Jael and Judith,' he urged them, 'Faith, like Sara, your holy mother; be zealous like Salomona, holy martyr. Prayer, prayer, that in Paradise they await you with crowns; joy, joy, that like Sheba you go to see the King of the Angels, to delight in his beauty and wisdom.'

Next day Luis scratched a message on a plantain and asked the jailer to take it to Catalina, not knowing that she was still free. He addressed her with the plural form *vosotras* in the hope she might be able to pass the message to her mother and sisters. 'Felicitations, felicitations, joy, joy!' he wrote. 'Because Paradise awaits us'. He recounted his dream of hunters pursuing ducks, and explained, as he had to Leonor, that the hunters represented the inquisitors, while his mother and sisters were the birds who had flown on wings of prayer to their Almighty God.

'This was revealed to me, my blessed ones of Adonay. He visits you and consoles you in your tribulation. Courage, courage, my Judith, my love, pray, pray.'

•

Some time that Saturday or Sunday Luis began to use the quill and ink and paper. He seems to have believed the writing materials the jailer had left him had been sent by Leonor and Isabel. Or perhaps that was what he wanted the inquisitors to think. In any case, on Monday morning, 22 May, he gave the jailer two long letters. One was for Leonor and Isabel, the other for Leonor alone.

To Leonor and Isabel he wrote: 'Loves of my life, *vidas de mi ánima*, by a miracle an inkwell and a quill came to me today so that I might send you a vignette, beloved ones of my heart. Whoever receives it first can wrap it with caution and send it on to my other dear blessed ones. I was arrested through the will and judgement of the Most High, and through the accusation of the good Lucena. I have confessed the truth about myself alone so as not to give testimony against anyone else, and I confess it hoping for God's true reward, of which I have had great and certain promise during my imprisonment. You, my dearest ones, my angels, my blessed ones, were arrested on suspicion only and I defended your innocence; may my soul be defended against Satan and his agents by the holy angel of my Lord, God.'

He told them he had been in Taxco a few days before his arrest. He alludes once more to the weeks he spent in darkness in the dungeon. 'They brought my food by candlelight, but then my blessed Lord God took me out of there, blessed be

His name, and brought me to a cell in this courtyard and I have a window through which I see the sky by night and day.' He told his sisters he had wept when he heard of their arrest. 'With bitter tears and on bended knees I sighed and cried to the Lord God for help from His merciful hand for the salvation of our souls—the most important thing—that I await with great confidence . . . I am in shackles,' he added, 'but neither these nor burning fire will separate my soul from the sweetness of the Lord my God.'

He urged Leonor and Isabel to accept their sufferings as God's will, and to remember that the Lord's intentions towards his people are always good, even when they do not seem to be. He reminded them that after years in slavery Joseph had become a prince of Egypt. And he recounted that tale of utmost faith from the Book of Genesis: the terrible moment when God commands Abraham to take his only legitimate son, Isaac, to the top of the mountain and sacrifice him. He urged his sisters to remember the sacrifice of the saintly Isaac, 'who awaited the thrust of the knife with such obedience' and 'the faith of his saintly father, our patriarch Abraham'. 'This is the road to the glory of Paradise,' Luis continued, 'where we are awaited, and there is no other road open to us, and a better journey it is than the road to Castile. And since our good Lord is opening the door for us, let us not hinder him.'

He told them that their mother was in a cell near theirs, hoping perhaps to comfort them with the thought that Francisca was close by. 'How I wish I could come to see you and be with you,' he added. 'I have asked my Lord God to let me do this and perhaps He will, but if it cannot be done I am comforted that we shall see each other before we die.' He meant that they would meet on the day of their execution. After that, he promised, they would be together in eternity, among the beautiful angels and saints. 'Oh, what a joyous expectation,' he told them. 'You shall live. You shall live beyond your death . . . Oh, my dearest flock,' he sighed, 'we are so scattered.'

He told his sisters he had heard them passing by his cell, and it is possible he did hear Leonor because she had been in prison for six days by then.

'I know it is you from the sound of your *chopines*,' he said, referring to the elevated clogs Spanish women used to wear to keep their gowns above the mud of winter and the dust of summer.

'I will keep a cloth in my little window,' he added, 'so that when you pass by you will see it.' He wanted his sisters to know which door was his, and that he was there, behind it, listening for their footfall as they passed.

He concluded by reminding them that as children of Adam they were all born to die. 'Happy is he who leaves the prolonged death of this life in order to live the true life.' He finished with uncharacteristic suddenness: 'In the quill and raisins you sent me I saw what you wanted.'

To Leonor alone he had written: 'Sister of my heart, you cannot know the comfort I felt to see in my hands the plantain that you, whom I so love and cherish, had held in yours. Believe me dearest, *alma mya,*' he continued, 'if you think, as you appear to, that I was a good son and brother when required to be during our life . . . with the help of my Lord God I shall be a better one in this greater need.'

So Leonor had got a note to him inside a plantain. She would later admit this to the inquisitors, but the text of her message is not recorded in the transcripts, which suggests that the jailer did not intercept this one. But that is not the only revelation in Luis's letter to Leonor.

'Although you remain in Egypt,' he wrote, 'and I go to the Promised Land, I shall respond to your request, my angel, in every way I can.' He was using Egypt, that ancient land of Jewish exile, as an allegory for Spain. The metaphor was a commonplace among the clandestine Jews of Spain and Portugal. The striking thing about Luis's words is that until this point he had presumed that Leonor would die with him, yet now he speaks of going alone to the Promised Land while she lives on in Egypt. What had changed his way of thinking? It seems that Leonor herself had changed it in her little note.

'You have consoled me by telling me that these gentlemen have treated you with mercy,' Luis wrote. This allusion to the inquisitors is puzzling, given that Leonor had not yet appeared before them, but it is possible they had visited her in her cell and spoken kindly to her. In any case, Luis told his sister that he was also comforted to learn of her determination, 'because these gentlemen are very merciful, and God, Our Lord, sees that we are made of flesh'. And quoting from the Book of Proverbs he assured her that even the just person falls seven times a day. 'He gives his hand to the sinner who wishes to rise up. May He extend His to you.'

Determination to do what? Luis meant 'decision'. The word can convey that sense in Spanish, as it can in English, and Isabel will later use it in precisely that way when referring to her decision to confess. Meanwhile Luis urged Leonor to calm herself, sleep, and eat. 'God is great,' he assured her. 'After all, Jonah was in worse peril and in a far worse prison, yet God saved him. And Hezekiah had given up all hope, yet the Great Physician granted him fifteen more years of life . . . Remember,' he told her, 'that the soul that truly acknowledges and laments its guilt and repents, receives God's reprimand with loving devotion, just as the blessed David did when he went about barefoot and weeping, even though he was king, at the time when his son was pursuing him.

'I have drenched your gift with my tears, my dearest,' he concluded. By 'gift' he surely meant the plantain she had sent him. He concluded by saying that although he had no inkpot the Lord was providing him with ink. As for food, he was refusing meat or broth. 'With fruit, cheese and tears I get by.'

Men and women who live their lives in fear must find ways of communicating essential messages to those they trust without betraying their inner beliefs and feelings to those they do not. It is a skill born of dread and apprehension and Luis had learned it as a boy in Medina del Campo. He had used it when he filled the pages of his book of miracles with the story of his life, and he drew on it again as he wrote to his mother and sisters.

Leonor had shown him in her little note that she didn't want to die. Now that he understood this he wanted to help her live. Yet he knew he must also prepare her for the likelihood of martyrdom, so in his letters from this point on, he continued to evoke the joys that awaited her in Paradise. 'What music there will be!' he wrote on 28 May. 'What dancing! And after eating that delicious food, that milk sweetened with God's love and wisdom, we shall all dance together with our saintly mother to "Let Us Sing for Joy".' It was the song they used to sing together in the house in Santiago Tlatelolco. 'What delightful castanets,' Luis continued, 'and blessed David will make music for us with his beautiful songs. And we will join the chorus of the angels and saints and dance to the words: "Bless the Lord, Oh my Soul!"'

What were Leonor's chances of another reprieve? Inquisitions throughout the European world functioned according to a common set of rules, and Mexico, or New Spain, had been part of that world for seventy years. Clemency in the form of reconciliation had to be granted to penitent heretics, but usually only once. Leonor had been reconciled five years earlier, but she may have hoped a second reconciliation might be possible given that she had been so young—just sixteen—at the time of her first arrest.

How could Luis both encourage and console her? He did so by invoking that story he had read so often beside the river in Tampico and, later, in the library at Santiago: the binding of Isaac. Luis had alluded to this story in his first letter on paper and he would return to it often in his letters from now on. It provided him with an exemplary tale of courage and perfect faith that ended with a reprieve when God sent his angel to rescue Isaac.

•

Luis wrote nineteen letters to his sisters between 21 May and 3 June. Seven were for Leonor, and the lyricism of his writing never falters. At times it seems to echo King Solomon's enchanting Song of Songs, or the poetry of St John of the Cross. But Luis's letters are remarkable for another reason. As far as we can tell he handed them to the jailer without attempting to conceal them. We have seen him act incautiously before and have witnessed the consequences of his rashness. But this time he seems to have known exactly what he was doing.

On 26 May he wrote to Isabel telling her he had suffered for God's truth, 'which I clearly confess about myself alone, so as not to lie'. In a second letter that day he wrote, 'My blessed one, may Almighty God be with you and all his children who believe. Amen. Remember you were arrested on suspicion only.'

To Catalina and his other sisters two days later he went further.

'Although in front of you, my dearest ones, I feigned another thing, the truth is that never in my heart did I depart from the Law of God, and so I have confessed and confess about myself alone because to say anything else would be to give false testimony; you, my angels, were arrested on suspicion alone and I have defended and defend your innocence like a true brother . . .'

On 3 June, he reminded little Anna, who he mistakenly believed to be in prison, that she had been arrested on suspicion only. 'If your innocence is wounded,' he wrote, 'consider it a certain sign, not of displeasure, but of the great love that the Lord God, your Celestial Father, bears for you.' That same day, in one of his final prison letters, he wrote to Mariana, 'I have confessed His truth about myself alone so as not to bear false witness against anyone ... you, *vosotras*, were arrested on suspicion alone ... In front of you, my dearest ones, I feigned another thing ...'

It seems clear that he was sending his letters without concealment because he wanted their message—that he alone was guilty—to be read and understood by the inquisitors.

On Friday 25 May Leonor wrote another note to Luis. She concealed it in a piece of cheese and asked the jailer to take it to Luis. Instead the jailer took it to the inquisitors.

'Brother, advice is necessary, whether life or death,' Leonor had written, 'because I am in great debate whether no or yes or no, because I haven't gone upstairs yet, and before I go pray, everyone pray to God.' To this plaintive cry for help she had added, 'I didn't read the pear because I didn't look.'

Leonor knew she had only two alternatives. She could confess and ask for mercy, or deny everything for as long as possible. Denial would mean death if the truth emerged from other sources, which it almost certainly would. Confession might just win her clemency, but in confessing she would have to betray both her family and her faith, so that even if she survived she would live a life filled with remorse and shame. That was Leonor's dilemma, the 'great debate' with which she was struggling, alone in her cell.

The inquisitors read her note and told their scribe to copy it into the record. When he had done this they instructed the jailer to take the original to Luis, still pinned inside the cheese, so that he would not guess it had been intercepted. They had further instructions for the jailer. Wrap a sheet of blank paper and a quill in some linen, they told him. Hide it inside a plantain, or plantains, and give it to Leonor to encourage her to write to her brother again. They told Reyes to do this with great care, 'so that the truth may be discovered and justice administered'.

Luis received Leonor's note. He wasn't sure which one of his sisters had written it, but he responded, as the inquisitors hoped he would.

'I cannot tell from whom the little note comes,' he wrote. 'If it is from my Anica you are not to blame, my love, nor are any of you, because you have already done penance for the past. This has been the will of the Almighty who wanted to take us to heaven and not to Castile, and to me it seems a better journey than remaining here, dying a thousand deaths each day and offending God.'

He repeated his assertion that he alone was guilty. 'I have confessed the truth of God about myself alone,' he wrote. 'You, my loves, *vosotras*, were arrested on suspicion only, because, thanks to the Lord God, I have not given false testimony about anyone because you are not at fault . . .' Then, shifting into the singular form of address, he wrote, 'I do not know what to tell you, *no sé que te diga*. I think that to deny is useless but if you ask for mercy I think they will grant it a second time, that is, if you do not dare to leap into heaven with me through the passage of death . . .' He added that in his own case he had chosen to die for God's holy Law in order to live eternally. He concluded by saying that if 'the little crazy one' had not uttered any lies about them, there was no witness who could hurt them. The allusion to Mariana was intended to support his claim that his sisters were innocent.

On Monday 28 May the jailer showed Luis's reply to the inquisitors. Next morning, Dr Lobo Guerrero sent for Leonor.

# 11

# MORE LIKE AN ANGEL
# THAN A MAN

Dr Lobo Guerrero sat behind his polished desk. Leonor sat on a wooden chair in front of him. He was a man of fifty with dark hair, heavy brows and that solemn face which looks down at us from the walls of the cathedral museum in Lima today. She was a young woman of twenty-one, although Susana Galbán had said she still slept with her mother, which suggests that Leonor was still very much a girl. As for her looks, no portrait of her exists, but Luis had said in his journal that her beauty was 'slight' at the time of her marriage. She had been just twelve at the time, however, and a brother is not always the best judge of his sister's looks, so she may have been prettier than he thought.

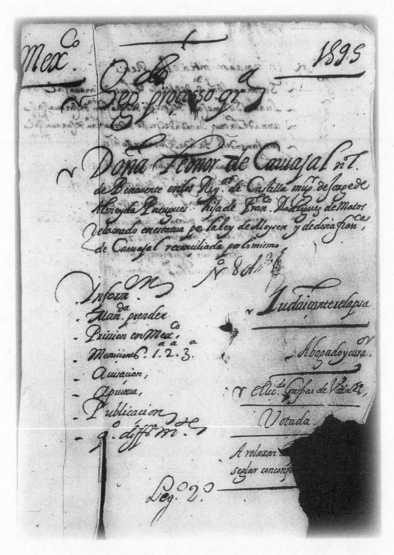

FRONT SHEET OF LEONOR DE CARVAJAL'S TRIAL TRANSCRIPT,
1595–1596. COURTESY OF THE BANCROFT LIBRARY,
UNIVERSITY OF CALIFORNIA, BERKELEY, USA.

'My name is Leonor de Carvajal,' she began, in answer to
the usual preliminary questions. 'I am a native of Benavente
in the kingdom of Castile from where I came as a little child,
*muy niña*, to this New Spain. I am twenty-one years old, a
little more or less, and I sustain myself by my needlework.
I am married to Jorge de Almeida, Portuguese, who is now
in Castile, and my parents are called Francisco Rodríguez
de Matos, who was burned in effigy by this Holy Office
for having observed the Law of Moses; my mother is doña
Francisca de Carvajal, reconciled for the same Law.'

After that Leonor faced the same formal questions that
Luis had faced in February.

'Have you been a prisoner of the Holy Office before, and
been punished by it?'

'Yes,' she replied. 'I was a prisoner a little over five years
ago for having believed and observed the dead Law of Moses,
its rites and ceremonies, and in the *auto* celebrated in the
cathedral of this city on the day of St Matthew five years
ago, I went out reconciled and wearing a penitential habit.'

Her description of the Law of Moses as 'dead', superseded,
suggests she was anxious to prove her Christian credentials.

'And did you abjure and detest the heresy and apostasy of
which you were accused and to which you testified and for
which you were reconciled and promised never more to return
to, on pain of being considered relapsed and impenitent?'

Leonor replied that it was true she had abjured and detested the heresy and apostasy of which she was accused and to which she testified. 'And I went out reconciled and promised never more to return to it, and to remain in the unity and communion of our Holy Mother Church on pain of being considered relapsed and impenitent. And I made the said abjuration promising never to return to the Law of Moses but to persevere in the belief in Our Redeemer, Jesus Christ. But I didn't sign the abjuration because at that time I had not yet learned to write.'

The scribe read her abjuration oath to her. She listened and said that what was contained in it was true.

Dr Lobo Guerrero asked Leonor whether she had understood when she took her oath that if she returned to her heresy she would be considered a relapsed impenitent and be released without mercy, *relaxado*—that terrible word—to the justice of the secular arm.

'I don't remember,' Leonor replied.

And so it went throughout the early stages of that first hearing. Leonor was asked, as all prisoners were asked, whether she knew or presumed why she had been arrested.

'No.'

Dr Lobo Guerrero responded in the usual way by reminding her that the Holy Office did not arrest people on a whim, and as she was a prisoner it followed that she must have done something against the Holy Mother Church. It would be better, therefore, if she relieved her conscience by telling what she knew without giving false testimony against anyone, so that her case could be treated with brevity. He did not mention mercy and Leonor probably did not know enough about inquisitorial proceedings to understand what this omission meant for her. In any case the response she gave was far too candid.

'For about a year, until this point,' she told him, 'I have had some doubts about whether I have been right to observe the Law of Our Redeemer, Jesus Christ, and whether it was good or bad to draw apart from the Law of Moses.'

'Which of the two things do you doubt most,' he asked her, 'that the Law of Moses is good and the Law of Our Redeemer, Jesus Christ, is bad, or that the Law of Jesus Christ is the good one and the Law of Moses the bad?'

This convoluted query sounds designed to confuse but Leonor's reply was firm and confident.

'I believed the Law of Jesus Christ to be the good Law and so I drew apart from the Law of Moses.'

He pressed her further. 'Why did you ever have doubts about the Law of Jesus Christ being the good Law?'

'Because I heard my sister doña Mariana recite some commandments of the Law of Moses, one of which said: "I am your Lord and God who with infinite power liberated you from Egypt where you lived in sorrow and bitterly afflicted. Do not have strange gods before me, or make and worship false idols."'

Dr Lobo Guerrero asked what it was in this commandment that had made Leonor doubt the Law of Our Redeemer, Jesus Christ, and observe the Law of Moses instead.

'Those words "do not have strange gods",' she replied.

She was stumbling into dangerous territory.

'Are there any strange gods in the Law of Our Redeemer, Jesus Christ?' he asked.

'The crucifixes are strange gods,' she said. It was a disastrous answer, so disastrous that we imagine an abrupt silence in the audience chamber.

'In whose memory are the crucifixes made?' Dr Lobo Guerrero continued.

'In memory of Jesus Christ.'

'Is Jesus Christ a strange god?'

'No,' Leonor said.

He pointed out the contradiction in her responses.

'If the *"Cristos"* are strange gods then given that they represent Jesus Christ, does that mean you believe that Jesus Christ himself is a strange god?'

'I was referring to the fact that there are so many figures of Jesus Christ,' Leonor replied.

He explained that the painted and sculpted Christs represented just one Christ, Our Redeemer, God and Lord, and that just because they were so many didn't mean they were strange gods.

Leonor replied in her youthful, artless way. 'Well, this was the doubt that troubled me, because it had seemed to me that to have so many Christs was to have many gods.'

Was Lobo Guerrero touched or angered by her responses? We read his words but cannot hear his voice or see the expression on his face. He left this subject for the moment.

'Have you heard your sister doña Mariana say anything else that caused you to doubt that the Law of Jesus Christ was a good law?'

'No, I have not heard her say anything else.'

'Have you heard any other person say anything about the Law of Moses that caused you to doubt the Law of Our Redeemer, Jesus Christ?'

'No, except that on two occasions in our house I saw my brother Luis de Carvajal reading the Bible and some psalms to Manuel de Lucena, Pedro Enríquez and Diego Enríquez, the brothers-in-law of Manuel de Lucena, and reciting them in Romance.'

'Do you think Manuel de Lucena, Pedro Enríquez and Diego Enríquez believe and observe the Law of Moses?'

'I do not know.'

'And does your sister, doña Mariana, observe the Law of Our Redeemer, Jesus Christ?'

'Yes,' Leonor replied. 'When she was sane I saw that she observed it, but after she lost her reason she recited many prophecies of the Law of Moses and said what I have told you about the commandment: "I am your Lord and God."'

Leonor's first hearing ended with that. She read the scribal transcript and signed her name 'doña Leonor'. Her handwriting on the parchment has a childlike quality. She had not been educated at the Jesuit school in Medina del Campo like her brothers, and had only recently learned to write.

Luis had spent that day in his cell with his quill and ink and his precious sheets of paper, and next morning he gave two letters to the jailer. He wanted the first to go to Catalina and as usual he addressed her with the singular '*tú*' before moving to the plural '*vosotras*' in the hope that she could pass the note on to her mother and sisters. He reiterated his claim that he alone had been guilty of following the Law of Moses. He urged his mother and sisters to have faith like Sara, to pray like Hannah and Esther, to have courage like the blessed Judith and Salomona. 'And when you leave your imprisonment in Egypt'—again that metaphor for Spain—'you will sing of victory like Miriam and Deborah in Paradise, where they wait to dance with you in chorus when the Lord crowns you.'

His second letter was for Leonor. 'Dearest, *alma mya*,' he wrote, 'If you have some white paper with which you can write me a note, hold a dish to the candle, then take a feather and write with the soot, as if with ink, and tell me if you are alone or not and if you know anything about the blessed lamb, our mother, who is there, because when I sent her the raisins you sent me they took them upstairs. The edge of my quill causes pain to my flesh,' he added, 'but great consolation to my spirit.'

He used the plural form *'vosotras'* for the remainder of that letter as he again urged his mother and sisters to emulate the valiant women of the scriptures: Judith, Susana, Hannah, Esther and 'your Holy Mother, Sara'. And he composed a variation on that old Castilian blessing he had carved into an avocado stone a few weeks earlier: 'Blessed the day you were born,' he wrote, 'the bread you ate, the earth you trod, the torments you suffered and the womb from which you came.' As always he evoked the pleasures of Paradise. 'The Lord will give you white satin skirts, brocade jackets, rich headdresses and garlands of flowers,' he told them, and he promised they would bathe in fragrant waters before dressing in these lovely clothes. But he ended this letter on an anxious note: 'They have not given me any more ink.'

•

Next morning Leonor went upstairs again. It was the last day of May and Licenciado Alonso de Peralta, with his elegant face and small, precise mouth, had joined his older colleague in the audience chamber.

'Have you remembered anything in relation to your cause?'

'No,' Leonor replied.

They read her the second admonition, warning that she should speak the truth about what she knew so that her case could be treated with brevity. Again they offered only brevity, not mercy.

'I have nothing more to say,' Leonor told them, and the hearing ended. She signed the transcript in her childlike hand and the guard returned her to her cell.


They sent for her again two days later.

'Have you remembered anything relevant to your cause?'

She had. In the hours that had passed since her last hearing Leonor had resolved her great debate. She fell to her knees in tears, and begged for mercy.

'I wanted to confess the truth before and confess as I was advised to do,' she sobbed, 'but the devil had put it into my imagination that if I confessed my husband, Jorge de Almeida, would leave me and not want to live with me, but now I want to tell what has happened, having consideration for God alone and for no other reason, because I want to convert sincerely to the Evangelical Law of Our Redeemer, Jesus Christ.'

The words poured out of her. 'And the truth is that about one year ago my brother Luis de Carvajal asked me whether I had departed from the Law of Moses and I replied "Yes", and my brother told me, "Don't do that, don't believe in the Law of Jesus Christ because it is a nonsense; only believe in the Law of Moses, as you did before you were reconciled, and hope for the Messiah promised in the Law."

And he told me I must fast in observance of the Law of Moses on Mondays, Wednesdays and Thursdays of each week, from sunrise to sunset, without eating all day until night-time, and observe Saturdays as I did before I was reconciled and not eat bacon fat, nor things of pork. And I should fast on the Great Day of the Lord that the Jews call *"de Penitencia"* and take the grease from the meat by way of keeping the said Law and believe in one God only and commend myself to him alone.

'And Luis said to me that the sacraments of the Law of the Church and the mysteries it celebrates are things of nonsense, *del aire*, and he advised me that I must save myself through the Law of Moses because it was the good and true Law and not in that of Jesus Christ, which was not. And through the persuasion of my brother, Luis de Carvajal, a year ago, as I have said, I decided to leave the Law of Jesus Christ and pass to the Law of Moses and believe in it, thinking I would save myself through it like before I was reconciled by this Holy Office, and so since that time a year ago that I have declared I have believed in the Law of Moses and have kept it and thought to save myself through it and not in that of Jesus Christ, Our Lord, and I understood through what my brother told me that the true Messiah who had to come was the anti-Christ of whom the Christians speak, who would gather the people of Israel who had been dispersed and taken them out of captivity and their cells, and carry them to Mount Sinai where he would give them palms and crowns for having kept the Law of Moses, and although I wore good clothes on Fridays and put clean linen on the bed, when I had the chance I didn't think about it as observing the Law of Moses because I was only concerned with observing the Sabbath. And on Saturdays my brother used to read to me and my mother doña Francisca de Carvajal and my sisters doña Isabel and doña Mariana the psalms of David in Romance that he had taken from the Bible in the college of Santiago Tlatelolco, and on Fridays at sunset, to commence the observance of the Sabbath, my brother sang to me and to my mother and my sisters a canticle that went: "If with great care each day, We sang praises to the Lord . . ."'

She sang Luis's song for them, and then she sang four more. Her second canticle began, 'It is right to give praise to the Lord . . .' The third began, 'The holy and blessed name of the Lord is glazed upon my heart . . .' The fourth, in praise of Moses, began, 'On the high and beautiful hill of Mount Raphardi the first most holy prophet was speaking . . .' The fifth recalled how the six tribes of Israel were raised up, 'and responded with clear voice and loud cries to the Levites . . .'

Leonor was singing for her life, or thought she was.

Leonor sang another four songs that afternoon but the scribe recorded only the first verse of each. Her sixth praised the beauty of God's Law and warned that those who blaspheme will be blasphemed in the afterlife. Her seventh promised new songs of praise to the Lord in the communion of his saints. The eighth warned against being deceived by the enemy of 'the good human state' and thereby losing the blessing of the Omnipotent and Holy Sovereign. Her ninth and final song said that if believers called to God, in order to glorify His name, their understanding would be illuminated and their souls, tongues, hearts and wills would be touched.

'My brother Luis prayed and sang these nine canticles on Friday nights,' Leonor explained, 'so as to prepare us to observe the Sabbath, and when we could not pray them on

Friday nights, because of some hindrance or obstacle, we prayed them on Saturdays. And as he said them my sisters doña Isabel and doña Mariana and I responded; but although my mother, doña Francisca, was present and heard them, she did not respond because she didn't know them from memory; and also, on the Sabbaths, in their honour and in praise of the Lord, my brother recited the Law of Moses in couplets and my sisters doña Isabel and doña Mariana and I responded because we knew it by heart also, as we did the nine canticles; and my mother, doña Francisca, was present but she didn't respond to this either because she didn't know it from memory.'

The fact that Francisca did not know these songs suggests they were not a family tradition she had handed down to her children. The biblical themes may have been familiar but the songs were new to her. Someone had composed them; probably Luis. After Leonor recalled those nine canticles she sang a lament that began, 'To you Lord God we cry, with voices and moans, see our afflictions and our despair . . .' She sang of defenceless orphans and afflicted widows, spirited maidens and harsh prisons, of hearts filled with fear by constant tribulations. She ended with an admission 'of the sins we have committed', a promise to do penance, and a plea to the Lord to grant his people clemency as he had in the past.

When she had finished she recited the Ten Commandments. Luis had turned them into rhyming couplets to make them easier for his sisters to remember:

*Yo soy tu Dios y Señor,*
*que con poder infinito,*
 *te liberté del Egipto*
*donde vivías con dolor*
*y ásperamente aflicto.*

And so it went. Leonor recalled those ancient edicts from Mount Sinai and as she did she mingled Portuguese and Spanish words and phrases, saying *'meu nome'* instead of *'mi nombre'*, *'muyta'* for *'muy'* and *'pay y may'* for *'padre y madre'*. Perhaps she and her family always spoke that way, in a melange of the two Iberian tongues they had been speaking since 1492.

When Leonor had finished reciting the Ten Commandments the inquisitors asked her to explain clearly and succinctly what the Law of Moses commanded.

'We must celebrate the Passover of the Lamb for seven days with unleavened bread,' she replied, 'and the feast of the Great Day of the Lord, that is called *Penitencia,* on which day God judges sinners and pardons souls; and we must observe the Passover of the Booths, *la Pascua de las Cabañuelas*—she meant Sukkot—and not eat food from unclean animals like pigs, or those with cleft hooves or that do not chew their cud, or fish without scales, or animals that drag their chests across the earth or eat other animals, or black animals with four feet.

'And on Saturdays and other days, by way of observing the Law of Moses, we sang prayers like this: "Lord of the world, I come before you"; and another that begins, "You are Blessed, my God, Lord of the world"; and another that begins, "Our God, God of our Fathers . . . "; and another that begins, *Shema Israel*".' Leonor gave a poor rendition of this moving prayer. Either that, or the scribe transcribed it badly. But as he was the same man, Pedro de Mañozca, who had recorded Luis's more accurate recitation in February, it may have been Leonor, in her anxious state, who stumbled over it.

'And we said another prayer that begins, "Our king, strength of Jacob . . . " And another that begins, "Lord God All Powerful, help of souls . . . " and another that we pray when we fast, that begins, "Receive my fast in penitence . . . " And I prayed in observance of the Law of Moses on Saturdays and the other days of the week, directing my prayers to the God of Israel, excluding from my heart his son Our Lord Redeemer, Jesus Christ, and the Holy Spirit. And I also prayed penitential psalms, in Romance, saying only "Glory be to God" at the end of them, and excluding mention of the persons of the Son and the Holy Spirit.'

It must have been late afternoon by the time this long and fateful hearing ended. Leonor signed the transcript and after that the guard returned her to her cell. Her feelings as she descended the stairs and walked along the corridor past her brother's cell are not recorded; nor do we know whether he heard her footsteps on the flagstones as she passed, as he thought he had a few weeks earlier.

While she had been upstairs confessing he had written six more letters: one for Anna, another for Catalina, a third for Mariana, none of whom were yet in prison. Three of the notes had no particular designation, but the briefest and the saddest letter was almost certainly for Leonor. 'Blessed one,' he wrote, 'May Adonay, the Lord God be with you. They no longer want to take anything from me. I don't know why.' It seems that the jailer was now refusing to carry any more messages to Leonor. 'Perhaps they have suspected you,' Luis continued, 'or your companion has said something during her hearing. I make this sweet, delicious *guisado* for God, and perhaps the Lord will take it to you as consolation for your solitude, my love. I send it to you, commending it to God.'

What was this sweet *guisado*? The word usually signifies a casserole or stew, but Luis had no way of preparing such a thing. Perhaps it was a metaphor for the blessing he was sending Leonor. Whatever he meant, there is no evidence of any further letters. He was alone now, isolated in his cell, cut off from any hope of written communication with his beloved Leonor, as she was from him.

Six days later, on Wednesday 7 June, his eldest sister Isabel was imprisoned in the Holy Office cells. His youngest sister Anna was still so gravely ill with quinsy that the inquisitors placed her in the home of one of their officials. They did the same with Mariana who they saw was clearly mad. As for Catalina, her trial transcript is missing from the archives so we do not know precisely when they took her into custody, but Anna would later say that Catalina was arrested some time after Isabel.

Although most of Luis's letters were intercepted by the jailer, it is clear that one or two did reach Leonor within days, perhaps even hours of his writing them, because many months later, on 24 October, she talked to the inquisitors about them. They began by asking whether she had communicated with any other person since being imprisoned.

'Yes,' she replied. 'I communicated with Manuel Gómez Navarro, who was in a cell close to mine. And what happened was that he heard me singing a song that goes,

I say with great sorrow,
Ay! In the midst of my days,
I returned to the shadowy doors of this jail
Through my error and my misdeeds.'

Navarro had asked Leonor why she was singing this sad song and she had told him it was because her brother was in shackles and wanted to die in the Law of Moses. She had begun to cry and Navarro asked why she was crying. Leonor had explained that it was because she had condemned her mother and her sister but feared they were still denying everything and would be tortured.

This moving glimpse of a young girl singing to herself and weeping in the solitude of her cell was not the response the inquisitors had wanted. They put their question a different way.

'Did you write a paper or papers to any person in this jail, and how did you send it and with whom?'

'Yes,' she replied, 'I wrote three notes to Luis de Carvajal my brother and sent them with dissimulation, hidden in a plantain and inside cheese and fruit, and asked the jailer to take them as gifts to him.'

The inquisitors showed her two notes. She admitted that they were hers.

Reading aloud from Leonor's plea to Luis in May the previous year they asked her, 'And what did you mean, when you wrote to Luis de Carvajal saying, "Brother, advice is necessary, whether life or death, because I am in great debate whether no or yes or no, because I haven't gone upstairs yet and before I go pray, everyone pray to God. I didn't read the pear because I didn't look"?'

'I wrote to my brother,' Leonor replied, 'because I was in great turmoil about whether to confess and ask for mercy, or deny everything, and I asked for his advice. And what I meant about the pear was that I hadn't seen the writing on it and so had eaten it.'

They asked her, 'Who wrote a note to you that began, "Sister of my heart, may the Almighty God guide you and free your soul and your life . . ."? And in another part it says, "I do not know what to tell you. I think that to deny is useless but if you ask for mercy I think they will grant it a second time, that is, if you do not dare to leap into heaven with me through the passage of death."'

'It came from my brother,' Leonor replied, 'and he wrote it in response to my plea for advice.'

'And what did your brother Luis de Carvajal mean in another note when he said, "You cannot know the comfort

I felt to hold in my hands the plantain that you have held in yours."

'The plaintain was the fruit I confessed to having sent my brother, in which I placed a piece of cheese with a note inside.'

'What did your brother Luis de Carvajal mean when he said in that same letter, "To your petition, my angel, I will respond with deeds"?'

'I had asked him whether I should die professing the Law of Moses, or say I had parted from it and ask for mercy, and he replied, saying that he would respond to my request as far as he could.'

Paraphrasing Luis's words they asked Leonor, 'What did your brother, Luis de Carvajal, mean in the same letter when he said, "I feel consoled to learn of your determination because those gentlemen are merciful and God, Our Lord, sees that we are made of flesh and that even the just person falls seven times a day and He raises up the sinner by the hand"?'

'I had written to my brother,' Leonor replied, 'saying that I had confessed and asked for mercy and he responded that he felt comforted to know that the inquisitors are merciful; and that God, Our Lord, sees that we are flesh and that even if we deny His Law in order to save our lives he forgives us, because even the just person falls seven times a day.'

Luis had said nothing about denying God's law when he assured Leonor of God's divine capacity for forgiveness.

This may have been his subliminal message and she may have read him correctly. After all, she knew her brother far better than we can ever hope to do. In any case, that is what she understood him to mean. Yet there is one other apparent incongruity in her recollection of his message. She says he wrote her a note after she told him she had confessed, yet the jailer presented it to the inquisitors ten days before she made her confession. How can we account for this discrepancy?

The most plausible explanation seems to be that Leonor confused the sequence and the content of their letters. Six months had passed by the time she talked about them. She was young and lonely and desperate to live and she needed to believe that Luis, and God, would forgive her for confessing and denying the Law of Moses. She had not been physically tortured. Her anxiety and her solitude were torture enough. She confessed because she believed that Luis had given her permission to do so.

For us the most unbearable aspect of this melancholy riddle is the knowledge that both Leonor and Luis seem to have thought she might be spared if she confessed. They could not see what we see with the benefit of hindsight: that those admonitions offering brevity, but not mercy, meant she had no chance at all.

•

Isabel never received any of Luis's letters because she was not in prison when he wrote them. But she learned about them later, some six months after he wrote them. On the morning of 9 October 1595 Inquisitor Peralta summoned her to the audience chamber, and told her, after the usual preliminaries, that in May that year a certain person had asked that a tablet of caramel conserve be delivered to her along with a plantain. Peralta did not name that person. He said only that a letter had been found inside the plaintain. The scribe had copied its text into the record and Peralta directed Isabel to read it.

'Loves of my life, *vidas de mi ánima*,' she began, 'by a miracle an inkwell and quill came to me today so that I might send you a vignette, beloved ones of my heart . . .' It was one of the letters the jailer had intercepted on 22 May.

Isabel read on while the inquisitor watched, and the scribe recorded that when she reached the words, 'bent low I pray to Adonay, my great God, that we may be with Him in the glory of His holy kingdom, Amen, Amen,' she murmured 'Amen' several times in response.

After that Peralta showed her the letters Luis had written to her on 26 May. 'Adonay be with us,' she read. 'You will live my martyrs, joy, joy . . .' And, 'My blessed one, may Almighty God be with you and all his children who believe. Amen.'

When Isabel had finished reading Peralta asked her who she thought had written the letters.

'They are from Luis de Carvajal, my brother,' she replied, 'whom I know, and know to be a saint. And everything contained in them is good because it is intended to console his sisters.'

The scribe noted that Isabel read the third letter with particular care. Weeping, she said, 'I know his life has been good,' and then, 'I do not deserve such a gift as this, that my brother sent me.' And when she reached the part where Luis told her he was in shackles she said, 'It cannot be because of anything bad he has done in this life, because he has lived more like an angel than a man.'

# 12

# FRAGILE SEED

ON THE MORNING OF 10 JUNE LUIS RETURNED TO THE AUDIENCE
chamber. It was his first hearing since March and Dr Lobo
Guerrero sat alone at the great polished table. The prosecutor
was also present. He had come to present his formal accusation
and he began by reminding Luis that on St Matthew's Day
five years earlier he had promised to abandon the Law of
Moses and stay firm in that of Jesus Christ. 'Yet after taking
that sacred oath,' the prosecutor intoned, 'you returned to
the belief and observance of the Law of Moses like a dog that
returns to its vomit.'

This analogy, borrowed from the Book of Proverbs,
suggests a deep hostility towards Luis on the part of the
prosecutor, but it was a commonplace among European

theologians at that time. In England Sir Thomas More had used it to describe the Protestant heretics he wanted burned. Even Jewish authorities had been known to employ it from time to time: the rabbis of Barcelona, for example, had used it to describe their brethren in southern France who had condemned the philosophical works of the great Maimonides.

The prosecutor read the charges against Luis and, although we cannot hear the tone of his voice, his words sound cold and derisive. He said that Luis was deluded by the same 'ridiculous hope' held by Jews for centuries: that the Messiah had not yet come. He called Luis a blind man, 'without light', and so drunk with observance of the Law of Moses that he dreamed about it all day long and interpreted simple, ordinary events as miracles. His beliefs were inanities and errors, the prosecutor said, that had inspired him to write a book to his brothers who were Judaising in Rome and Salonika, to tell them about those miracles. 'And delighting in Jewish names and abhorring those that are Christian and from the Law of Grace, he calls himself "Joseph Lumbroso".' As for Luis's dream that God, through Solomon, had placed a precious liquid in his mouth, the prosecutor derided it as 'errors and nonsense of the Jews who defend their law with chimeras, dreams, trickery and imaginings'.

When the prosecutor had finished Luis was told to respond to the charges against him. To the first, that he was a baptised and confirmed Christian who observed the Law of Moses but had been reconciled on Saint Matthew's Day on 24 February 1590, he replied, 'This charge is true.' To the second, that after being reconciled he had returned to the Law of Moses like a dog that returns to its vomit, he said, 'The second charge is true.' Then with quiet defiance he added, 'But one cannot call someone a dog if he believes in the Law of God that promises not just temporal rewards but eternal life.'

He did not attempt to deny the next nine charges. He had already confessed to everything contained in them so there was no point. To item twelve, which accused him of observing the Jewish Sabbath by singing and praying in observance of the Law of Moses, he said, 'It is a very great truth, what this charge contains.'

'In whose company did you sing the canticles referred to in number twelve?' they asked him.

'I prayed in my room, and closed the door', he replied.

'Did you sometimes pray in the company of other people?'

'No, Señor,' Luis answered.

They had already moved on to charge thirteen, which dealt with the fasts he observed in the middle of the week, when he announced that he had something to add to the previous charge. The prosecutor, the inquisitor and the scribe, with quill in hand, paused to listen as Luis spoke.

'I did not sing and pray alone,' he admitted, 'but with my mother Francisca and my sisters, Isabel, Mariana, Leonor and Anica. And if I did not declare it before, it was out of love as a son and brother, and there is nothing strange in my not having done so.'

His words leap from the pages of his transcript. Why would he give this sudden testimony against his family after going to such lengths to protect them? He explained his change of heart like this.

'I understand that you have been shown the notes and letters I sent from my cell to my mother and sisters, and I want to tell the truth because I abhor lies and don't wish to lie, and because I understand that they have confessed about what is said in charge number twelve—that I sang and prayed nine canticles and other rhyming Jewish prayers when we observed the Sabbath. But I sang and prayed them only with my mother and sisters and with no other person that the Holy Office can show.'

As so often in Luis's story it is difficult to know what he was trying to do. It is significant, however, that he did not mention Catalina. As far as we can tell she had not yet been arrested and if he had learned this through the prisoners' network he may have been attempting to save her. But why had he implicated Anna and Mariana? Their circumstances were different. Anna was very young and very ill, Mariana had lost her mind, and Luis probably believed, correctly as it turned out, that their lives would be spared.

Late that afternoon, after Luis had responded to all the accusations, the time came for the prosecutor to recommend a sentence. There could be only one for such an impenitent heretic. The prosecutor proposed that Luis should be released, *relaxado*, to the secular authorities and burned alive as a punishment and an example to others of the fate they would meet if they followed his path.

Luis did not beg for mercy. He had been preparing for this moment since the day of his arrest. 'I desire as salvation the day when I must die,' he declared, 'not as a vile hanged man but burned alive, because it has more glory.' He meant he wished to be burned rather than garrotted, which was the usual death for penitent heretics. 'Because in that way,' Luis continued, 'I will leave this prison and these shackles and ascend into heaven.' He was thinking, perhaps, of the prophet Elijah, who was said to have ascended into the heavens in a chariot of fire.

In England and much of continental Europe heretics were frequently burned alive. But few people in Spain and its dominions seem to have suffered this terrible fate. With the merest sign of contrition—the nod of a head, the closing of one's eyes in apparent assent, the kissing of a crucifix, or the mumbling of a prayer—condemned men and women could avoid this agonising death, even at the very last moment, and most did avoid it. They were garrotted instead, and after that their bodies were slowly reduced to cinders. But Luis de Carvajal did not want that more merciful death. He wished to die in the flames, bearing witness to his faith.

He fought on with words, audaciously and fervently— stirred, no doubt, by the mockery he had endured that morning.

'I pray to God Our Lord to discover the true heretics and have pity on these blind sons of Adam and enlighten them,' he said, referring to the prosecutor and the inquisitors. 'By being burned I will go to enjoy the eternal glory of God, Our Lord, like the blessed martyr, Eleazar, and Salomona and her seven Maccabean sons.'

He meant 'Hannah' but it didn't matter. Like those Jewish martyrs of ancient times and many martyrs since he was trying to embrace death in order to deprive his tormenters of a victory over him.

Ever since his childhood Luis had needed deep and lasting courage to follow his ancestral faith. As a boy in Medina del Campo he had committed himself to the Law of Moses, knowing that to do so could get him killed. In Mexico ten years later he had forfeited the opportunity to escape in order to protect his mother and sisters. At the age of twenty-two he had survived his first encounter with the Holy Office by holding his nerve and using his wits.

He had achieved a great deal. He had converted the Franciscan to the Law of Moses beneath the noses of the inquisitors. He had spent four rapturous years in the library of the Franciscan college learning what he could about the Law of Moses. Now he was in prison once more and he knew that this time he would not survive. In February, when he danced in his cell, he had hoped the end would come quickly, but it did not. His incarceration lasted almost two more years, and throughout that time his courage ebbed and flowed.

In October 1595, around the time his sisters were shown his letters, he asked to meet with learned theologians. He said that he wanted to discuss his doubts about the Catholic faith with them. The inquisitors chose two men for this mission. They were Jesuits, like the maternal uncle in Medina whom Luis had never known, and they spoke with Luis for some time. They implored him to see the error of his ways, but when they had finished he announced that nothing they had said had altered his devotion to the Law of Moses. The luckless Jesuits tried three more times in the days that followed, but finally they admitted to Dr Lobo Guerrero that they had been unable to convince Luis to return to the Church.

Outside in the city life went on. In November 1595, as autumn drew to a close, Viceroy Luis de Velasco left for Peru. His successor arrived on horseback, passed beneath the triumphal arch prepared for him, and entered the cathedral on the plaza to the solemn cadence of the beautiful '*Te Deum*'.

In December Luis was brought from his cell to meet the lawyer appointed to advise him. Together they listened as the prosecutor read the testimonies he had gathered from Luis's imprisoned friends and family, as well as from the spies, Susana Galbán and the priest Díaz, who had betrayed him. The lawyer advised Luis to discharge his conscience by speaking the truth of what he knew. Luis did just that.

'I believe in one true God,' he said, 'creator of the sky, earth and sea, and of all things visible and invisible, and in his immaculate law and truths. And I don't believe in the Law of Jesus Christ because I believe it is false.'

He had something else to say.

'When I agreed to talk with the wise theologians and learned men it was not because I had ever doubted the truth of the law of God but because I wanted to confound and convert them by saying with truth what Psalm 128 and Psalm 118 say: "And I spoke of thy testimonies before kings: and I was not ashamed".'

He followed this defiant response with an unusual request. He asked to sign what he had just said. The inquisitors consented. The scribe handed him a quill. Luis took it and in firm and graceful letters wrote, 'Joseph Lumbroso, slave of the Highest, Adonay.' From that point on in the inquisitorial record the scribe refers to him always as 'Luis de Carvajal (alias) Joseph Lumbroso'.

Early the following year, when frost lay on the flagstones outside the Holy Office jail, the inquisitors took Luis to the torture chamber and ordered him to reveal other Judaisers or suffer the consequences. He refused. The torturer entered, tied him to the rack and gave the wheel one turn. As the ropes cut into Luis's flesh he began naming names. Until that moment he had denied that Catalina observed the Law of Moses, and had been vague in his replies about young Anna. Now he said that both his sisters observed the forbidden faith, although he still insisted that Anna did so in a childlike way because she lacked the capacity to understand.

He endured four more turns of the ropes that morning but after that no further physical harm was done to him. There was no need. Fear of pain rather than pain itself caused him to capitulate. He spent the next five days in that subterranean chamber, knowing that his tormentors could return him to the rack at any time. He kept on talking and by the end of the week he had named his mother, all five of his sisters, and some ninety of their friends as Judaisers.

On 14 February the inquisitors met with their advisers on the Holy Office council to consider whether or not to resume Luis's torture. Dr Lobo Guerrero voted against continuing. The archdeacon and one of the three secular judges on the panel agreed with him. Inquisitor Peralta, on the other hand, voted that Luis be made to suffer three or four more turns of the ropes. The two other judges from the secular courts agreed the torture should continue, but did not say to what degree. The mayor suggested that they merely threaten Luis, and as he held the casting vote Luis was saved from further physical torment.

Luis's courage had failed him in the torture chamber but on 15 February it returned. The inquisitors summoned him upstairs that day to ratify the confessions he had made. Without ratification his testimony could not be accepted, which suggests that the Holy Office understood the inherent untrustworthiness of information obtained by inflicting pain on prisoners.

Luis refused to ratify.

'I protest against the torture,' he said, 'because by the love of God His Holiness, I should not have been made to tell lies, and everything I said was a lie from the hour the torture began.'

He added that he said this by way of discharging his conscience, in case he died under torture and went to hell for his lies.

'What can have caused you to declare that everything you have said so far was a lie,' they asked, 'given that you confessed of your own free will and with little more than one command in the torture chamber, during the sessions on Thursday the eighth, Friday the ninth, Saturday the tenth, Monday the twelfth and Wednesday the fourteenth day of this month of February, in the year 1596?'

Their question sounds like a taunt designed to remind Luis of his weakness, and perhaps it was. But Luis replied with great simplicity.

'Because you have not tortured me this time.'

They asked whether his mother, his sisters, his two absent brothers and the many family friends he had named, including Manuel de Lucena, observed the Law of Moses and were Jews.

He told them his mother, his sisters and brothers and their friends Justa Méndez, Manuel de Lucena and Manuel

Gómez Navarro were indeed Jews who observed the Law of Moses. 'But against all the rest I have given false testimony for fear of torture.' He signed the transcript, in a hand as elegant as any scribe, 'Joseph Lumbroso'.

The guard led him from the audience chamber. But as they walked along the gallery towards the staircase leading down to the cells Luis hurled himself into the patio below. The guard dragged him to his cell and the inquisitors went down to see what condition he was in. They found him alive and suffering no serious injuries. They decided to place two prisoners with him, to watch over him and report anything that happened.

'And this took place at three in the afternoon,' the scribe recorded.

Next morning Luis sent word to Dr Lobo Guerrero, asking him to come to his cell alone. He said he did not want to see Inquisitor Peralta.

'He makes my flesh tremble because he seems so severe and *rigoroso* in the way he plies me with endless questions,' Luis explained, 'although apart from this he has treated me with much love and visited me on visiting days all the time I have been in prison, trying in every way to return me to the Catholic faith.'

So Dr Lobo Guerrero went alone to Luis's cell and Luis told him he would ratify everything he had declared in the torture chamber.

'The devil must have tempted me to throw myself from the gallery,' he said sadly, 'because it is a major sin to kill oneself in despair.'

Dr Lobo Guerrero told Luis to pay attention while everything he had said in the torture chamber was read to him; that way he could see whether it was true or not, or if there was anything to add or amend.

Luis listened as the scribe read out what he had testified on 8, 9, 10, 12 and 14 February.

'It is recorded accurately,' Luis said, 'and I have nothing to alter, add or amend; because it is well written, and the mere and plain truth, and I didn't say it for fear of torture, but because it is the truth.'

'And it being eleven o'clock,' the scribe noted, 'the hearing ended and the Señor Inquisitor left the cell and returned to the audience chamber.'


'Under torture,' the historian Howard M. Sachar wrote of the Carvajal family, 'the womenfolk recanted all heresies. Not so Luis.' The family's trial transcripts show that was not the case. Leonor was not tortured. She recanted and confessed because Luis had assured her that God would forgive her if she did, and because she hoped that by telling the truth she might save her life.

Francisca's transcript is missing from the archives but the portions of her testimony copied into her children's transcripts show that she confessed in August 1595, four months after her arrest. There is no evidence that she endured physical torture this time. The Chilean historian José Toribio de Medina thought she had, but the episode he describes in his famous history of the Holy Office in Mexico took place during her first trial, not her second. It is the same ordeal that Luis recalled in his book of miracles.

In reality, of all the members of the Carvajal family it was one of 'the womenfolk' who proved the most heroic. Isabel maintained an attitude of defiance, even insolence, throughout her interrogations, even when she was taken to the torture chamber on 15 June 1596. She endured eight turns of the ropes that morning and suffered the horror of drowning as three jugs of water were poured down her throat. It was a precursor of the drowning torture known today as 'water-boarding'. The scribe in attendance recorded that she refused to confess about herself or anyone else and that between her cries she sang psalms in Latin in a loud voice, 'con brio'. Finally, after the contents of the third jug had been poured down her throat, she appeared so weakened that the torture was suspended.

Even strong people can be broken, however. Some kind of injury or illness did eventually shatter Isabel's spirit. On 13 July 1596 she sent word to Dr Lobo Guerrero, asking him to visit her in her cell.

'I am ill in such a way that I cannot climb to the tribunal,' she told him.

What had happened to Isabel? Four weeks had passed since her torture and during that time she had climbed the stairs to the audience chamber on five occasions with no apparent difficulty. Yet that afternoon in July the scribe recorded that she was ill and bloodied, *enferma y sangrada*. He did not say in what way she was bloodied. Had the lacerations where the ropes had torn into the flesh of her arms and legs broken open? Was she suffering a haemorrhage of some kind? Had she been beaten in her cell? If so, did the inquisitors know about her assault?

A few years after these events several officials of the Holy Office in Mexico City were investigated by the Supreme Council in Madrid and found guilty of corrupt practices. They included Inquisitor Peralta; the prosecutor, Martos de Bohorques; the notary, Pedro de Mañozca; and the jailer, Gaspar de los Reyes. Most of their corrupt practices involved the taking of bribes, but Peralta was also reprimanded for

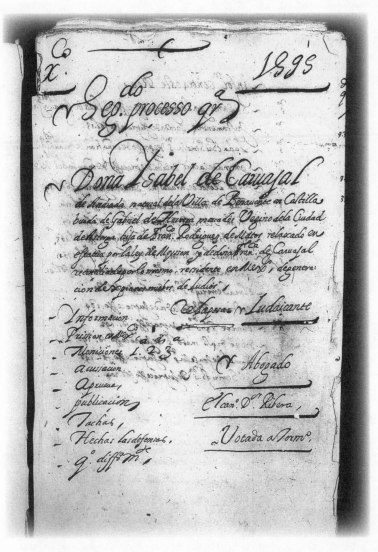

FRONT SHEET OF ISABEL DE CARVAJAL'S TRIAL TRANSCRIPT,
1595–1596. COURTESY OF THE BANCROFT LIBRARY, UNIVERSITY
OF CALIFORNIA, BERKELEY, USA.

excessive cruelty in the treatment of an elderly male prisoner. His misconduct suggests that he might not have been averse to an off-the-record beating of a recalcitrant prisoner like Isabel. Whatever it was that caused her bloodied state, she told Dr Lobo Guerrero that some days earlier she had made a decision, *una determinación*, to confess because she wanted to discharge her conscience and save her soul.

Confess she did, in fourteen pages of testimony. She told him what he already knew: that she and her family had continued to observe the Law of Moses after being reconciled five years earlier. She described the way they kept the Sabbath every week from Friday until Saturday evening, the way they wore clean clothes and put clean linen on their beds, the fasts and the feasts they celebrated, the foods they ate and did not eat, and the songs and psalms they used to sing together. She mentioned several of the sacred songs that Leonor had sung for the inquisitors the year before. The proceedings ended with the usual note that 'being given the hour the hearing ceased and she read and approved the transcript'. But she did not sign this one. The scribe recorded that her right hand was injured so she could not.

By 4 September Isabel was able to climb the stairs once more. Dr Lobo Guerrero sat at the polished desk in the audience chamber and she told him she regretted not having confessed earlier. She said she was now a true Christian and wanted to save herself in the Law of Our Redeemer, Jesus Christ. She asked him to grant her mercy. He said he would present her request to the advisory council.

That afternoon he met with Inquisitor Peralta, the prosecutor and the members of their council to vote on what should be done with Isabel. Was it time to close her case? Apparently it was not. They decided to submit her to torture once again, but in moderation this time, because of her weakness. On 6 September they carried out the sentence. Isabel endured four turns of the ropes this time, but she had nothing more to say.

In June that year of 1596 the inquisitor-turned-bishop, Francisco Santos García, passed away in Guadalajara. In July Gregorio López, the mystic Christian hermit whom Luis had believed to be a secret Jew, died at the Hospital de Santa Fe. By autumn the end was drawing near for the imprisoned members of the Carvajal family as well.

On the morning of 12 September Dr Lobo Guerrero summoned Luis to the audience chamber. His lawyer, who was waiting there, urged Luis to discharge his conscience. 'You are blind,' he said, and he begged Luis to open his eyes to understanding and not persist with this blindness, because in following the Law of Moses rather than that of Jesus Christ he would be condemned.

We know how Luis responded: by presenting his spiritual testament to Dr Lobo Guerrero.

'I have shown in a note written and signed in my name and by my hand,' he said, 'in which I have written the commandments that I obey, and my testament, that I wish to live and die in the belief of those commandments. And therefore I request and submit that this paper be placed with my trial documents, as my last will, so that it will be recorded for all time.'

Dr Lobo Guerrero accepted the note. He ordered the scribe to place it in Luis's trial transcript and it is still there, covered back and front with beautiful letters so small that they are difficult to read without magnification. In some two thousand tiny words Luis listed the fundamentals by which he had lived and intended to die. Like a lawyer arguing his case before the court, which in a sense he was, he invoked passages from Deuteronomy, Exodus and Psalms, from Ezekiel, Baruch, Jeremiah, Isaiah, David, Daniel, Job, Tobit and Maccabees to demonstrate that the Law of Moses was the true faith, that the Messiah promised in that Law had not yet come, and that therefore Christianity was an error and a heresy.

Luis repeated what he had said in his earlier hearing: that when he consented to speak with theologians it was not because he had ever doubted the truth of the Law of Moses. On the contrary, he had asked to speak with them in order to acknowledge that truth more fully, as recommended in the Book of Tobit: 'Confess him before the Gentiles ye Children of Israel, for he hath scattered us among them.' He added that there was another reason he had agreed to meet the theologians. He had wanted to see whether he could convert them, and the inquisitors too, given that they had shown such sincere desire for his salvation.

As he drew his testament to a close he rehearsed his coming death.

'By God's exalted name I again swear that I will live and die in this faith,' he wrote. 'May God give me the grace to imitate the holy zeal of Hananiah, Azariah, Mishael and Mattathiah and joyfully surrender my soul for the faith of the holy covenant in which they died. I look to the Lord for strength,' he continued, 'lacking all confidence in my own, for I am flesh born of fragile seed.' *Flesh born of fragile seed.* These are sad words. Luis had learned in the torture chamber that his physical courage was brittle. He feared that it might fail him once again at the hour of his death.

He knew that on his way to the burning place he would have no peace. The priests and the watching crowds would be exhorting him to deny the Law of Moses and return to the Catholic Church. If he did he would be strangled with a garrotte before being burned in the fire. But he did not want a merciful death. He wanted to die like a martyr, like old Eleazar the scribe, in the second book of Maccabees, bearing witness and sanctifying the name of the Lord.

'And even as I have placed a mother and five sisters in danger because of that Law,' he wrote defiantly, 'if I had one thousand I would give them too, out of faith in each one of the holy commandments. In witness whereof I have written and signed this, my testament, and with this final deposition in which I affirm and confirm my faith I conclude the process of my trial.'

He could not stop while he still had space left on his sheet of paper. Speaking directly to his God he declared, 'I commend this soul which Thou hast given me to Thy most holy hands, solemnly affirming that I will not change my faith until I die, nor when I die. I most humbly beg you to confirm me in your love and not abandon me: and may it please you to send to my help and defence that holy angel Michael, our prince, with his holy and angelic army, to help me persevere and die in your holy faith and free me from the hands and temptations of the enemy.'

Luis had almost finished. 'Have mercy my good God and Lord upon the glory of Thy name, Law and people, and upon the world Thou hast created. Fill it with Thy light and with the true knowledge of Thy name, so that heaven and earth may be filled with praise for your glory. Amen. Amen.'

Luis concluded by mingling his approximation of Hebrew time with a concept of the afterlife borrowed from Catholic theology.

'In *Purgatorio* this fifth month of the year of our creation, five thousand three hundred and fifty-seven.'

At the bottom, in the only space remaining, he wrote, 'Perpetual slave of the Highest, Adonay'. Then he signed with the name he had adopted to exemplify his Jewish soul: 'Joseph Lumbroso'.

Luis made seven more appearances in the audience chamber before he died; five at his own request. Perhaps he felt a genuine desire to unburden his conscience and argue his theological case further before he died; he was, after all, a profoundly religious young man. Or he may have simply wanted to escape his cell for a few hours and glimpse the sunlit city through those upstairs windows.

At all but one of those last seven hearings he found himself before Licenciado Alonso de Peralta, who made his flesh tremble. Peralta began each session by asking why Luis had requested it. Luis replied each time that after searching his memory he recalled that some years ago such and such

a person had approached him in the silver mines at Taxco, or in Zimapan, or in the college at Santiago Tlatelolco, and had said this or that thing.

On 28 September 1596, for example, he told Peralta about the day seven years earlier when his brother Balthasar had come to him in tears to say that their sister, Isabel, had been arrested by the Holy Office. Luis said he had wept too, and after that he and Balthasar had gone to the house of Manuel de Lucena where Manuel and his wife, Catalina Enríquez, had tried to comfort them by saying that perhaps Isabel would be released. The actor Antonio López had been there too, Luis said and, 'being an understanding man', he had assured Luis that God punishes those he loves. Catalina's mother had brought a plate of raisins to Luis, embraced him, told him not to worry anymore, and in the early hours of the following morning he and Balthasar had set out for Mexico City.

In another hearing some weeks later Luis recalled how one day in Santiago he had read his family chapter 39 of Jeremiah, 'which deals with the final bringing together of the people of Israel'. He had translated it from Latin into Spanish and Manuel de Lucena, who loved to play the harp, had embraced him and said, 'I would give all my music just to know a little Latin.'

•

Luis made his last journey upstairs on the morning of 7 November. This final hearing was as brief as the others, yet the biblical allusions encoded in his testimony that morning suggest that even at this late hour he was determined to prove to his Christian captors that they were the heretics and blind ones, not him.

He told Inquisitor Peralta that a friend of a friend had once asked him why, if the Law of Moses was the one in which men would be saved, the Jews were so hounded and battered about? Luis had told that person to read chapter 49 of Isaiah if he wanted to understand why the Jews were so constantly persecuted.

Luis then recounted for Peralta a time when Manuel de Lucena had looked at a crucifix and recited the psalm that went:

> The idols of the people
> Are silver and gold
> Made by the hands of men.
> They have eyes but do not see,
> Feet but do not walk,
> Hands but do not touch . . .

'And this is the truth,' Luis concluded. 'And I do not say it out of hatred, and it is for this that I requested this hearing.'

Isaiah chapter 49 promises the Jews revenge against their oppressors and restoration of their homeland, while the psalm that Manuel de Lucena recited, number 115, warns against false gods, urges the Jews to trust in the Lord as their help and shield, and promises that in return God will bless the house of Israel, the house of Aaron.

Both are deeply messianic readings. But as far as we can tell from the scribal record Inquisitor Peralta showed little interest in what Luis had to say. He asked few questions, as if he had grown tired of listening to this unyielding and impenitent heretic.

We hear occasional reports of Luis's sisters from other prisoners in the Holy Office jail. In October 1595 a young man called Francisco Rodríguez told the inquisitors that while he was in a cell on the principal patio he had called out to see if anyone was nearby. A woman had responded but refused to give her name. When he tried again a few days later she had told him she was doña Isabel de Andrada. It was the surname she had used before acquiring the generic family name 'Carvajal'. Later she had called to Francisco and asked about his health. After that she had begun to speak more openly, telling him about her parents and the fact that she had once been a rich married woman. She said she had come to this land thinking it would be good but it had all gone bad for her.

Five months later, in February 1596, a prisoner called Andrés Rodríguez admitted communicating through the wall with doña Leonor. When he told her he observed the Law of Moses she had recited psalms and prayers to comfort him. On 6 April 1596 another Rodríguez, Manuel this time, admitted to the inquisitors that he had been communicating with Catalina in her cell. Manuel said she had told him that she didn't dare confess because she believed the inquisitors would not grant her mercy.

The imprisoned Carvajales made many journeys to the audience chamber during 1595 and 1596. Their transcripts show that they sometimes went upstairs on the very same morning or afternoon. They may have heard each other's footsteps in the corridor, but as far as we can tell they never managed even the most fleeting glimpse of each other.

Leonor was summoned twenty-three times, Isabel thirty, and Luis made forty-one appearances, nine of which he himself requested. As Francisca's trial documents are missing we do not know for certain how many hearings she faced. The portions of her testimony included in her children's transcripts account for several hearings, but there were almost certainly others of which no record is available at present.

Catalina's transcript is also missing and not one word from her appears in the transcripts of her mother and her siblings. This is very strange, and yet something Luis said during one of his final interrogations suggests that she may have decided to stay silent. In August 1596 he asked the inquisitors for a quill and ink and paper. He said he wanted to write to Catalina because he had heard from another prisoner that she was being held in a dungeon. He assumed from this that she was refusing to confess.

In June the previous year he had described her to the inquisitors as very closed, *'cerradisima'*. From our perspective too she is the closed one, the silent one, and until her transcript is one day recovered she will remain so.

# 13

# SILENT FOR A
# THOUSAND STEPS

WINTER RETURNED TO MEXICO CITY. FROST LAY ON THE CRIMSON
leaves of the cuitlaxochitl plants, and in the central plaza
an army of carpenters began work on a large wooden stage.
The inquisitors had announced that an auto-de-fe would
take place there on the feast of the Immaculate Conception,
8 December. It would be the twelfth such ritual act of faith
in the twenty-six years since the Holy Office arrived in the
conquered city.

On the night before the auto-de-fe Dominicans moved
slowly through the jail in their black and white robes,
informing the condemned prisoners that they were to be
*relaxado*, released, to the secular authorities. Luis had known
from the moment he was arrested that he would have to die;

Francisca, Isabel and Catalina had probably understood this too. Only Leonor, the youngest, had dared to hope for mercy. But that night of 7 December she learned that she would not be spared and her distress must have been profound.

At dawn next morning the guards led the Carvajales from their cells for the last time. Young Anna had been brought to the prison four nights earlier. Perhaps she called to them. Perhaps they called back to her knowing they would never see each other again, or not in this life anyway. Out in the Plaza de Santo Domingo, Luis, Francisca, Isabel, Catalina and Leonor joined the other sixty-four penitents who would take part in the ritual of faith. Green candles were placed in their hands, and when everything was ready they began their procession to the great central square.

As always, the officials of the Holy Office walked ahead beneath their green banner. The bigamists, blasphemers and sexual offenders followed, and behind them came the heretics. Most of these had been granted mercy and would be reconciled to the Church during the auto-de-fe, but not the five Carvajales. They walked at the very back of the procession of infamy along with Manuel de Lucena, his mother-in-law Beatriz, her son Diego, and their cousin Manuel Díaz. All nine wore penitential habits and tall conical hats painted with red flames so that everyone who saw them would understand that they were to be released to the secular authorities for execution.

What did the spectators see as they watched that tragic group pass by? Apostates, heretics, perverse Jewish enemies of the state? Or simply two harmless old women—Francisca and Beatriz were elderly by the standards of the time—being sent to their deaths with their children? In his book of miracles Luis had mentioned several acts of kindness on the part of their gentile compatriots—acts that suggest those thoughtful patrons felt sympathy for the Carvajal family. Whether their sympathy had vanished now that Luis, his mother and sisters had been unmasked as persistent Judaisers we do not know. But we can be certain that a number of secret Jews stood among the spectators who watched the procession to the plaza. And, although they could not show it, their hearts were filled with grief and sorrow over the fate of their friends.

The high stage in the plaza had been divided into the usual two sections: the right side for the righteous, the left for the sinners, with a passage in between leading to the pulpit at the front of the stage. The penitents' benches formed a tall triangle so that the spectators in the plaza could see them clearly. Luis sat at the apex of the triangle, gagged and unrepentant in his conical hat, like one of the melancholy figures Francisco de Goya would evoke two centuries later in his *Los Caprichos* etchings.

The ceremony began with mass. After that the bishop of Manila preached the sermon, and when he had finished the penitents were called to the pulpit one by one to hear their sentences. Justa Méndez was among those granted clemency; so was Catalina Enríquez, the wife of Manuel de Lucena, and also Manuel Gómez Navarro, whose brother had denounced Luis to the Holy Office. The young man known as Diego Díaz Nieto, who had come from Spain with Balthasar's letter in 1594, had been arrested some months earlier. He was granted reconciliation, and so were the Rodríguez brothers who had communicated with Isabel and Leonor in their cells.

A young tailor known as Daniel Benítez was also reconciled. Daniel's trial transcript notes that he was born in Hamburg, had been arrested on suspicion of being a Lutheran heretic but, 'through the teaching of a certain companion' had begun to believe in the Law of Moses instead. The 'certain companion' was Luis. Daniel had shared his cell in recent months and during that time Luis had convinced him that the Law of Moses was the true faith. So while a prisoner in the Holy Office jail Daniel had shifted from one heresy to another. It was his first offence, however; he had repented and promised to abandon the Law of Moses, therefore the Holy Office allowed him to live.

As the afternoon shadows lengthened Francisca and her daughters were called one by one to the centre of the stage to hear their sentences. They listened as the public notary announced that they were to be carried on beasts of burden to the burning place in the market of San Hipólito, where they would be executed. They had agreed to return to the Christian fold, however, therefore they would be garrotted, and after that each woman's body would be burned to ashes 'so that no memory of her will remain'.

Luis was the last to be sentenced that day. The notary announced that he too would be carried on a beast of burden to the marketplace of San Hipólito. But as he was still refusing to abandon the Law of Moses he would be burned alive. He would die in the flames and after that his body too would be reduced to ashes so that no memory of him would remain. Luis did not necessarily have to die that terrible death, though. A special clause had been appended to his sentence, as it was to the sentences of all impenitent heretics in the Spanish-speaking world. The notary read it aloud for all to hear: 'If the said Luis de Carvajal, before being executed, demonstrates his repentance and conversion he will be garrotted first, before being set on fire.' It was a final temptation for Luis. It was also one last chance for the authorities to induce him to accept the principal role in their theatre of penitence: that of the heretic who finds redemption and salvation through the Holy Mother Church.

When the sentencing was over the five members of the Carvajal family and the friends who were to die with them were taken from the stage to begin their journey to the burning place. We cannot know their state of mind as they were led through the crowds. We can only guess at the terror they felt in all that noise and dust, as hundreds of people pressed around them, and the priests prayed and preached beside them. They were led slowly along what is now the Avenida de Madero to the marketplace of San Hipólito on the western edge of the Alameda gardens.

There, on a specially constructed platform made of limestone and pebbles, they were tied to stakes, and as darkness fell they were garrotted one by one. All of them, Luis as well. The official record of his death shows that he was not burned alive as he had wanted. Instead he died like a 'vile, hanged man', and many hours later, when his body and the bodies of his family and his friends had been burned to cinders, their smouldering ashes and any remnants of bone among those ashes were thrown into the canal like so much rubbish.

●

Later that night the chief constable of Mexico City made out a formal report about the executions. This is what he wrote about Luis's death:

In the city of México, the said day, month and year, in compliance with the said sentence, the said Luis de Carvajal was carried through the usual streets on a beast of burden with a crier announcing his crime, and on the way he showed that he had converted by taking a crucifix in his hands and saying certain words by which it was understood that he had converted and repented; therefore, having arrived at the burning place in the market of San Hipólito he was garrotted until he appeared to have died naturally; and his body was set on fire and left burning in live flames until it was turned into ashes. Being present as witnesses: Balthasar Mexía Salmerón, Chief Constable, and Pedro Rodríguez, Juan de Budia and Francisco de Benavides, his lieutenants, and many other persons. Before me: Alonso Bernal, Public Notary.

The following day the chaplain who had accompanied Luis to the burning ground presented his own report to the inquisitors. Their scribe placed it in the back of Luis's trial transcript, where it remains. The chaplain gave his name as Alonso de Contreras and his age as thirty-seven. He said he was a member of the Order of Santo Domingo and the vicar of 'Eztapaluca', probably present-day Ixtapaluca to the east of Mexico City. Fray Alonso wrote that it had pleased Jesus Christ Our Lord, through him, to convert and return to the Holy and Evangelical Faith, Luis de Carvajal, Joseph Lumbroso by other name, and that Luis had proceeded with his conversion with all the truths and effectiveness morally possible and evident, and had acknowledged the indefinable mystery of the Holy Trinity and the infinite worth of the Passion of Jesus Christ, Our Redeemer.

That declaration of 9 December 1596 is not the last we hear of Fray Alonso de Contreras. The following year he prepared a far more detailed description of Luis's last hours for the Holy Office. It is still there among the inquisitorial records in the Archivo General, and its defensive tone reveals that not everyone in Mexico City at that time believed that Luis had truly been converted before his death. Whether or not we believe what Fray Alonso had to say, he has left us the only eyewitness account of that caravan of death as it travelled through the streets of Mexico City.

Fray Alonso called his narrative 'The True Relation of the Conversion and Catholic Death of Luis de Carvajal, by Other Name Joseph Lumbroso, Released to the Secular Arm by the Holy Office in Mexico City.' He began by explaining that when the day arrived for the auto-de-fe confessors were appointed to comfort the relapsed Jews who had to die. It is interesting that he said 'Jews' not 'Judaisers', something the inquisitors never did, not on paper anyway. They had jurisdiction only over baptised Christians, so to acknowledge that the accused people brought before them were Jews would have negated any heresy proceedings against them. In any case, Fray Alonso recalled that a certain Padre Medrano had been appointed confessor to 'the relapsed Jew, Luis de Carvajal', who had shown himself to be 'the hardest, most heretical, blasphemous and worst enemy of Jesus Christ Our Lord'. Therefore, although Medrano had spent the night in Luis's cell, he had failed to convert him, and when they set out next morning in procession to the central plaza everyone knew that.

Fray Alonso said that as they entered the great plaza where the stage had been constructed, Luis began calling to his mother and his sisters, urging them to die in the Law of Moses. The guards gagged him, and Fray Alonso, who wrote that he had never seen such a wilful and obstinate heretic, watched Luis with interest from then on. He noticed that as they approached the stage Luis glimpsed an effigy of a Jew that was to be burned later. It was possibly that of his brother Miguel, whose effigy was indeed incinerated that day. Fray Alonso said that Luis looked at it with great tenderness and sighed. 'And lifting his eyes to the sky he seemed to commend his soul to heaven, although he did not speak because he could not.' Fray Alonso noticed also that whenever someone held a crucifix in front of Luis's eyes, Luis looked away towards the east. It was the direction in which he had knelt to pray in his cell each day; the direction of the Jerusalem of his imagination.

While the sentencing was taking place Luis sat listening in his place at the top of the penitents' benches. When he heard the name of Justa Méndez called he slipped his gag and cried, 'Let me hear the sentence of that fortunate and blessed girl!' Later, when he stood at the front of the stage to hear his own sentence, he received the terrible news with a smile. What kind of smile? Triumphant or ecstatic? Fray Alonso does not tell us. He says only that when Luis's mother and sisters heard his sentence they wept and called to him, imploring him to convert. 'But he remained deaf to their cries and to the good counsel of his wise chaplain, as if he were a marble column.'

Why did Francisca and her daughters beg Luis to convert? So that he would suffer a merciful death? Or because their chaplains had convinced them that if he did not embrace Catholicism he would burn in hell? In that terrifying age, when Christians and Christianised Jews alike lived in fear of damnation, either or both explanations are possible.

As Luis was being taken down from the stage, Fray Alonso pushed his way towards him. He got so close that Luis's horse stepped on his foot, but despite his pain he studied Luis carefully. 'And I saw in his face a certain courage and insouciance, as well as great haughtiness and pride which he showed many times by laughing and mocking the holy reasoning of the religious persons who approached him.'

Fray Alonso watched as another Dominican pushed a green crucifix in Luis's face and urged him to kiss it. Luis spat at it and asked, 'Is there some law this thing commands? You should take it to the inquisition and punish it severely. It deserves it more than I do.'

The monk with the green cross asked him, 'Do you know what the Holy Office of the Inquisition is?'

Luis replied, 'The counsel of the ungodly and the chair of pestilence.'

He was quoting from the first psalm, and Fray Alonso said that everyone who heard his words considered them blasphemous, and many loud, confused voices erupted in the crowd.

Suddenly, amid all this turbulence and noise, Luis turned to Fray Alonso and asked, 'Is there any greater torment in the world than to be a bound man surrounded by rabid dogs?'

It sounds like an allusion to verse 16 of Psalm 22 and Luis, who knew and loved the psalms, may well have made it.

Fray Alonso saw his chance. He urged Luis to have patience and forbearance, as Christ had done when the high priests and Pharisees wanted to take his life.

'Padre mio,' Luis replied, 'I have much affection for Christ, but Christ is not God.'

Fray Alonso said that when the people pressing around them heard this they spat in Luis's face.

The sad procession continued to push its way through the crowds. Suddenly Luis's official chaplain, Padre Medrano, appeared, brandishing a cross and imploring Luis to kiss it. Luis looked up at the sky. 'Lord, my God, my helper,' he prayed, 'I will not fear what man can do to me.'

It was a fragment of Psalm 55; the kind of comforting mantra we can imagine him reciting as he prepared himself for the ordeal ahead.

They were still in the plaza at this point, barely able to move because of the hordes of people around them. But at last their procession made its way into Calle San Francisco, which is now Avenida Madero. Fray Alonso said that as they entered that narrow street he felt exhausted in both body and spirit because so many people were shoving and pushing him. He paused to wipe his face and lost his position beside Luis. When he tried to regain it a tall and corpulent monk from another order had taken his place.

Fray Alonso felt helpless and exasperated. He said that as the monks walked their habits brushed the ground, and the dust they raised filled his mouth and nose and eyes. 'The Lord knows how much I suffered,' he wrote. But at last the tall and corpulent monk moved away and Fray Alonso resumed his place beside Luis and continued his efforts to convert him. Luis responded with a scriptural passage to every argument he put forward, so that it seemed to Fray Alonso that Luis knew the entire Old Testament by heart and could counter any line of reasoning. Finally, in desperation, he decided to try a passage from Jeremiah. Praying for Our Lady's intercession he said, 'Luis, I only want to say one thing to you which I think, through the virtue of Jesus Christ, you will yield to; and if not I promise I will turn away and not tire you anymore.'

He told Luis there was a text in divine scripture that related clearly to Jesus Christ. He recited it in Latin: '*Spiritus oris nostri, Christus dominus, captus est in peccatis nostri cui diximuys, in umbra tua vivemos inter gentes.*'

Fray Alonso claimed that Luis looked puzzled and asked, 'Where does that come from?'

'From the prophet Jeremiah,' Fray Alonso responded, although he admitted in his account of this conversation that at the time he had not been sure of its exact provenance.

It is in fact verse 20 from chapter 4 of the Lamentations of Jeremiah, and although it refers to the anointed one of God, *Christus dominus*, there is nothing in this passage to prove that Jesus was that anointed one. Yet Fray Alonso claimed it had a dramatic impact on Luis, who exclaimed, 'Jeremiah is the prophet I venerate above all others, but I have never read or heard that passage.' Hearing this, Fray Alonso hoped he might finally have broken through 'the diamond heart' of Luis de Carvajal.

He says that Luis asked to see the text. Fray Alonso did not have a Bible with him but someone placed one in his hands, 'and with much anxiety I began to leaf through the prophecies of Jeremiah'. He wrote that by now the dust had almost blinded him, and he had been pushed and shoved so much that his habit was torn. He says that Luis began to laugh at him. Can this possibly be true? Could Luis really have been laughing on his way to the burning place? Perhaps he was laughing in confusion and despair, or not laughing at all, but sobbing. In any case, Fray Alonso found the place in Lamentations and told him, 'Read, my son.'

Luis read Jeremiah's words and Fray Alonso claimed that 'a gentleness new and strange' came over him, after which he lowered his eyes and said, 'I will keep my word and yield to the Holy Mother Catholic Church and confess truly that the prophet Jeremiah, or rather God through him, spoke here of

Jesus Christ, God and Man, Spirit and Soul of all the faithful, anointed, imprisoned, captive, whipped and killed by men, in whose shadow, that is his grace, we Jews can be yoked and deserve among the Gentiles the goodness of the sacraments, through which we can reach eternal life.' According to Fray Alonso Luis paused after that and declared, 'I confess it. Give me a crucifix.'

Fray Alonso wrote that at that very moment he suffered a painful blow from Luis's horse. He wondered whether it was really a blow from the devil, angered at his priestly intervention. Ignoring the pain he placed a crucifix in the hands of 'the good Luis de Carvajal' and Luis received it, he said, with many sobs and sighs, kissing its feet and its wounded side and speaking to it tenderly. Then Luis rested his head on Fray Alonso's shoulder saying, 'Oh angel of my safekeeping, restorer of my spirit, mouth of God! Who put into your mouth those words you said to me? Who taught you that?' Fray Alonso said that Luis clung to him and begged him with many tears not to leave him. Fray Alonso promised he would not leave, although he had to draw aside a little at this point in order to wipe the dust and tears from his face.

Some of this may be true: the tears, the embraces and Luis imploring Fray Alonso not to leave him. A young man on his way to a terrible death might well have responded like this to a kindly stranger. But as Fray Alonso had himself remarked, Luis knew the Old Testament by heart. He had been studying it intently since the age of eighteen and during his interrogations he had quoted Jeremiah more than any other prophet. It seems most unlikely that he had never before encountered that verse from Lamentations, and equally unlikely that he would suddenly accept that Jesus was the anointed one referred to in it. That was Fray Alonso's story, however, and he wrote that after Luis's capitulation the crowds lining the narrow street watched admiringly as he and Luis continued on their slow way towards the marketplace of San Hipólito.

He said that Luis had begun speaking to his crucifix and reciting, 'Sprinkle me, O Lord, with hyssop, and I shall be cleansed.' The words, although originally from Psalm 51, were used in the Latin mass at that time. In any case, Fray Alonso saw an opportunity in them.

'Luis, my son,' he said, 'in order to be truly cleansed you must not just receive the faith but show it with words and deeds. Do you now think that Christ Our Lord is the true God?'

According to Fray Alonso, Luis replied, 'Yes, I do believe.'

'Then do you also think that all the things he made gave virtue like God, especially the Holy Sacraments instituted by

His Church? And do you believe they bring grace to those worthy to receive them?'

'Yes, I believe.'

'Well you also have to believe that nobody can be saved without confessing their sins and being absolved of them, and that it is a mercy from God that He listens to them Himself so as not to cause you shame.' In a reference to Jesus, Fray Alonso added that it was likewise a mercy that God had not sent a pure angel to save mankind, but a man 'who had perhaps sinned more than you'.

Fray Alonso counselled Luis to examine his memory well and make the best confession possible at the place where he would die. 'And I will help you in that death.' He said that in response Luis bent his head, kissed the crucifix, and recited those most beautiful words from the Song of Solomon, 'My beloved is mine and I am his.'

After that, Fray Alonso said, Luis closed his eyes and continued on in silence. 'And for the space of a thousand steps he did not respond to anyone who spoke to him.'

A difficulty now arose. Fray Alonso was not Luis's official confessor and therefore he feared that one of the Jesuits in attendance might try to take his place, because they were keen to hear Luis's confession. But Luis would have nobody else, Fray Alonso wrote, 'and I would not leave him for anything'. And so they stayed together: Luis on his horse in his pointed hat and sanbenito, Fray Alonso beside him in his torn and dusty robes as they made their way along the Calle San Francisco.

Fray Alonso said that when they reached the marketplace of San Hipólito Luis was speaking with great devotion to the crucifix in his hands and had begun reciting the Catholic prayer of contrition, the *Miserere mei*. Luis may in fact have been reciting Psalm 51 once more, on which the *Miserere* is based. Meanwhile, the magistrate's men took him down from his horse. Fray Alonso held his hand and together they climbed onto the limestone platform where the stakes had been erected. Luis asked permission to speak with his mother. Fray Alonso said he could.

Francisca was already tethered to her stake with the iron garrotte around her neck. Luis knelt before her and, according to Fray Alonso, he addressed her thus, 'Mother of mine, the mother until now of a hard and obstinate sinner, now the mother of a son converted to the faith of Christ through his charity and love, I ask your pardon and blessing, in the virtue of the passion of Christ. I hope to see you in heaven through the faith in which I die.'

That final sentence, with its poignant echoes of Luis's prison letters, sounds like something Luis might well have uttered as he knelt before his mother. But the rest of this ornate speech, with its references to Jesus, is surely Fray Alonso's invention. In any case Fray Alonso said that he embraced both Luis and Francisca and then led Luis to his own stake. Luis knelt before it to make his last confession, and as he did the executioners began to garrotte Manuel de Lucena. Luis turned to look at his friend, and here begins the defensive part of Fray Alonso's report. Ever since that night some spectators had apparently been asserting that Luis and Manuel made secret Jewish signs to each other before they died, signs that suggested the two had not truly returned to Christianity. Fray Alonso did not explain in his narrative what those signs might have been. He said only that he did not take his eyes from Luis's face at this point, and therefore he did not see them.

Meanwhile, as Manuel was dying, Luis began his confession which, according to Fray Alonso, went like this: 'By the sign of the Holy Cross on which my redeemer Jesus Christ died, free me Lord from my enemies, especially those who have until now held me captive and blinded my understanding. In the name of the Father and His Son, my Lord Jesus Christ, and the Holy Spirit who comes from both, Amen Jesus. I, Luis de Carvajal, great sinner, confess to God the Father and Jesus Christ His Son and His Holy Mother my Lady the Virgin Mary and all the confessed saints who are in heaven, and to you, Padre, in place of God, that I have sinned gravely against my Lord and Redeemer, Jesus Christ, and against my understanding because it being such a noble power disposed to know God I did great injury in obstructing it for so long, and for all that I did and said.'

Fray Alonso wrote that he had never encountered such a confession in any other Christian in all his life. 'Heroic, concise, clear, plain and true,' he called it. He added that Luis then asked him to give the inquisitors the names of several people he had falsely testified against. Fray Alonso promised that he would and that he would also say twenty masses for the repose of Luis's soul. They had been kneeling together all this time, but now the moment had come for Luis to die. Fray Alonso said he wept as they embraced. He asked Luis not to forget him in heaven and Luis promised he never would. They moved towards the stake. According to Fray Alonso Luis announced that he wanted to clearly profess the faith in which he was going to die, and as he could no longer talk very loudly he asked that witnesses draw close to listen.

The watching people pressed close against the limestone platform. Luis began to speak, 'and I helped him,' Fray Alonso wrote. He became Luis's death-hour interpreter, or his ventriloquist. He wrote that Luis made a long and moving profession of his faith in Jesus Christ and asked pardon of those he had injured or upset with his bad life. 'And after that the poor man could say no more.' They embraced again and Luis said many tender things that Fray Alonso could no longer recall when he wrote his account. The executioner approached Luis's stake, stood behind him and began to twist the iron garrotte. Fray Alonso said Luis was holding the crucifix and praying the Apostles' Creed in a loud voice as he died. Then his hands dropped, 'and his soul was released'.

His hands dropped, his soul was released. It sounds like a peaceful death, but it was not. Fray Alonso added that as the executioners were not very skilled they garrotted Luis 'with a great deal of trouble'.

'And this was the end of Luis de Carvajal, with this understanding and this confession, for which I envy him.'

In concluding, Fray Alonso declared that he felt sure in his heart that Luis de Carvajal had died a good Catholic and was now with God. At the beginning of his narrative he said that Luis was such a good Jew 'that if he had lived before the incarnation of Our Redeemer, he would have been a heroic Hebrew, and his name would be as famous in the Bible as the names of others who had died in defence of their law'. It was a tribute that would have filled Luis with joy.

How much, if any, of Fray Alonso's story can we believe? He said himself when he wrote it that ever since the night of 8 December some people in Mexico City, even priests and monks, had expressed their doubts about Luis's conversion. Fray Alonso spent the remainder of his narrative attempting to refute those doubts, and in the course of his refutation he noted the placement of the stakes. He felt that this was necessary because some gossipers were alleging that before dying Luis de Carvajal had turned his head, looked at his sisters and made secret Jewish signs to them. Fray Alonso argued that this was impossible: that they could not have seen each other or communicated in any way. He pointed out that Luis had been tied to a stake facing west, Francisca had been facing north, and Isabel had faced south. Catalina had looked east toward the volcanoes, and young Leonor, tethered to a stake beside her, had been the last to die.

So did Luis really convert, or 'show signs of conversion', during his final journey to the burning place? It is possible. He may well have succumbed to fear and recanted, as most people did then, and most of us would now. In his final testament he had described himself as 'flesh born of fragile seed'. He remembered his capitulation in the torture chamber and knew he might lack the strength to die the glorious martyr's death he desired. That is why he asked the Lord to send the Archangel Michael, 'our prince, with his holy and angelic army', to assist him as he died. But what if the doubters were correct and Fray Alonso did, in fact, lie about Luis's conversion? Why would he do such a thing?

He may have been a humane man who wished to spare Luis unnecessary suffering, or a vain man who lied in order to cover himself with glory as the only priest capable of 'turning' this impenitent heretic. It is also feasible that he was acting on orders from the magistrate, for as the historian Brad Gregory noted in *Salvation at Stake*, his study of Christian martyrs in sixteenth-century Europe, the public death of an unrepentant heretic was always a defeat for the authorities and one they went to great lengths to avoid.

It is possible, of course, that Luis's brother Gaspar played an unseen part in Luis's death by garrotte rather than by fire. He and Fray Alonso were fellow Dominicans of about the same age. Both resided in the monastery of Santo Domingo and Gaspar may have implored Fray Alonso to find a way to spare Luis from being burned alive. Perhaps Gaspar provided his fellow monk with a bribe to ensure that he did just that. In those days of public executions throughout the European world, money paid to the executioner or chaplain could often save a victim from an excruciating death.

Fray Alonso could have lied for any or all of the above reasons; they are not mutually exclusive. The only thing we can say for certain is that Fray Alonso ensured that Luis was garrotted before being burned.

Was Luis any less a martyr if he truly did capitulate in order to avoid being burned alive? No. Implicit in the idea of martyrdom is an element of choice, of choosing death, or the risk of death. Luis had made that choice as a boy in Medina del Campo, and he had confirmed it later, after his reconciliation, when he continued to follow his forbidden faith, knowing that the consequences would be fatal if he were caught.

In the end, like the Maccabees he so admired, Luis had used his own death as a form of resistance. And whether or not Fray Alonso and his fellow clerics understood, he had lived and died bearing witness, and sanctifying the name of the God he loved.

# 14

# CODA

THE PLACE WHERE THE CARVAJAL FAMILY DIED IS NOW A QUIET
lane between the western edge of the Alameda gardens
and the former Church of San Diego. Most afternoons an
ice-cream seller sets up her stall at the end of the lane, and it
is a scene so peaceful that it is hard to imagine the suffering
that occurred there on the night of 8 December 1596. The
former Hospital de San Hipólito, where Luis washed the floor
with his tears, still stands just a few hundred metres away
across the busy Avenida Hidalgo. Luis would have been able
to see it from his stake on the night he died, had it not been
for the crowds and the smoke-filled air.

We do not know whether Gaspar witnessed his family's
executions. As a Dominican he would normally have attended

Site of former
*Quemadera*
(burning ground)
in Mexico City,
January 2006.

such judicial killings, but the prior of his order may have spared him the sight of his mother, his sisters and his younger brother being strangled on that limestone platform. Gaspar was never again arrested by the Holy Office and as far as we can tell he lived out the rest of his life in his monastery on the Plaza de Santo Domingo and was buried in its grounds.

Fray Pedro de Oroz died the year after Luis, and his body was interred in the Church of Santiago, beside the college for Aztec boys where he had spent his life. One of Fray Pedro's

Nahuatl epistles made its way to the British Museum, where it is held today, while a history he wrote of the Franciscan mission in New Spain is preserved in the Latin American collection at Tulane University in New Orleans. Whether Fray Pedro watched his protégé die in the marketplace of San Hipólito in December 1596 is not recorded.

Mariana lived on for five years after her family's execution, and for much of that time she continued to suffer the torments of mental illness. But gradually her symptoms abated, and in May 1600, when she was twenty-nine, she requested a hearing at the Holy Office. Dr Lobo Guerrero was no longer in Mexico City, but Licenciado Alonso de Peralta was still there and on the afternoon of 29 May he received Mariana in the audience chamber.

She explained that for three years she had been living in the house of doña Maria de Peralta, mother of Bernardino Vázquez de Tapia. 'During the first year I was taken very badly by the illness that I succumbed to in my mother's house,' Mariana said, 'where I lost my reason through a great melancholy caused by the troubles I had, and through my sins.' She added that in recent months she had recovered her reason and had begun to pray the rosary and attend mass and live like a good Catholic.

Mariana told Inquisitor Peralta that after her reconciliation in 1590 she had continued to observe the Law of Moses, but now felt deep regret and guilt at having done this—so much so that she had told her confessor Fray Juan de Santiago that she wanted to go to the Holy Office and admit what she had done. Fray Juan had begged her not to go. 'It is madness to think you have to die in order to save yourself,' he had counselled her. But Mariana had insisted. 'And I am very content to have been brought here yesterday morning,' she told Peralta.

During the hearings that followed she described her life in her mother's house in Santiago Tlatelolco and sang the very same canticles that her sister Leonor had sung for him in June 1595. Mariana sounds lucid and coherent throughout her hearings—no babbling or confused muttering—and her signature at the end of every transcript is firm and clear. Her voluntary confession and her professed desire to live as a Christian did not save her, however. Her insanity had protected her from prosecution in 1595, but back in 1590 she had used her single chance for clemency, and so on the morning of 17 October 1600 the Council of the Inquisition voted that she should be released to the secular authorities as an impenitent and relapsed Judaising heretic.

Five months later, on 25 March 1601, Mariana walked to the Plaza Mayor dressed in a yellow sanbenito and long pointed hat, just as her family had done five years earlier. Perhaps, after all her sufferings, this was what she wanted: to follow literally in their footsteps. During sentencing that afternoon the magistrate announced that Mariana would be led through the streets on a beast of burden until she reached the marketplace of San Hipólito. There she would be garrotted, and after her death her body would be burned to ashes 'until no memory of her remains'. Next day the magistrate filed the usual official report to say that the sentence had been carried out.

Anna, the youngest Carvajal daughter, appeared in the same auto-de-fe of 1601. She had been arrested on the basis of Mariana's testimony and readily confessed to the crime of Judaising, but as this was her first offence Inquisitor Peralta granted her reconciliation and allowed her to go free. Anna was eighteen at the time of her release. She married, had six children and resided quietly in Mexico City until the age of sixty-three, when she was imprisoned once again. Six years later she was released to the secular authorities for execution in the marketplace of San Hipólito. She was the last of her family to suffer that fate.

•

Balthasar and Miguel, now known as Jacob and David Lumbroso, lived on in their respective sanctuaries in Ferrara and Salonika. No doubt they lamented and wept when news of their family's deaths at the end of 1596 reached them. The following year Ferrara erupted in political turmoil, and many of its Jewish residents fled north to the relative safety of the Venetian ghetto. Perhaps Balthasar and his family went with them. He had said in his letter of 1594 that his wife was expecting another child. We can only hope that Esther and her infant survived, whether in Ferrara or Venice, and that in Salonika Miguel achieved his desire to become learned in the Law of Moses.

There was one member of the Carvajal family who has not yet appeared in this narrative. She was the only child born of Catalina and Antonia Díaz de Cáceres. Her name was Leonor de Cáceres. She was fourteen when her aunt Mariana surrendered herself to the Holy Office in 1600, and at Mariana's urging Inquisitor Peralta brought young Leonor in for questioning.

On the afternoon of Thursday 14 December Leonor told him that she, like Mariana, was living in the house of doña Maria de Peralta. He asked Leonor if she knew or presumed why she had been called to the Holy Office, and she replied that she imagined it was in order to say and declare what she knew about *'la Ley Judaica'*. She called it that— the Jewish Law—rather than the Law of Moses, as her family had always done. She added that for some time she had wanted to come and discharge her conscience by telling the Holy Office about the things her mother doña Catalina, her grandmother doña Francisca, her aunts doña Isabel, doña Mariana and doña Anna had taught her since the age of five, and also her uncle Luis de Carvajal. She did not mention the aunt after whom she had been called—Leonor—perhaps out of nerves, or simple forgetfulness. But she proceeded to describe in minute detail the feasts and fasts her family had observed, the prayers they had prayed, and the songs they had sung, including those that her aunt Leonor had sung for the inquisitors in May five years earlier.

Young Leonor recalled sitting with her grandmother, her mother and her aunts and listening as her uncle Luis read to them from a little black notebook that he had been writing at the 'school for Indians'. She meant his book of miracles. She also recalled how her family had dressed in clean clothes on Saturdays, the foods they prepared—she said they always soaked their poultry in basins of water until it was drained of blood—and the foods they avoided, like pork and bacon. She mentioned that her father, Antonio Díaz de Cáceres, liked to eat bacon and kept some for his own consumption, but her mother, doña Catalina, used to feed it to their little dog whenever she could. Leonor also told Inquisitor Peralta that her mother used to beat her and refused to feed her unless she said her Jewish prayers.

This may or may not have been true. It was important, after all, that Leonor present herself as free of any Jewish leanings. In any case Inquisitor Peralta believed her story. He granted her mercy on the basis that as a child in her mother's power she had not been capable of understanding which faith was the true faith, and he ordered her to take part in the auto-de-fe of March 1601. It was the same 'act of faith' after which her aunt Mariana was garrotted. But Leonor, like her aunt Anna, was reconciled to the Church that day and lived.

Diego Díaz Nieto, the young man who had brought Luis those precious letters from Balthasar and Jorge de Almeida in 1594, was rearrested in 1601, also on the basis of Mariana's testimony. The warrant for his arrest describes him as a man of about twenty-five, tall, neither fat nor thin, with a good beard, a pale face and blue eyes, and dressed in blue clothes. This second incarceration—he had been reconciled five years earlier—should have meant the end for him. But it didn't, and the reason he survived is an intriguing story in itself.

During his first trial in 1596 Diego had declared that he had been born, baptised and raised as a Christian in Portugal.

However, on Wednesday 10 January 1601 he told Inquisitor Peralta that none of this was true. He declared this time that in reality he had been born and raised in Ferrara, in Italy, that his real name was *Ysaque*—Isaac—Neto, that he had been circumcised in the Portuguese synagogue of Ferrara when he was eight days old, and was not a *'forzado'*—a forced one—as he had previously stated. In fact, he said, he had never been baptised, adding however that if his doubts about the Christian faith could be satisfied he would like to be.

Diego's new claim must have startled Inquisitor Peralta. Nevertheless Peralta said that he would summon some learned theologians to see if they could satisfy Diego's doubts, and sure enough, two days later, two Jesuits did indeed come to the audience chamber to talk with him. Diego explained to them his uncertainties about the Christian notion of a Trinitarian god, and the question of whether Jesus had truly been the Messiah, and they discussed these complex issues with Diego at some length. On Sunday 14 January 1601 he told Inquisitor Peralta that his doubts had now been satisfied. The scribe in attendance recorded that in tears Diego knelt, took a crucifix in his hands with great tenderness, declared that he wanted to live and die in the Holy Catholic Faith and asked to be granted mercy.

After listening to this plea Inquisitor Peralta sent a formal request to his Holy Office colleagues in Ferrara and asked them to investigate Diego's claims about having been born and raised in the Portuguese-Jewish community there. To assist them in their inquiries he explained that Diego had testified that he had been born and raised in his father's house near the street called Gioveccha; that he had spent ten years studying Hebrew, Spanish and Italian under the tutelage of one Rabbi Moysen Cohen, and had also taken lessons from a woman known as Sara. Inquisitor Peralta asked his colleagues in Ferrara to try to find Rabbi Cohen and the woman called Sara in order to verify what Diego had told him. 'And if it can be verified,' Peralta wrote, 'he will be granted mercy and his case will be definitively concluded.'

The Holy Office in Ferrara received Peralta's letter in 1602 and in June that year the Inquisitor General of Ferrara himself—Fray Juan Bautista Scarella de Gaydo de Brescia—interviewed three Jewish witnesses to see whether he could authenticate Diego's story. Each witness took an oath on Jewish prayer books, 'libros hebraicos', and each was asked whether he knew a rabbi called Moysen Cohen, a woman called Sara, and a family known as Nieto. It emerged from the witnesses' replies that although both Rabbi Cohen and Sara were now dead, the details of their work as teachers of Hebrew, Spanish and Italian accorded with what Diego Díaz Nieto had told Inquisitor Peralta in Mexico City.

Furthermore, all three witnesses had known the Nieto family and testified that the father's name was Jacob, his son was called Isaac, and they had indeed lived in Ferrara. The third witness, one Moysen Carabon, who gave his age as fifty-seven, said he had known the Nieto family quite well. The inquisitor general asked where the boy Isaac had been born, and approximately how long ago. Moysen replied that Isaac had been born in Jacob Nieto's house close to the street called Gioveccha. 'And that would be about twenty-four years ago, more or less.'

'And do you believe that the said Isaac was circumcised,' the inquisitor asked.

'Father, I think he was,' Moysen replied, 'because I recall that we went to visit his mother on the Saturday of the week he was born . . . and on the eighth day after his birth he was circumcised.'

The inquisitor asked Moysen whether he knew where Jacob and Isaac Nieto were now. Moysen said he didn't know because it had been a long time since they left Ferrara.

'Do any of Isaac Nieto's relatives still live in Ferrara?' the inquisitor asked.

'No sir, none.'

The interview was over. Moysen Carabon signed his statement and the notary copied it out, along with the statements of the other two witnesses. Although they did not know it they had saved Isaac/Diego's life.

Diego remained in the Holy Office prison in Mexico City while the copies of those life-saving testimonies made their slow way from Ferrara to Seville, and then across the Atlantic to New Spain. Those must have been anxious days for him, but in the end he won his reprieve. On 26 March 1605 he was reconciled for a second time—an almost unheard of privilege—and sentenced to a period of seclusion in the Jesuit College in Mexico City. On 29 May that year he was baptised in its chapel by one of the Jesuits who had converted him. At his baptism Isaac/Diego acquired yet another name—the name of his godfather, 'Alonso Guerrero'.

The following year Isaac/Diego/Alonso benefited from yet another general pardon for Jewish New Christians, this time issued by Pope Clement VIII. When Diego learned about the pardon he begged leave of the Holy Office to allow him to travel to the kingdom of Portugal. Inquisitor Peralta granted his request, and in a declaration of 3 June 1606 Diego expressed his gratitude for this clemency. He was released from his confinement at the Jesuit College that day, and although his movements after this point are unknown, we can safely assume that he left New Spain, and probably all Spanish territories, forever.

•

Jorge de Almeida, the husband of Leonor de Carvajal, did not return to Mexico City after her death in 1596. The Holy Office tried him in absentia in 1607 and two years later they burned an effigy of him in public. After that he too disappears from the inquisitorial records. Whether he stayed on in Spain or settled in Ferrara, or Venice, or even in Salonika, we do not know, but given his tough and wily character it is easy to imagine that he prospered wherever he happened to end up.

Catalina's husband Antonio Díaz de Cáceres did not escape the Holy Office. He was arrested in March 1596, and spent the next five years in the cells, successfully denying everything, even under torture. During the auto-de-fe of March 1601 he walked to the Plaza Mayor in the 'procession of infamy' with his daughter Leonor and his sisters-in-law Mariana and Anna. He was reconciled that day and released from prison with a hefty fine. After that he, like Jorge de Almeida and Diego Díaz Nieto, disappears from the Holy Office records.

In 1944, when the Mexican historian Alfonso Toro wrote his study of the Carvajal family, he described the inquisitors, Bartolomé Lobo Guerrero and Alonso de Peralta, as 'monsters of cruelty, unworthy of being called men'. But were they?

Peralta's persistent and meticulous questioning made Luis's flesh tremble, and there may well have been a sadistic coldness in his manner which cannot be discerned through the written texts. It is also true that while other members of the advisory council, including Peralta's fellow inquisitor, Lobo Guerrero, voted to cease Luis's torture, Peralta voted to continue it; and that during the inquiry held several years after Luis's death, Peralta was reprimanded for excessive cruelty towards an elderly prisoner. Yet he appears to have treated both Leonor de Cáceres and Diego Díaz Nieto correctly in accordance with Holy Offices rules.

Dr Lobo Guerrero, on the other hand, was exonerated of any malpractice in his role as inquisitor, and the fact that Luis and Isabel chose to unburden their souls to him, rather than to his colleague, Peralta, suggests that he seemed to them a more sympathetic man. Making moral judgments about people in the remote past is notoriously difficult. It is particularly so when we think about a subject as prone to polemics and exaggeration as that of the Holy Office. The stern old nineteenth-century historian Henry Charles Lea described inquisitors in general as 'prisoners of time'; not monsters, but bureaucrats operating according to an ideological framework deemed now to have been monstrous, but which was not considered so in the sixteenth century.

However we may judge them, both inquisitors involved in the Carvajal family's second trial did well in their subsequent careers. Peralta remained in Mexico City long enough to preside over the trials of Mariana and Anna de Carvajal, Antonio Díaz de Cáceres, his daughter Leonor, and Diego Díaz Nieto, alias Isaac Neto. But in 1609 Peralta's role as inquisitor ended. That year he was elevated to the post of archbishop in the diocese of La Plata in present-day Bolivia, and he died there seven years later.

Dr Lobo Guerrero left Mexico City in 1599 to take up an appointment as archbishop of Santa Fe de Bogotá in what is now Colombia. He appears to have been a music lover, for in Bogotá he provided scholarships for choristers, purchased an organ for his cathedral and commissioned several works of plainchant. In 1609 he was appointed archbishop of Lima, and made the long and difficult journey across the Andes to that foggy coastal city. Although no longer an inquisitor, he took an active interest in the extirpation of Andean religious practices, which he naturally considered to be idolatry. In doing so he became an authority on those practices and inadvertently helped record them for posterity.

In March 1997 the San Diego Opera in California presented a work based on the life of Governor Luis de Carvajal de la

Cueva. In this work, entitled *The Conquistador*, he is depicted as a kindly protector of the Indians, and a friend of the great Franciscan linguist and ethnologist Bernardino de Sahagún. When the inquisitorial authorities come for Governor Carvajal, it is because he has been far too kind to the natives.

The governor would not have recognised himself in the opera in San Diego. He might even have been insulted to see himself aligned on stage with a pious intellectual like Sahagún, who spent his life with ink-stained fingers in the Franciscan college in Santiago Tlatelolco, learning and recording what he could of Aztec culture and religion. It is difficult to think of a more implausible friendship in sixteenth-century Mexico, but art is not bound by the same conventions as history, and the opera was received with quiet acclaim.

The auto-de-fe of 1649 at which Anna de Carvajal died was the last big event of its kind in Mexico City. After that the Holy Office returned to prosecuting the usual plethora of cases concerning bigamy, blasphemy and sexual misconduct. By the time it was abolished in Mexico in 1813 it had conducted a little over two thousand trials, of which three hundred and fifty were for alleged Judaising. Many of those latter investigations concerned people like Luis's brothers who had escaped to Jewish communities in the Old World, or had already died. Of the accused Judaisers who did appear in person before the inquisitors twenty-seven were executed by garrotte and four by fire. It is impossible to know how many secret Jews lived on, undisturbed and undetected, in Mexico City. The only ones we know about are those who came to the notice of the authorities. They were relatively few and were by definition the most fervent believers—those least capable of compromising their beliefs; people, in other words, like Luis de Carvajal and his family.

The parchments that record the tribulations of the Carvajales and their friends have made many journeys of their own since December 1596. At some point during the nineteenth century the records of the second trials of Francisca, Isabel, Catalina, Leonor and their friend Manuel de Lucena went missing from the archives in Mexico City. Francisca's and Catalina's have not yet been found, but in 1990 those of Isabel, Leonor and Manuel de Lucena turned up at an antiquarian book fair in Los Angeles. The University of California's Bancroft Library purchased the three transcripts and they have remained together in the quiet and scholarly atmosphere of the Bancroft ever since. It is a place their friend and brother Luis would have loved.

Some of Leonor's notes to Luis have survived within her transcript: pitiful remnants of her young life, covered back and front with her childlike letters. The largest note begins, 'May God be blessed, *Sea Dios bendito*, I intend to confess my sins and ask for mercy.' Leonor tells Luis she hopes that she will be granted penitence and that Jorge de Almeida, her husband, will not leave her. She says she feels the pain of her loneliness and begs Luis to ask God 'who freed us before to free us now'. She ends by telling him that she is disconsolate. Although Leonor did not date this note she must have written it shortly before she made her confession on 2 June 1595.

Leonor wrote her smallest note on both sides of a scrap of paper so narrow that she found it necessary to split her words across two or sometimes three lines. It is possible to make out *'mandamiento'*—commandment —*'en casa dos beces'* [sic]—in the house on two occasions—*'como es berdad'* [sic]—and the names of her sister Mariana and friend Manuel de Lucena. But Leonor's awkward lettering, along with her irregular word divisions and occasional ink blots, make it difficult to decipher the overall meaning of what appears to be the first side of the note. The text on the reverse side is clearer. It contains just ten words: *'y si estan aca mis ermanas [sic] por algun falso testimonio'* – 'and if my sisters are here through some false testimony'.

Leonor did not date this fragmentary and apparently
unfinished message, but she probably wrote it some time in
May or June 1595, and there is poignancy in her allusion to
false testimony. It suggests that, like Luis, she realised that
her communications were being intercepted, and was hoping
to convince the inquisitors that she and her sisters were
innocent of the charges against them.

•

The small black journal in which Luis wrote his book of miracles while he was living in Santiago Tlatelolco went missing from the archives in Mexico City early in the 1930s and has never been recovered. In the preface to his study of the Carvajal family Alfonso Toro claimed that a visiting scholar from Brazil known as Jacques Nachbin removed it from Luis's transcript in 1932 and took it with him to the United States. According to Professor Toro, Nachbin also removed Luis's letters from the transcript and, although he later returned them by post from New York City, they are still missing.

Soon after this alleged incident of scholarly theft the Spanish Civil War broke out. Jacques Nachbin went to Spain as a reporter, disappeared there and is presumed to have died during that conflict. It is possible that Luis's book of miracles was buried with him. Fortunately Professor Toro had already prepared a palaeographic transcript of its text so that we can still read the passionate words that Luis wrote so furtively over four hundred years ago. But the original black notebook that he described as his book of miracles, and in which he recorded the story of his life, has never been recovered.

•

The name *Carvajal* or *Carabajal* and its Portuguese variant *Carvalho* can still be found around the borderlands of north-west Spain and north-east Portugal, and people in those parts will sometimes mention in passing that their forebears were once Jews. They do so with a certain sadness. They know about the terrible events of long ago and sense their loss. But they can admit their lineage now, as their ancestors could not.

Life goes on in the Portuguese province of Trás-os-Montes. In the town of Mogadouro, where Francisca de Carvajal and her brother the governor were born, snow envelopes the old Templar castle in winter and pomegranates hang like red baubles in the plaza. Just a short drive away, across the Spanish border in Fermoselle, villagers till the soil and tend their grapevines while the great River Duero glistens in the canyon far below. Royal eagles and peregrine falcons glide high above them, wood smoke drifts on the air, and the solitary tolling of the church bell and the distant barking of a dog are the only sounds that disturb the silence.

But these days if you look up into the sky you may see the silver trail of a jet flying south to Lisbon. And as night descends the lights of the villages across the river in Portugal begin to shimmer in the darkness. They look so close that you could almost touch them, if not for that river and the sheer, soaring cliffs that have for centuries separated the kingdoms of Iberia.

In the village of Carbajales de Alba, not far from Fermoselle, life is also very quiet. In 1546, when Francisca de Carvajal fled to Carbajales from Portugal with her daughter-in-law and little grand-daughter, it was a thriving town with seven churches and numerous inns. It has just one church now and no inns. It is famous throughout the province for its exquisite embroidery, and during carnival each year the women and girls of the village parade and dance in shimmering costumes sewn with pearls and tiny mirrors. But visitors to Carbajales are rare now, apart from the children and grandchildren who return from afar on feast days, and during Holy Week and Christmas.

In April 1767 the Jesuits were expelled from Spain and all its dominions. They left Medina del Campo but their former school remained beside the Santiago gate until the twentieth century, when it was demolished to make way for new apartments. The chapel that once adjoined it has survived, however. It is now known as the Church of Santiago and large white storks build their nests of twigs and grasses on its bell tower as they do on every tower and chimney pot in this part of Spain.

At least once each year the parish priest tells his congregation the story of St Paul's fateful journey along the road to Damascus, and the moment when a blinding light transformed him from a persecutor of Christians to a Christian himself.

If you happen to be sitting there and listening to that story, as I was one icy night in January 2008, you may remember that somewhere not far beyond the austere walls of the church the young Luis de Carvajal—a far less famous *converso* than St Paul—underwent his own transformative experience.

Except that in Luis's case the light that filled his eyes drew him away from Christianity, and illuminated his journey towards the Law of Moses.

# NOTE ON TRANSLATION
# AND SPELLING

All translations from Spanish and Portuguese in this text are my own.
I should point out that although the scribes at inquisitorial hearings
recorded what they heard in third person, I have returned them to first
person for the purposes of this book. I have left Luis's autobiographical
'book of miracles', in third person, however, just as he wrote it.

I have also left the Spanish orthography of the sixteenth century
unaltered. Therefore readers will see 'cossa' instead of 'cosa' and
'compassión' instead of 'compasión', 'mya' instead of 'mia', and will
occasionally encounter other forms of spelling that have long since
disappeared from modern Spanish.

The Carvajal surname has a number of variants, both in Spain
and Portugal. Its several forms are reflected in the original sixteenth-
century trial transcripts where the name is sometimes written
'Caravajal' or 'Carabajal', but mostly 'Carvajal'. Luis himself spelled
it 'Carvajal' and I have used that form throughout this book.

In his letters to his sisters Luis spelled the Hebrew word for Lord
as either 'Adonay' or 'Adonai'. In this text I have chosen to stay with
just one: 'Adonay'.

# BIBLIOGRAPHY

## Manuscript sources

*Lisbon: Arquivo National da Torre do Tumbo*

Several members of the Carvajal family were tried by the Holy Office tribunal of Évora in Portugal during the 1540s. In this book I have touched on only one case—that of the first Luis de Carvajal of Fermoselle—but have listed below a selection of the others for the benefit of readers who may wish to locate them in the Arquivo Nacional da Torre do Tumbo in Lisbon. I have included details of the case of their friend Antonio de Valença, whose late father had been a rabbi in Zamora, and whose trial transcript alleges that he taught Judaism to the Spanish exiles in Mogadouro.

- Luis de Carvajal (listed as 'Carvagalo' in the Torre do Tumbo index), Inquisicão de Évora, No. 8976.
- Álvaro de Leão, Inquisicão de Évora, No. 1545. Son-in-law of Luis.
- Duarte de Leão, Inquisicão de Coimbra, No. 543. Brother of Álvaro. Tried in absentia.

- Jorge de Leão de Andrada, Inquisicão de Évora, No. 11267. Brother of Álvaro.
- Antonio de Leão, Inquisicão de Évora, No. 9023. Father of Álvaro, Duarte and Jorge.
- Isabel Nunes (sister of Álvaro de Leão?), Inquisicão de Évora, No. 3314.
- Antonio de Valença, Inquisicão de Évora, No. 8232.

*Note:* Lyanor de Carvajal, daughter of Luis de Carvajal, was arrested with her husband Álvaro de Leão during the mid 1540s. She is referred to as a prisoner in his transcript, but her records cannot presently be located.

## *Madrid: Archivo Histório Nacional*

The letter from the inquisitors in Mexico City to the Supreme Council in Madrid, in which they describe Luis's case as *una cossa de compassión*, is held in Volume 1049/762, *Cartas de la Inquisición de la Nueva España al Consejo de Inquisición desde el Año de Mil y Quinientos y Noventa y Quatro*.

Trial transcripts from the tribunal of Valladolid are also held in the Archivo Histórico Nacional. I have not, however, been able to locate the trial transcripts of the first Francisca de Carvajal who, according to her brother, was imprisoned by the Holy Office in Valladolid at some point prior to 1546.

## *Mexico City: Archivo Histórico Nacional*

The majority of manuscripts relating to the Carvajal trials during the final decade of the sixteenth century are held in the Archivo General de la Nación in Mexico City. Their details are as follows:

- Luis de Carvajal de la Cueva, Governor of Nuevo León, Inquisición Vol. 11, Exp. 3, Colección Riva Palacio. Year 1589–1590.
- Luis de Carvajal (alias Joseph Lumbroso), Inquisición Vol. 11, Exp. 2, Colección Riva Palacio. First trial, year 1589–1590.

- Luis de Carvajal (alias Joseph Lumbroso), Inquisición Vol. 14, Colección Riva Palacio. Second trial, year 1595–1596.
- Francisca Nuñez de Carvajal, Inquisición Vol. 12, Exp. 1, Colección Riva Palacio. First trial, year 1589–1590.
- Gaspar de Carvajal, Inquisición Vol. 126. Year 1589–1590.
- Isabel de Andrada de Carvajal, Inquisición Vol. 558, Colección Riva Palacio. First trial, year 1589–1590.
- Leonor de Andrada de Carvajal, Inquisición Vol. 12, Exp. 2. First trial, year 1589–1590.
- Mariana Nuñez de Carvajal, Inquisición Vol. 126, Exp. 13. First trial, year 1589.
- Mariana Nuñez de Carvajal, Inquisición Vol. 15, Exp. 3. Second trial, year 1600.
- Balthasar Rodríguez de Carvajal, Inquisición Vol. 12, Exp. 3. Colección Riva Palacio. Year 1589–1590. Tried *in absentia*.

## Bancroft Library, University of California, Berkeley

The transcripts of the second trials of Isabel and Leonor de Carvajal, and that of their friend Manuel de Lucena, who died with them, can be found in the Bancroft Library of the University of California in Berkeley:

- Isabel de Andrada (Carvajal), Vol. 4, BANC MSS 96/95m, year 1595–1596.
- Leonor de Andrada (Carvajal), Vol. 3, BANC MSS 96/95m, year 1595–1596.
- Manuel de Lucena, Vol. 2, BANC MSS 96/95m, year 1594–1596.

## Huntington Memorial Library, San Marino, California

The transcript of the trial in 1601 of Leonor de Cáceres, daughter of Catalina de León (Carvajal) and Antonio Díaz de Cáceres, is held among the Mexican Inquisition Papers at the Huntington Memorial Library: H. Ms. 35101, Vol. 11.

## Printed sources relating to the Carvajal family and their circle

A paleographic transcript for the trial records, autobiography and letters of Luis de Carvajal, alias Joseph Lumbroso, was published in Mexico in 1935 by Luis Gonzalez Obregón and Rodolfo Gómez for Publicaciones del Archivo General de la Nación. This work, entitled *Procesos de Luis de Carvajal (El Mozo)*, provides an excellent resource for readers who would find it difficult to read the original transcripts, or who are unable to visit Mexico City.

Dr Martin Cohen and Dr Seymour Liebman have each published English translations of Luis's personal writings as follows:

Cohen, Martin, 'The Autobiography of Luis de Carvajal, the Younger' in *American Jewish Historical Quarterly*, 55, 1965–1966, pp. 277–318.

——'The Letters and Last Will and Testament of Luis de Carvajal the Younger', *American Jewish Historical Quarterly*, 55, 1965–1966, pp. 451–520.

Liebman, Seymour, *The Enlightened: The Writings of Luis de Carvajal El Mozo*, Coral Gables, University of Miami Press, Florida, 1967.

As there are significant differences in Dr Cohen's and Dr Liebman's interpretations, readers might like to compare them with Luis's original words, as I did at times while preparing my own translation.

The following books and essays have been of great assistance to me:

Adler, C. 'The Trial of Jorge de Almeida by the Inquisition in Mexico' in *Publicaciones of the American Jewish Historical Society*, Vol. 4, 1986, pp. 29–70.

Bodian, Miriam, 'A Conquistador's Nephew in New Spain' in *Dying in the Law of Moses: Crypto-Jewish Martyrdom in the New World*, Indiana University Press, Bloomington, 2007.

Cohen, Martin, *The Martyr: Luis de Carvajal, A Secret Jew in Sixteenth-Century Mexico*, The Jewish Publication Society of America, University of New Mexico Press, Albuquerque, 2001.

——'Antonio Díaz de Cáceres: Marrano Adventurer in Colonial Mexico' in *American Jewish Historical Quarterly*, 60, 1970–71, pp. 169–84.

——'Don Gregorio López, Friend of the Secret Jew' in *Hebrew Union College Annual*, Vol. 38, 1967, pp. 259–84.

Goldmann, Jack, 'The Tragic Square of Don Luis de Carvajal de la Cueva' in *The Historian*, Vol. 1, 1938, pp. 69–82. Note that in this interesting paper Goldmann confuses Governor Carvajal with his nephew Luis.

Hamilton, Michelle, 'La Poesía de Leonor de Carvajal y la Tradición de los Crypto-Judeos en Nueva España', *Sefarad*, 60:1, 2000, pp. 75–93.

Mott, Margaret McLeish, 'Leonor de Cáceres and the Mexican Inquisition' in *Journal of the History of Ideas*, Vol. 62, No. 1, January 2001, pp. 81–98.

Toro, Alfonso, *La Familia Carvajal: Estudio Histórico sobre los Judios y la Inquisición de la Nueva España en el siglo XVI, basado en Documentos Originales y en su Mayor Parte Inéditos, que se conservan en el Archivo General de la Nación de la Ciudad de México*, Editorial Patria, S.A. Mexico, D.F. 1944.

Uchmany, Eva, *La Vida Entre Judaismo y Cristianismo en la Nueva España 1580–1660*, published by Fondo de Cultura Económica y Archivo General de la Nación, Mexico, 1992. In this excellent work Professor Uchmany provides a detailed account of the trials of Luis's friend Diego Díaz Nieto who, against all odds, survived his second encounter with the Holy Office in Mexico.

## Suggested reading

An exhaustive list of the many other books and essays that helped to shape this book would require a separate volume in itself. The complete bibliography and other background information can be found on the website of the Institute of Latin American Studies at La Trobe University, Melbourne: www.latrobe.edu.au.

Meanwhile, in the section that follows I have compiled a thematic selection of works that may interest general readers. Most are in English, but as some of the most important studies, particularly on the Jews of Portugal, are available only in Portuguese or Spanish, I have included several pieces in those languages, along with one or two in French.

## Anti-semitism in Western Europe

Davies, Alan (Ed.), *Antisemitism and the Foundations of Christianity*, Paulist Press, New York, 1979.

Kisch, Guido, 'The Yellow Badge in History' in *Historia Judaica*, Vol. XIX, No. 2, pp. 91–122.

Moore, R.I., *The Formation of a Persecuting Society: Power and Deviance in Western Europe 950–1250*, Blackwell, Oxford, 1987.

——'Anti-Semitism and the Birth of Europe' in *Christianity and Judaism*, Diana Wood (Ed.), Eccesiastical History Society, Cambridge, Massachusetts, 1992, pp. 33–57.

Oberman, Heiko A., *The Roots of Anti-Semitism in the Age of Renaissance and Reformation* (translated by James I. Porter), Fortress Press, Philadelphia, 1984.

Owen Hughes, Diane, 'Distinguishing Signs: Ear-Rings, Jews and Franciscan Rhetoric in the Italian Renaissance City' in *Past and Present*, No. 112, August 1986, pp. 3–59.

Radford Ruether, Rosemary, *Faith and Fratricide*, Seabury Press, New York, 1974.

Yuval, Israel Jacob, 'Jews and Christians in the Middle Ages: Shared Myths, Common Language' in *Demonizing the Other: Anti-Semitism, Racism and Xenophobia*, Robert Wistrich (Ed.), Vol. 4, Studies in Antisemitism, pp. 88–107, Harwood Academic, Amsterdam, 1999.

## Jewish life in Spain prior to 1492

Baer, Yitzhak, *A History of the Jews in Christian Spain*, Jewish Publication Society of America, Philadelphia, 1966.

Beinart, Haim, 'La Formación del Mundo Sefardi' in *Actas del Primer Simposio de Estudios Sefardies*, Jacob M. Hassan (Ed.) with the collaboration of Maria Teresa Rubiato and Elena Romero, 1970.

Cantera Burgos, Francisco, *Sinagogas Españolas con especial estudio de la de Córdoba y la Toledana de El Transito*, Instituto Arias Montano, Madrid, 1955.

Carrete Larrondo, Carlos, 'Hacia un mapa de las Aljamas y Juderías Castellanas en 1492' in *Proyección Historico de España en sus Tres Culturas, Castilla y León, América y Mediterraneo*, Vol. 3, 1993, pp. 61–6.

Kedouri, Elie, *Spain and the Jews: The Sephardi Experience 1492 and After*, Thames & Hudson, London, 1992.

Roth, Norman, *Jews, Visigoths and Muslims in Medieval Spain: Cooperation and Conflict*, E.J. Brill, Leiden, 1994.

## The expulsion of 1492 and its aftermath

Bernaldez, Andrés, *Memorias del Reinado de los Reyes Católicos*, Madrid, 1962.

Cantera Burgos, Francisco, 'Fernando de Pulgar y los Conversos' in *Sefarad*, IV, 1944, pp. 295–348.

Haliczer, Stephen H., 'The Castilian Urban Patriciate and the Jewish Expulsions of 1480–1492' in *American Historical Review*, 78, 1973, pp. 35–61.

Kamen, Henry, 'The Expulsion: Purpose and Consequence' in *Spain and the Jews: The Sephardi Experience 1492 and After*, Elie Kedouri (Ed.), Thames & Hudson, London, 1992.

——'The Mediterranean and the Expulsion of Spanish Jews in 1492' in *Past and Present*, 119, May 1988.

———'Toleration and Dissent in Sixteenth-Century Spain: The Alternative Tradition' in *The Sixteenth Century Journal*, Vol. 19, No. 1, Spring 1988, pp. 3–23.

Raphael, David (Ed.), *The Expulsion of 1492 Chronicles: An Anthology of Medieval Chronicles Relating to the Expulsion of the Jews from Spain and Portugal*, Carmi House, California, 1992.

## The Jews of Portugal and Trás-os-Montes

Paulo, Amílcar, *Os Judeus em Trás-os-Montes*, N.P., 1965.

———*A Disperção dos Sephardim: Judeus Hispano-Portugeses*, Porto, Editora Nova Crítica, 1978.

Pimenta Ferro Tavares, Maria Jose, *Los Judios en Portugal*, Editorial Mapfre, Madrid, 1992.

———'Para o Estudo dos Judeus de Trás-os-Montes no Seculo XVI: A Primera Geração de Cristãos Novos' in *Cultura Historia e Filosofia*, Vol. 4, pp. 371–417.

———'Judeus e Conversos Castelhanos em Portugal' in *Anales de la Universidade de Alicante*, No. 6, 1987, pp. 341–68.

Sousa, Fernando de, 'The Silk Industry in Trás-Os-Montes During the Ancient Regime' in *e-JPH*, Vol. 3, No. 2, Winter 2005.

## The mental world of the Judeo-Conversos

Cohen, Martin, 'The Religion of Luis Rodríguez Carvajal' in *American Jewish Archives*, 28, 1968, pp. 33–62.

Gitlitz, David, *Secrecy and Deceit: The Religion of the Crypto-Jews*, Jewish Publication Society, Philadelphia and Jerusalem, 1996.

Graizbord, David L., *Souls in Dispute: Converso Identities in Iberia and the Jewish Diaspora 1580–1700*, University of Philadelphia Press, Philadelphia, 2003.

Lazar, Moshe, 'Scorched Parchments and Tortured Memories: The "Jewishness" of the Anussim' in *Cultural Encounters: The Impact of the Inquisition in Spain and the New World*, Mary Elizabeth

Perry and Anne J. Crutz (Eds), University of California Press, Berkeley, 1991.

Pimenta Ferro Tavares, Maria José, 'Cristãos-Novos: Um Barco com Dois Lemes (Diaspora Judaica no Seculo XVI)' in *Estudos e Ensaios em Homagem a Vitorino Magalhaes Godinho*, 1992, pp. 239–49.

Ricard, Robert, 'Pour une etude du judiasme portugais au Mexique pendant la periodo coloniale', *Revue d'Histoire Moderne*, 14, 1939, pp. 516–24.

Uchmany, Eva, 'El Judaismo de los Cristianos Nuevos de Origen Portugués en la Nueva España' in *Society and Community*, Misgav Yerushalayim, 1991, pp. 119–37.

Wiznitzer, Arnold, 'Crypto-Jews in Mexico during the Sixteenth Century' in *The Jewish Experience in Latin America*, Vol. 1, The American Jewish Historical Society, Martin Cohen (Ed). Waltham, Massachusetts.

## The Holy Office in Spain and Portugal

Alcalá, Ángel, *The Spanish Inquisition and the Inquisitorial Mind*, Columbia University Press, New York, 1987.

Coelho, Antonio Borges, *Inquisicão de Évora* (Dos Primordios a 1668), Editorial Caminho, Colecção Universitaria, 1987.

Henningsen, Gustav, and Contreras, Jaime, 'El Banco de Datos del Santo Oficio: las Relaciones de Causas de la Inquisición Española 1550–1770', *Boletin de la Real Academia de Historia*, Vol. 174(3), pp. 547–70.

——'Forty-Four Thousand Cases of the Spanish Inquisition (1540–1700): Analysis of a Historical Data Bank' in *The Inquisition in Early Modern Europe: Studies on Sources and Methods*, Gustav Henningsen and John Tedeschi (Eds), Dekalb, Northern Illinois University Press, 1986.

Kamen, Henry, *Inquisition and Society in Spain in the Sixteenth and Seventeenth Centuries*, Indiana University Press, Bloomington, 1985.

Peters, Edward, *Inquisition*, University of California Press, Berkeley, 1989.

Rawlings, Helen, *The Spanish Inquisition*, Wiley–Blackwell, 2005.

## *The Holy Office in Mexico*

Alberro, Solange, *Inquisición y Sociedad en México 1571–1700*, Fondo de Cultura Económica, Mexico, 1998.

Greenleaf, Richard E., *Zumarraga and the Mexican Inquisition*, Academy of American Franciscan History, 1961.

——*The Mexican Inquisition of the Sixteenth Century*, University of New Mexico Press, Albuquerque, 1960.

Uchmany, Eva, 'La Vida en las Cárceles del Santo Oficio en la Ciudad de México entre 1589 a 1660' in *Memorial I.S. Revah: Etudes sur le Marranisme, Heterodoxie Juive et Spinoza*, H. Mechoulan and G. Nathan (Eds), Peeters, Paris and Louvain, January 2000.

Medina, José Toribio, *Historia del Tribunal del Santo Oficio de la Inquisición en México*, Ediciones Fuente Cultural, Mexico, 1952. *Note:* This classic work on the Holy Office in Mexico is a valuable resource, but readers should bear in mind that in the section dealing with the Carvajal family Professor Medina confused the younger Luis with his uncle, the governor of Nuevo León. Furthermore, the details he gives of Francisca's second trial in fact relate to her first.

## *Autos de fe*

Bethencourt, Francisco, 'The Auto da Fe: Ritual and Imagery' in the *Journal of the Warburg and Courthauld Institutes*, Vol. 55, 1992, pp. 155–68.

Flynn, Maureen,'Mimesis of the Last Judgment: The Spanish Auto de Fe' in the *Sixteenth Century Journal*, Vol. 22, No. 2, Summer 1991, pp. 281–97.

Avilés, Miguel, 'The Auto de Fe and the Social Model of Counter-Reformation Spain' in *The Spanish Inquisition and the*

*Inquisitorial Mind*, Ángel Alcalá (Ed.), Columbia University Press, New York, 1987, pp. 249–64.

## Medina del Campo

Barrosa, Efrén de la Peña, *Los Judios de Medina del Campo a Finales del Siglo XV*, Fundación Museo de las Ferias y Diputación de Valladolid, 2008.

Benassar, Bartolomé, 'Medina del Campo: Un Exemple des Structure Urbaines de l'Espagne au XVIe Siecle', *Revue d'Histoire Economique et Sociale*, 4, 1961, pp. 155–68.

Sánchez del Barrio, Antonio, *Estructura Urbana de Medina del Campo*, Junta de Castilla y León, Consejeria de Cultura y Bienestar Social, 1991.

——*Guia Breve del Museo de las Ferias*, Fundación Museo de las Ferias, Medina del Campo.

## Mexico City in the sixteenth century

Altman, Ida, 'Spanish Society in Mexico City After the Conquest' in *The Hispanic American Historical Review*, Vol. 71, No. 3, August 1991, pp. 413–45.

Kubler, George, *Mexican Architecture of the Sixteenth Century*, New Haven Press, Connecticut, 1948.

O'Hara, Matthew D., 'Stone, Mortar, and Memory: Church Construction and Communities in Late Colonial Mexico City' in *Hispanic American Historical Review*, 86:4, 2006, pp. 647–80.

## Santiago Tlatelolco

Barlow, Robert, *Tlatelolco, Rival de Tenochtitlán*, Instituto Nacional de Historia e Antropologia, Mexico, 1987.

Carreno, Alberto Maria, 'El Colegio de Tlatelolco y la Educación Indigena en el Siglo XVI' in *Divulgación Historica*.

Steck, Francis Borgia, *El Primer Colegio en América: Santa Cruz de Tlatelolco*, Mexico City, 1945.

## Martyrdom

Boyarin, Daniel, *Dying for God: Martyrdom and the Making of Christianity and Judaism*, Stanford University Press, Stanford, 1999.

Gregory, Brad S., *Salvation at Stake: Christian Martyrdom in Early Modern Europe*, Harvard University Press, Cambridge Massachusetts, 1999.

Henten, J.W. van, and Avemarie, Friedrich, *Martyrdom and Noble Death: Selected Texts from Graeco-Roman, Jewish and Christian Antiquity*, Routledge, London and New York, 2002.

Shaw, B., 'Body, Power, Identity: Passions of the Martyrs' in *Journal of Early Christian Studies*, Vol. 4, No. 3, Fall 1996, pp. 269–312.

## Inquisitorial trial transcripts as historical sources

Beinart, Haim, 'The Records of the Inquisition as a Source of Jewish and Converso History' in *Proceedings of the Israel Academy of Sciences and Humanities*, 2, pp. 211–27.

Ginzberg, Carlo, 'The Inquisitor as Anthropologist' in *Clues, Myths and the Historical Method*, translated by John and Anne Tedeschi, John Hopkins University Press, Baltimore, 1986, pp. 156–64.

Rosaldo, R. 'From the Door of His Tent: The Fieldworker and the Inquisitor' in *Writing Culture: The Poetics and Politics of Ethnography*, J. Clifford and G.E Marcus (Eds), Berkeley and Los Angeles, 1986.

# Further reading

Around the time the Carvajal family were facing their inquisitors in Mexico City, a miller from the Friulian region of northern Italy was tried by the Venetian Inquisition, not as a Judaiser, but for making heretical statements about Jesus Christ that suggested Catharist influences. His name was Domenico Scandella and he has been the subject of two fine case studies:

Del Col, Andrea, *Domenico Scandella, Known as Menocchio: His Trials before the Inquisition 1583–1599*, translated by John and Anne Tedeschi, Medieval and Renaissance Texts and Studies, Binghampton, New York, 1996.

Ginzberg, Carlo, *The Cheese and the Worms: The Cosmos of a Sixteenth-Century Miller*, Penguin, New York, 1982.

*Note:* The Hassidic tale that gave this book its principal title was retold by the poet Deborah Masel in one of her *Faith* columns for the *Sunday Age* during 2009. Deborah Masel's other works include *In the Cleft of the Rock*, a series of meditations on *The Five Books of Moses*, published by Black Pepper Publishing in 2009, and *Sacred Fire: Torah from the Years of Fury 1939–1942*, published by Jason Aronson in 2002.

# INDEX